World Volunteers

The World Guide to Humanitarian and Development Volunteering

Green Volunteers
Publications

World Volunteers
The World Guide to Humanitarian and Development Volunteering

Editors:	Fabio Ausenda, Erin McCloskey
	Roberta Di Matteo (Assistant Editor of the current edition)
Cover design:	Studio Cappellato e Laurent srl, Milano
Cover photo:	International volunteer and the children of the Abura Literacy School, Abura (Ghana)
	© Projects Abroad (see listing)

This Guide is not an annual publication: the useful websites section, the suggestions for contacting the organisations in the introductory pages and the updates page of our website (see bottom of next page) allow the reader to find continuous new opportunities and to keep the information in this Guide always up to date.

Published by: Green Volunteers di Fabio Ausenda
Via Canonica 72
20154 Milano, Italy
www.greenvolunteers.com
E-mail: greenvol@iol.it

US & Canada distribution:	Universe Publishing
	A division of Rizzoli International Publications, Inc.
	300 Park Avenue South,
	New York, NY 10010
UK distribution:	Crimson Publishing
	A division of Crimson Business Ltd
	Westminster House, Kew Road,
	Richmond TW9 2ND, England
Australia & NZ distribution:	Woodslane Pty Ltd
	Unit 7/5 Vuko Place
	Warriewood NSW 2102
Printed in Jan. 2008 by:	Consorzio Artigiano L.V.G. srl, Azzate (VA), Italy

ISBN: 978-88-89060-13-1

Library of Congress Control Number: 2007943560

The Editors highly recommend the following introductory pages are read. These pages explain what humanitarian and development volunteering involves and will increase the volunteer's chances of being accepted by an organisation.

HOW TO RECEIVE ANNUAL UPDATES FROM THE INTERNET:

Regular annual updates of this guide will be available at no cost to the reader. In order to obtain the updates from the Internet, the reader should carefully read the following introductory pages and in particular the section dedicated to useful websites and the **Important Note on pages 35–36**. Free annual updates of this guide will be available on the Internet unless the Publisher ceases operating for any reason.

TABLE OF CONTENTS

INTRODUCTION 5
    VOLUNTEERING OPTIONS 11
    USEFUL WEBSITES 18
    HOW TO READ THE GUIDE 24
    TIPS FOR CONTACTING AN ORGANISATION 32

IMPORTANT NOTE 35

ORGANISATION LIST 39

APPENDICES 237
    ANALYTICAL TABLE BY GEOGRAPHICAL AREA
    AND VOLUNTEER TYPE 238
    ANALYTICAL TABLE BY SECTOR 244

ORGANISATION ALPHABETICAL INDEX 251

Before joining any project or organisation prospective volunteers should carefully read the Warning on page 3 and the Important Note on pages 35–36.

INTRODUCTION

The growing gap between North and South

In the past decades, the division between North and South has deepened. The industrialised world—Europe, North America, and Japan—is running towards a consumerism that knows no limits. Seemingly limitless technological advancement is growing so fast that we had to coin a new phrase and "invent" a new branch of the economy: the *New Economy*. This economy is based on things virtual and potential—not only on technology but also on new forms of consumption, science, and biotechnology. However, the rest of the world is being left behind.

Up until the '80s, the East was undoubtedly tied to an image of totalitarian regimes without democracy. However, there was never an image of an economy in ruin, with hunger, poverty, and spreading diseases, or pro-capita income worst than many third-world countries. Increasingly we see frightening ethnic wars closer to our borders (such as in the Balkans) and poverty in many countries that previously were able to boast acceptable standards of living. Even countries not affected by war have been reduced to unimaginable poverty since the collapse of the Soviet block—think of the citizens of Moldova or Belarus, or of the street kids of Romania.

In the '90s, following the collapse of the Soviet Union, we came to realise that the South's boundary had moved closer and, tragically, the gap had become bigger. Today, many people are discovering this boundary, that was once at a comfortable distance, now only hundreds, at times only tens, of kilometres away. While in the past the western perspective of poverty and underdevelopment was perhaps only associated with the famines in Africa; today in many western European countries, it is not uncommon to see children, from countries such as Albania, begging for money from people stopped in their cars at traffic lights or taking the subway to work or to go shopping.

In Africa the situation has become even worse. Following the famine caused by climate conditions or conflicts triggered by the Cold War there are now also ferocious local conflicts with effects that are mostly ignored by the rest of the world. These conflicts, since they don't have any external support, leave entire countries devastated and abandoned. Previously, at the end of a conflict, the prevailing superpower attempted to extend its political influence by helping the local economy and infrastructure. This is no longer the case: the wars are bloody and cruel and are caused by ethnic, tribal, religious, or economic reasons. This all happens often with complete indifference from the wealthy countries. Africa is ravaged by diseases such as Aids or Ebola. At the same time, western pharmaceutical companies care more about preserving profits

5

and protecting patents than about the overwhelming number of deaths—a death toll that they have contributed to.

Finally, terrorism, such as the events of 11 September 2001, is a fanaticism, which can be the most dangerous by-product of poverty and underdevelopment and that increases the gap between the rich and the poor. Ultimately this justifies war by some countries and creates an isolationist attitude by others.

Thankfully, not everyone is insensitive to what is happening. The media are making the distances shorter and bringing to the attention of the western world the incredible gap in resource distribution and the consequential tragedies, such as natural disasters and wars, in the world.

Today, it costs much less to travel to far places and communication time and costs have decreased dramatically with the Internet and e-mail. All of these reasons have not only increased awareness, but also a willingness "to act". In addition, citizens in wealthy countries have more time and resources to allow them to travel or move abroad more easily. When a person does go abroad the ease of communication makes home feel less distant. Therefore, the increased awareness has caused a collective desire to act, with low transportation and communication costs making this desire more feasible.

Moreover, in the last few years, a "political" movement has emerged. In reality, it is a movement common to many ideologies: the political left, environmentalism, and various religious beliefs. This is the "anti-global" movement characterised (with some exceptions) by a strong, inspirational solidarity. It is not by chance that in the last few years, part of this desire to act has been directed towards developing countries. This Guide is a tool for those people (even without previous volunteer experience in poor countries) that no longer just want to be spectators but instead want to "act".

What can we do?

We have seen how the awareness of this gap between the North and South, and the growing number of catastrophes (more or less of human cause— even natural disasters can often be traced to human error, such as negative development, deforestation and other contributors to climate change, etc.) has awakened the desire to "do something" to help those who are less fortunate. Help can be given in many ways:

1)   **by donating money**
2)   **by donating material objects**
3)   **by donating time**

Donating money

It is an easy solution especially if you have limited time available. In effect, by donating money you delegate your willingness to act to others. The only difficulty is in deciding which organisation to choose. Many people are hesitant to donate because they are unsure of how their money will be spent. This topic is debatable: it would be like a dog biting its own tail. Small local organisations are able to use a higher percentage of donated money for projects as opposed to operating costs, however, because of their small size, the effectiveness for the cause is limited. The communities they help are quite small. Alternatively, large organisations with high administrative costs have a greater impact on the projects they support. Often these organisations are able to obtain additional funding from governmental or Inter-Governmental sources, ultimately supporting projects for many years. It is very rare that organisations divert funds from the original cause. The more common case is that of organisations spending a large portion of donated funds on excessive administrative costs. A good control method for someone who wants to regularly donate funds is to ask to see an organisation's certified financial statements. The larger organisations have balances that are certified by auditing firms. In almost all fiscal systems, donations to non-profit organisations are tax deductible, further facilitating the act of giving. Regardless, donating money to large or small organisations is always the right thing—without donations, many non-profit organisations would cease to exist.

Donating material objects

In the last few years there has been a decline in this action. We are in a time of abundance, globalization enables the production of items (such as clothing) in the far east at extremely competitive prices. Therefore, it is much cheaper and easier for aid organisations to purchase clothing—new, packaged, and sorted in the right sizes—directly from the producers, as opposed to selecting, washing, packing, sorting, and transporting used items from households. Up until a few years ago, used items had more value and donating objects was more common.

Other actions, such as donating food, have an impact if they are donated to organised programmes. Donating food items according to what an organisation requests, as opposed to casually giving extras from your kitchen cupboards, is much more efficient. Donated groceries are used to supply soup kitchens for the homeless in our own cities. When intervening in developing countries for emergency purposes and hunger relief, often times the food is donated by large producers and governments. It is much easier for large aid organisations, as with the clothing, to ship groceries well packaged and preserved, than to collect, select, and pack groceries donated by private individuals. Actions such as donating used toys, much like clothing, is often not a priority on a global scale, although there are exceptions. Systematically organised collections, such as the ones performed by many organisations, can be useful if they generate funds.

Donating time – Volunteering

Volunteering is the third donation possibility, which in the context of this Guide, is obviously the most important. Since it is not always true that volunteering is the best way to help those in need, with this book we try to give the potential volunteer the tools and advice that will make volunteering enriching for the participant, useful for the aid organisation, and essential for the cause.

Volunteering in developing countries, contrary to what most people think, is not always unpaid, but, in many cases, the volunteer, especially the professional volunteer, is paid for by the sending NGO. These funds are used for providing pocket money or a stipend. This stipend is sometimes equivalent to what would be earned in the volunteer's own country, or some times even higher.

Situations can vary from contract to contract and they also depend on the paying institution. Often salaries are in US dollars (not in local currencies) and are tax free. Volunteers may receive a good salary or an additional indemnity because the paying NGO must compete for a qualified professional within the private sector. For those who may be concerned by the fact that volunteers will be paid a salary for staying a few months abroad, we can point out that these salaries are only for the most qualified people, working in development projects financed by large NGOs.

The majority of volunteers in the long-term humanitarian projects receive a salary just enough to fulfil the basic needs. In this Guide we have included organisations that offer paid positions for qualified professionals because many still require unpaid volunteers. We will therefore provide information on finding a professional position, considering that a few months (or years) away from home, even if paid, is always a sacrifice—of family and friends, hobbies, sports, and comforts.

Time can be donated occasionally (e.g., for a fundraising event), regularly (for a few hours a week), or by going overseas (for a few weeks, months, or even years). This last case is the focus of this Guide, which aims to be a useful instrument for those who, for short or long term want to become volunteers. We give suggestions in order to have this experience fulfilled and also to help every prospective volunteer find the organisation nearest to his or her needs. We will talk about local volunteering in the following section, "how to start" (see page 11).

Volunteering organisations

Generally speaking, volunteering in developing countries is done with non-profit organisations that supervise and train the volunteers, allowing them to serve in a structured way and, most of all, guaranteeing continuity to the efforts of the organisation. If a volunteer wants to be more autonomous, we suggest joining a non-profit organisation directly that is working in a developing country. These organisations are greatly in need of help, both economically and in management because they are located in poor countries with limited resources. It may also be convenient to apply with an organisation from a developing country because if a volunteer is financially self-sufficient and can cover the travel and living expenses, they are often more easily and willingly accepted by the organisation.

The common classifications of international development organisations are: Government Organisations, Inter-Governmental Organisations (IGOs) and Non-Government Organisations (NGOs). The IGOs include all the national aid agencies. Almost all wealthy countries have their own development agency. In the US, for example it is USAID – the US Agency for International Development. Among the IGOs, the major donors are: the European Union, the World Bank, the Organisation of American States, and the numerous UN agencies acting independently or together with other NGOs such as UNDP (United Nations Development Programme), FAO (Food and Agriculture Organization), UNICEF (United Nations Children Fund), WFP (World Food Programme), and UNHCR (United Nations High Commission for Refugees).

This Guide does not consider Government or Inter-Governmental Organisations, either because they don't offer volunteering programs, or because they are managed in conjunction with NGO's. The United Nations have established one agency, UNV (United Nation volunteers) headquartered in Bonne, Germany, which recruits and sends volunteers to various UN agencies. UNV has been listed in this Guide. NGOs make the bulk of the organisations listed, although it is not a comprehensive list because the number of humanitarian NGOs is so large that surpasses the scope of this Guide. A thorough list of NGOs of a given country can be easily found on the web—the richest source of information (see "useful websites" page 18). In this Guide the reader can find a studied selection of organisations from all around the world (many of them from developing countries). There is a great variety of choices: from workcamps (for those with little or no experience) to professional contracts (for specialised doctors). Organisations listed have headquarters and projects in countries all around the globe. The type of organisations range from large religious organisations to small rural projects in a developing countries. There are many organisations from the developing countries that are in extreme need of help, such a hospital in Cameroon or an orphanage in Kenya. This Guide is a useful instrument for finding an organisation to volunteer for or for starting a search for other organisations on the Internet.

VOLUNTEERING OPTIONS

How to start: local volunteering

Whatever is the motivation to volunteer in a developing country it is important to keep in mind that one cannot improvise oneself into a volunteer. Motivation must be strong because the sacrifice is considerable and a good adaptability is recommended. Work is often done in difficult conditions, with little or no comfort, often by helping people in desperate situations and witnessing tragic realities. It is highly advisable to test this motivation before hand. The NGO itself must be aware of the volunteer's motivation, otherwise it would risk losing time and resources, and, worse of all, the unmotivated volunteer could negatively influence the project he or she is working on. However, the volunteer's motivation is generally perceivable from the volunteer's resume and interview.

If this is your first volunteering experience abroad, it is recommended to start local. This may turn out to be a practical activity such as visiting the elderly or the homeless or working in a food distribution centre for the poor in your own home town, or, if possible, you may choose to start working locally with the NGO you would later be interested in volunteering for on an overseas project. This can be a great occasion to get to know the work environment and to show your skills, initiative, and spirit of sacrifice. Activities can be of all kinds: from simple office work to fundraising or public awareness activities about the goals of the NGO. Every NGO, whether large or small, normally uses local volunteers and it always welcomes a person's intention to form a local small chapter or fundraising group, if an office of the organisation is not located nearby.

It is not absolutely necessary to volunteer locally with the NGO you will be joining overseas. Any social or humanitarian organisation is fine, the important thing is to be confident in your decision. If the local volunteer experience proves that your motivation is less than anticipated, you may reconsider the idea of a becoming volunteer overseas. Or you may discover that your sector of interest has changed. The "useful websites" section (see page 18) may be very useful in finding the organisation operating locally that is right for you.

Volunteering from home

With the increased use of computers, it is now possible to volunteer comfortably from home. Some organisations, such as NETAID (www.netaid.org) or Interconnection (www.interconnection.org), give you the opportunity to become a "virtualvolunteer" for an NGO in a developìing country with extreme need of tecnological help. A typical example of the work a virtual volunteer can provide is the construction of websites but there are many other tasks that can be performed with a computer communicating by e-mail. Some organisations from poor countries needing computer help are listed in this Guide. The section "useful websites" (see page 18) shows how to find other organisations on websites featuring international directories such as www.idealist.org.

Being a virtual volunteer allows you to become familiar with the NGO from a developing country with which a volunteering period is forseen. Volunteering directly for an NGO from a poor country is certainly a challenging choice as mentioned earlier. Such an organisation can have strong management difficulties and the working and living conditions may be very poor without having the help and the support of other expert volunteers. For this choice no particular prerequisites are needed. It is sufficient to have some professional qualification useful to a project and to be ready to bare all travel and living expenses. For these reasons this option must be strogley motivated and therefore a test period of virtual volouteering is advisable to start developing personal relations with the people you may laterbe working with.

The workcamp: an ideal experience for young people

A workcamp is the ideal setting for a volunteer with no previous experience who does not want to committ too much time. It is therefore particularly suitable for students and young people as a meaningful way to spend a summer vacation or visit a new country. It could be considered more of an alternative vacation than a true volunteering committment. Nevertheless workcamps are good introductory experience to volunteering, and they are an enriching life experience for the work accomplished and for meeting people from many different countriers and cultures who share the same interests and lifestyle.

The psychological commitment is minimal however, the risk of a workcamp is that it may not be taken very seriously by all the participants and the "holiday" aspect can takeover and shade the primary goal of the workcamp, which is to help those in need. This will depend on the motivation and dedication of organisers of the workcamp. If the organisation has a website, they may post feedback and often e-mail addresses from past volunteers. This is a good way to assess the philosophy or atmosphere of a particular workcamp. A balanced attitude towards "vacation" and the social or humanitarian commitment can be the best approach.

Often no previous experience is required for workcamps; the structure is organised to lodge and cater to a certain number of volunteers, the tasks to be accomplished are simple and the work is never in extreme situations. Often the only requirement is to know the language of the workcamp (most often English). For these reasons the workcamps are preferred by young people and students. Older volunteers may also be accepted, but they should first verify the kind of work to be done and the age group of other volunteers, in order not to feel too isolated from the rest of the group. More experienced volunteers can always apply for a coordinating position. In the Appendix Tables at the end of the Guide the organisations that offer workcamp opportunities are indicated.

Workcamps and unpaid volunteer positions obviously have less competition but they may not be able to take volunteers at the time you may apply. This may be owing to the available positions being already filled. They may also require specific qualifications to meet the needs of the association or project at that time. And even though volunteers may be financially self-supporting and willing to work, they still require considerable engagement on the part of the organisation. They require space, attention (in sometimes critical situations), coordination, assistance, transportation, and they must be provided with higher standards of hygiene and safety than what may be found in that country. A volunteer may become depressed, sick, or injured. An unneeded or, even worse, an unwanted volunteer can be of great hindrance. Make as large a search spectrum as possible to increase your chances of finding an organisation that is not only interested but ready to accept you to their project.

Short-term volunteering: for retired people or skilled workers

To volunteer in a developing country it is often not necessary to have extensive travelling experience, to speak a foreign language, or to have a university degree; tradesworkers such as mechanics, plumbers, electricians, brick layers, ironsmiths, carpenters, etc., who can teach their skills to others may be extremely desired by a project.

We recommend that only people with previous international experience apply directly to an NGO in a developing country. A considerable autonomy along with the ability to work independently in sometimes uncomfortable or unusual conditions may be necessary. For first-time volunteers with no previous travel or work experience in a developing country, it is advisable to apply with a larger, established sending organisation that coordinates projects with more provisions in place and larger groups of volunteers on site often with group leaders for support.

Religious missions are an ideal environment for skilled labourers or retired people to share their lifetime working experience. With these projects it is possible to work in a quiet environment and there is usually no necessity to speak a foreign language, since the resident missionaries act as interpreters and cultural mediators. Typically, volunteers accepted onto missionary projects are sent by a church or agency supporting the mission. There are countries with a strong Christian tradition, who have close ties with missions: Italy or Ireland are good examples. Volunteers on missions have typically already been involved with the church and its activities and events, such as fundraising, etc., to prove their skills, motivation, and faith. They become so acquainted with the group supporting the mission that going to work at the mission is a sort of spontaneous evolution.

Short-term volunteering: for skilled professionals

Many qualified professionals (medical doctors, engineers, architects, agronomists, etc.), during their professional life, may feel they want to help those in need through a professional experience working in a developing country. The response to this inclination can be short-term professional volunteering, which can last as little as one month or a summer vacation period. Obviously the professional volunteer can be engaged for longer periods by taking a leave of absence from work.

The qualified professional is very often accepted because of possessing necessary qualifications and sometimes for having the ability to bear all the travel and living expenses. Under these circumstances the professional volunteer can be accepted in a project even without previous volunteering experience abroad. The higher the qualifications of the volunteer the higher the chance of being accepted to a project basis. For example, a dentist with several years of professional experience is the ideal candidate for spending a month in a dental clinic in Africa. It will be very difficult for a professional to be paid for short-term volunteering (less than one month). This can happen for longer term engagements - at least 2-3 months - or if a relationship between the candidate and the NGO is well established or the application is in response to an employment offer.

Many NGOs will ask to have preliminary meetings or to perform short training courses (during weekends, for example). These requests are absolutely legitimate and allow the organisation better to know the prospective volunteer and vice-versa.

Medium-term volunteering

Medium-term volunteering may involve both professional and unskilled volunteers. Normally it lasts from two to six months. In general, medium-term volunteers are either students or professionals who are familiar with the world of cooperation and have already served as volunteers in the past. The most experienced are often employed with contracts issued by financing institutions, such as the European Union. Highly specialised professionals, e.g., medical doctors, often receive placement for few months with a salary, even without previous volunteering experience. The Guide lists a few European and American organisations, mostly in the field of health, that tend to select only experienced professionals, paying them with sufficient, if not competitive, salaries. Keep in mind that there are rarely any expenses incurred by the volunteer: board and lodging are supplied and there are few amusements that require money.

Long-term volunteering

Long-term volunteering is a true choice in life. In general, the minimum period lasts at least two years and is renewable. The economic treatment is regulated by specific contracts and conditions issued by the organisations that co-finance the projects, such as the European Union. The approach to a career in cooperation must be made in a systematic way, as for any other field, starting from proper courses of instruction, of which many are run by the NGOs themselves. Humana (see listing) is a one such example.

Volunteering with organisations in developing countries

The following outlines the main characteristics of NGOs situated and working in developing countries:

- NGOs in developing countries need a considerable amount of help in view of the very scarce resources to which they have access, especially if they are not helped by partner organisations residing in the "rich countries".
- NGOs in developing countries are the least selective in accepting volunteers and often the length of the volunteering period is negotiable. Also, the requested qualifications are not very strict: even generic qualifications may be enough (e.g., teaching basic computer skills).
- The volunteer must pay for all of his or her expenses: certainly travel, often board, sometimes lodging, and at times also give a contribution.
- The volunteer may be without other volunteers to share experiences with or ask advice from. The project leaders may also have very high work expectations.
- The volunteer may find conditions of considerable lack of organisation, extreme scarcity of means, or with few comforts, in other words, the experience may be a difficult test on the volunteer's capabilities.

In spite of all the possible problems described, we continue to recommend this type of volunteering to those who have courage and initiative. These points are not meant to deter but to make sure a potential volunteer is not naive to the difficulties that may be involved. However, the rewards are even greater because they give the opportunity for the volunteer to be instrumental in contributing to changing the existing situations of extreme precariousness, allowing those organisations to better help their own people. We especially advise volunteers with language skills, who are endowed with considerable initiative and autonomy, to address themselves to these organisations.

In this Guide we have listed a good number of NGOs of developing countries, especially African ones. In the section "useful websites" (see page 18) and also on our website (see page 19) we have selected a list of sites with excellent links to many other NGOs not listed in the Guide.

Responsible tourism

Responsible tourism deserves a separate mention. Indeed, it is not volunteering, but as the term suggests, "tourism made on tiptoe".
The tourist tries to understand the local culture, to live with the locals, and to visit their villages, schools, farms, and cooperatives using the services offered by the local communities as much as possible so that they may increase their revenues. Responsible tourism is for those who want to travel, understand,

and to be as little trouble to their host as possible. Several NGOs, in fact, are beginning to organise trips to the locations where their projects are carried out, so that the travellers may visit the volunteers and the communities being helped. Responsible tourism, in the context of this Guide, may be considered a gradual approach or introduction to volunteering.

Self-reflection before departure

Motivation is the best key to success in the volunteering experience, both for helping the project and oneself. Desire to leave should never be a flight or an escape from personal problems. Humanitarian volunteering means "to give oneself totally and sincerely" leaving behind, at least for a while, one's problems. A stressed and unhappy volunteer can cause many problems to a project where the objective is to help—not to be helped. For a meaningful and enjoyable experience and for the enhancement of the project, volunteers must pause for deep self-reflection before leaving to affirm their motivation and commitment and be ready to give their best effort.

USEFUL WEBSITES

The World Wide Web is the most comprehensive source of information on voluntary work worldwide. In this section we have highlighted the ones that we believe to be the most useful. However, if we were to list one book on voluntary work worldwide, *The International Directory of Voluntary Work* by Vacation Works Publications (Oxford UK), is the most comprehensive listing thousands of voluntary placements worldwide in different fields, many of them local, in the UK, the US, Europe, and other countries.

On the opposite page we have provided a links page from our website, to allow to reach easily the websites listed below. To obtain annual updates of this guide from the Internet please read carefully the "Important Note" on pages 36–38 of this guide. The links and the updates pages are not publicised to reserve them only for the readers of this Guide.

The Internet allows us to rapidly access information from almost anywhere in the world on practically every subject. The organisations involved in humanitarian volunteering are quite certainly a primary use of the Internet. Non-profit organisations in developing countries have little funding and considerable demand for communicating their calls for assistance, their needs, their public awareness campaigns, the collection of funds and, as concerns our field, their need for volunteers. After understanding which activity sector, the type of work, the country of destination, and the motivation behind volunteering, the Internet becomes a great tool in finding the most suitable volunteer opportunity.

Search-engines, links to other sites, and, for constant information without having to navigate the Internet, select organisation newsletters are valuable tools for researching volunteer opportunities.

Practically every organisation, be it small or large, has a website. The volunteer positions are nearly always listed in the menu under the sign "Get involved!" or "How to help us". Most often, after a section dedicated to fundraising, there is a section concerning volunteering, both locally and at national headquarters. The national and international NGOs, which mostly run financed or co-financed cooperation projects, have a section dedicated to "Personnel search". In this case they are looking for qualified or specialised professionals to be hired on a contract basis (longer periods) in cooperation projects in developing countries. Therefore, answer these announcements as you would answer any employment offer: send a CV and wait for the answer (which may not arrive). As in all searches for employment it is advisable to send your CV to as many associations as possible. There are sites specialising exclusively in personnel searches for non-profit organisations.

The Internet is a fundamental tool for widening the search field and finding less competitive organisations.Naturally, the Internet is also quite useful in finding an association with which to perform local volunteering. Use a good search engine and look for "association + volunteering + the city name" to quickly find nearby associations. A good way to find workcamp organisations is to use a search engine and type in the key word "workcamp" and the country name.

Most of the websites of the organisations listed in this Guide are useful and often provide good links, however, we have chosen to make available to the reader a wide variety of useful websites which we have included in a link page of our website, accessible only to those who have purchased this Guide, which we will update periodically. The address of our links (for updates, please see pages 36-38) page is:

www.worldvolunteers.org/links.html

Below we have highlighted a few websites from organisations already listed in the Guide as well as selecting (as an example of what can be found in our website) a certain number of additional websites that may link you to hundreds of associations all over the world. The following websites should not be overlooked:

www.idealist.org
In our opinion, number one: the site with the largest data base of associations in the world, divided by sector of intervention and country; one can subscribe to a newsletter to receive the announcements of searches for volunteers, or even for professional persons on the part of associations listed in the data base.

www.avso.org
The site of the AVSO, Association of Voluntary Service Organisations, with links to all associated organisations.

www.alliance-network.org
The site of the Alliance of European Voluntary Service Organisations, a group of several European NGOs offering workcamps.

www.vfp.org
The site of Volunteers for Peace; it has a list of workcamps with opportunities in 80 countries.

www.oneworld.net
The international site of the Oneworld organisation; it lists volunteering opportunities offered by organisations all over the world, job opportunities, and links to all other Oneworld websites.

www.cnvs.org
The site of the Catholic Network of Volunteer Service; it has an excellent page of linked Catholic volunteering organisations both in the USA and elsewhere.

www.netaid.org
This site is already mentioned in "Volunteering from home" (page 12). Even for those not interested in doing volunteer work with their computer from home this is an excellent resource with several links.

www.interconnection.org
The site of an organisation of "virtual volunteers"; it has several links and information for volunteering opportunities all over the world.

www.volunteer.org.nz
A New Zealand-based site that offers volunteer programs through partner organisations; it includes information about post secondary education in development.

www.volunteermatch.org
A US-based database of volunteering opportunities for local non-profit and public organisations. Run a search by entering a zip code, then sort according to interest. Well organised, with icons to represent opportunities for different age groups. Excellent for local volunteering opportunities.

www.kabissa.org
A non-profit organisation that seeks to further democratic change and social justice in Africa by providing a space on the Internet for the African non-profit sector. Features include volunteering opportunities, NGO directory, newsletters, and more. It is an excellent directory of organisation for volunteering in Africa.

www.visionsinaction.org
This site has excellent suggestions for raising funds for voluntary work.

www.nonprofitcareer.com
Volunteering and job opportunities in the non-profit market, mainly in the US. Includes a job centre, directory of non-profit organisations, and information on

workshops, conferences and job fairs, and a good list of volunteering organisations.

www.icva.ch
The website for the International Council of Voluntary agencies—a global network of human rights, humanitarian, and development NGOs, which focuses its information exchange and advocacy efforts primarily on humanitarian affairs and refugee issues. Great links to agencies worldwide, newsletters, and more. International Council of Voluntary Agencies. Good page of links worldwide.

www.ugandamission.org
The website of Mission to East Africa. The focus of this site is world missions, particularly in Uganda, East Africa, where they are based. There are over 1500 links to helpful Internet sites, including overseas missions, recent news articles, and extensive research topics.

www.bond.org.uk
BOND is a network of more than 250 UK-based voluntary organisations working in international development and development education. The site includes a current issues section, an extensive directory, a discussion room, and more. The website of a membership body for organisations engaged in international development work overseas or in the UK.

www.acfid.asn.au
An informational website for the Australian Council for International Development, that provides an overview of human rights activities in Australia It has an excellent directory, with links, to Australian Aid Organisations, as well as links by topic.

www.oneday.takingitglobal.org
A directory of 1514 international organisations. Browse by subject or by region and get a brief synopsis of the organisation or link to their website.

www.voluntario.org.br
Recife Voluntário - Centro de Voluntários do Recife   A well done website, with many links to partner organisation for volunteering all over Brazil. Only in Portuguese, English "under construction".

www.youthactionnet.org
An excellent website with many volunteering and job opportunities for young people all over the world.

www.volunteerafrica.org
A simple and friendly website providing many links and advice for volunteering in Africa.

www.ngovoice.org
Voluntary Organisations in Cooperation in Emergencies within the Liaison Committee of NGOs to the European Union. VOICE is the largest European network of non-governmental organisations (NGOs) who are active in the field of humanitarian aid.

www.nvoad.org
National Voluntary Organizations Active in Disaster, Cooperation, Communication, Coordination, Collaboration in Disaster Response. A very useful infocentre, of many US organisations.

www.americorps.org
The official website for the domestic Peace Corps, excellent resource for getting involved in local community, cooperation for the National Service, and programmes for senior citizens, and more.

www.csv.org.uk
Community Service Volunteers (CSV) provides opportunities for all young people to volunteer full-time helping in communities throughout the UK.

www.charitypeople.com
A very large database in the UK for finding a job in the Non-profit world, ideal for people who return!

www.ihe.org.uk
The website and magazine "The Health Exchange" for Health Professionals Interested in Working in Developing Countries!

www.nursingabroad.net
Extremely useful website with medical and nursing positions worldwide.

www.servenet.org
Excellent for finding volunteering positions in the US with excellent links. Through SERVEnet, users can enter their zip code, city, state, skills, interests, and availability and be matched with organizations needinghelp. SERVEnet is also a place to search for calendar events, job openings, service news, recommended books, and best practices.

www.miusa.org
As a US-based national non-profit organisation, the mission of Mobility International USA (MIUSA) is to empower people with disabilities around the world through international exchange, information, technical assistance and training, and to ensure the inclusion of people with disabilities in international exchange and development programs.

www.volunteerabroad.com
US website appropriate for Young people and students.

www.worldvolunteerweb.org
Extremely informative and updated UN Internet portal on worldwide volunteer resource established as a continuation of the International Year of the Volunteers (2001) web site. The site is maintained by UNV (see listing), the United Nations agency for Volunteering.

www.citizens4change.org
A very informative website from a group of Canadian organisations, with excellent information on how to choose a project and for pre-departure preparation.

www.isp.msu.edu/NCSA/volteer.htm
A substantial list of Organisations (both African and not) offering volunteering opportunities in Africa, with contacts and description, compiled by the National Consortium for Study in Africa at the Michigan State University

www.aboutistc.org/iaewep/contact_members.html
List Student travel organisations in 26 countries, members of The International Association for Educational Work Exchange Programmes (IAEWEP). Good for contacting the organisation in the desired country directly.

www.reliefweb.int/w/rwb.nsf
The website of the United Nations Office for the Coordination of Humanitarian Affairs (OCHA). It features a vast Directory of Humanitarian Organizations and a very updated and resourceful list of professional vacancies.

www.developmentgateway.org/
The website of the Development Gateway Foundation. It has a very good directory of current development project in every country.

HOW TO READ THE GUIDE

World Volunteers is a directory. It lists organisations of different natures offering volunteering opportunities in developing countries. The Guide gives examples of the different kinds of opportunities but it can not be considered comprehensive. If an organisation of interest can not be found among the organisations listed, the section dedicated to resources on the Internet gives the reader the possibility of finding hundreds or thousands of additional organisations. Organisations are listed in alphabetical order. Should an organisation have an acronym, as many do, the organisation is listed in alphabetical order by the acronym. For example, MSF (Médecins san Frontières), UNV (United Nations Volunteers), and EVS (European Voluntary Service) are listed alphabetically by their acronym.

At the end of the Guide, there is an Appendix with two analytical tables. The first table lists the geographical area of the projects of each organisation in the Guide. It also indicates whether the organisations run workcamps or offer non-professional or short-term opportunites (up to 3 months). The second table lists the sectors of activity for each organisation.

Meaning of recurrent acronyms:

NGO: Non-governmental Organisation

EU: European Union.

Meaning of abbreviations

For each organisation the Guide lists:

The **address** and the **telephone** and **fax** numbers with the international codes. Remember to change the local area code according to the country's telephone system. For example, to call the UK (listed as ++44 (20) XXXX-XXXX), people calling from the UK should not dial ++44 (the international code), but should add 0 (zero) before 20 (the local area code). Calling from Europe add 00 before 44 to call the UK, whereas from the US only dial 011, then 44, the international access codes from the US to the UK. **E-mail** and World Wide Web (**www**) addresses are listed where available. Some organisations in developing countries do not have a website: it can be useful to ask via e-mail if they have implemented one since the printing of this Guide. If not, a prospective volunteer with good computer skills can help this organisation to make one: it is a good way to begin volunteering and an excellent introduction to the organisation. Organisations who do not have a website, therefore do not have their e-mail address linked to a domain name and tend to change their e-mail address quite often. If, after a reasonable number of solicitations an organisation does not answer to the e-mail messages, or a message bounces back, a search with the most common Internet search engines (such as google, altavista, or yahoo) or a quick phone call or fax will indicate whether a new e-mail address exists. It is also possible to send an e-mail message to an organisation from the same country or of the same sector, which probably knows the organisation in question. If an organisation exists and still operates, it is always possible to trace it through the Internet, and with a bit of investigation it is always possible to find the new coordinates. The reader should also realise that projects are dynamic and details such as sectors, costs and benefits, project duration, start and finish dates, or countries in which the organisations operate may vary from year to year. New projects arise and old projects may end. Periodic verification of the websites of interest is highly recommended.

Desc.: This section is the description of the activities and main objectives of an organisation, along with some general information on their history, partnerships, or other information relevant to prospective volunteers. Information on specific projects run by the organisation may be elaborated.

Sector: This section helps show the scope of the organisations' actions by describing the sectors in which the organisations operate. At the end of the Guide there is an Appendix with an analytical index, formatted as a table, to allow the readers to easily select organisations operating within their sectors of interest. The difficulty of this categorisation has been the grouping of various definitions in order to standardise the categories. Therefore when, in our opinion, it has not been possible to include an area of action of a given NGO in one of the specific categories chosen, we have introduced the category: various. Unfortunately, it may be that an organisations listed may have specific sectors not outlined in the Guide. It is also easy to see how many sectors overlap: for example, a project that works with the rights of women can be considered to be working in the sectors of women's issues, education, human rights, child welfare, skills training, and even agriculture. Therefore, the reader should not consider this classification rigid or absolute, and should contact or consult the website of the organisations of interest to confirm the full scope of the project and whether it works in a sector that has not been classified here.

Agriculture: Farming projects, irrigation, livestock breeding, treatment and processing of products and crops, and shipping to markets of the final products or commodities. Relevant professions vary from agronomists to veterinarians to hydrologists.

Child welfare: The defence of children rights for shelter, education, nutrition; protection against abuse or violence, prevention of child labour and exploitation; assistance with orphanages; providing attention to street children; or prevention of child prostitution.

Community Development: The development of all products and services that foster a sound and peaceful coexistence of a community. The promotion of grassroots organisations, small entrepreneur unions, sport groups, basic democracy, public administration, economic organisation, etc.

Construction: The constructions of public or private buildings, schools, hospitals, etc., urban planning and servicing a community, such as the planning and construction of water and sanitation systems.

Culture: Ranges from intercultural exchange and awareness to archeological preservation.

Education: Basic literacy and language courses, hygiene and health education, social skills, technology, and computers.

Emergency: Short term immediate actions, disaster relief such as after an earthquake or other natural disasters, or initial response to refugees from a conflict.

Environment: Natural resources, pollution treatment and cleanups, solid and organic waste management, forestry, wildlife management, protected areas management, aqua-culture, etc.

Health: Basic healthcare; specialist medicine; health education and HIV/AIDS awareness; nutrition and hygiene; or first aid.

Housing: Homelessness, building homes, etc.

Human rights: This is a broadest sector and includes the defence and monitoring of human rights. These rights are legal as well as emotional and encompass prisoners' rights, torture prevention, labour and workers rights, as well as the rights of the elderly or disabled.

Hunger relief: Distribution of food in famine situations.

IT: Information Technology and communications, which also includes media.

Peacekeeping: Peace monitoring actions.

Refugee aid: Logistic assistance, providing food and shelter, health and administrative assistance, repatriation, and reconstruction of living conditions for refugees of political, conflicts, natural disasters, etc.

Religious: Religious worship, assistance, or practice; it usually pertains to the missions although it also may be a Christian organisation with a spiritual element that is not evangelical or a working component of the project.

Sanitation: Sewage treatment, potable water, etc.

Skills training: May or may not be exclusively related to working to earn a salary. Skills taught may be personal financing or economics, craftsmanship, trades, computers, etc.

Small-enterprise development: The development of basic entrepreneurial efforts, including small shops or retail activities, community services, small craftsmanship activities, farm products manufacturing or processing, or small lodging, restaurants, and guiding services within a sustainable tourism context. Included within the small-enterprise development is micro-credit development, which is a fundamental tool for enterprise development.

Women's issues: Work towards raising the role of women in their societies, women's rights in submissive conditions, family planning, creation of women's organisations, protection from physical violence, etc.

Various: Anything that does not fall in the previous classifications, such as tourism, and specific trades or professions that would be listed under qualifications.

Country: Countries are grouped by continent. For cultural and geographical activity Mexico is included with Latin America instead of North America and the Caribbean is a separate group. The Middle East is kept distinct from the rest of Asia. Projects in Oceania, due to the small number of countries, are few, whereas those in Europe take place mostly in Eastern Europe. Organisations finish and start new projects continuously, and therefore the list of countries is extremely dynamic. It is recommended to verify with the organisation directly or with their website that the country of interest has a project currently taking volunteers.

Qualif.: The qualifications and skills required of a volunteer who wants to join a project. As a general rule for the workcamps no special qualifications are needed, other than a strong motivation and enthusiasm. Adaptation to harsh work, basic accommodation and little comfort is almost always required. For professional volunteering (whether short, medium, or long term) volunteers are chosen according to their qualifications. Therefore, the major qualifications required by an organisation are specified. These requirements however, must be considered dynamic, particularly for larger organisations. Active organisation have many projects at different phases, and start new ones continuously, therefore new professional skills are always needed. Smaller organisations tend to specialise in a specific field, and therefore tend to select mostly specific professional figures. For organisations hiring young graduates, if they do not have a technical preparation, it is difficult to identify them with a professional qualification, which will be acquired with years of experience. In this case someone's motivation, maturity, ability to work autonomously are taken into consideration, because of the great dedication needed to live and work for a few years in a very different country from what a recent graduate is used to. Often candidates for long-term volunteering are exposed to specific training courses by the sending NGO. These courses focus on the local culture, language, and specific aspects of the organisation and the projects the volunteers will be involved with. Often also qualified professionals are required to attend these training courses particularly if they don' have previous experience in working in developing countries.

Nonpro: This abbreviation stands for 'non-professional'. It indicates whether or not non-professional or unskilled volunteers are accepted by organisation. All organisations providing workcamp opportunities by definition accept non-professional volunteers. Many NGOs accept recent graduate students for long-term positions or internships in order to introduce them to a career in international development with training opportunities. Other organisations, particularly those in developing countries, may accept short-term volunteers with experience or skills in activities and industries such as fundraising, managerial, or computer.

Age: Some projects impose a minimum and maximum age on the volunteer profile. Typically the minimum age is 18 for workcamps or generic volunteer positions. Minors may be accepted for certain programs or with a guardian. Seniors are almost always accepted unless the physical demands of the project are considered too high. Where a specific professional is needed the age becomes irrelevant and experience the more appropriate criteria for acceptance.

Duration: The duration of the volunteering period can span from weeks to months or years. Typically, workcamps last two weeks to one month at the most, short-term volunteering up to three months, middle-term volunteering is six to twelve months, and long-term volunteering can last well beyond one year.

Lang.: This important section states the languages that are required for a volunteer to work on a project. The importance of communicating with the project staff or with other local or international volunteers should not be overlooked. Often another international language (such as Spanish, Portuguese, or French) is used. It is very important to be able to speak at least a few words of the local language, especially when volunteering in the health sector. Prospective volunteers should never underestimate the importance of this aspect and never overestimate their ability to understand a foreign language in a working environment. It is often expected that long-term volunteers learn the local language in order to be more integrated in the project. Even a professional and experienced volunteer may not be accepted to a project if the foreign language needed is not spoken. In general, for unskilled volunteers, such as those participating in workcamps, English is sufficient.

Benefits: Volunteers working overseas receive many of the benefits provided in the private sector, but obviously with much lower standards. The benefits can vary greatly between the workcamp, short-term (professional or unskilled), and middle- or long-term volunteering situations. Middle or long-term volunteers often receive a salary, which will depend on the experience. It may seem to be a contradiction in terms to be a "paid" volunteer, but it is a necessity: Very few people can afford to leave home for months or years and return without any money, especially if the volunteers are young (and have little savings) or older with a family to support. NGOs therefore must offer a salary , even low, otherwise it would be very difficult to recruit the personnel to run the projects. Many NGOs, when possible, hire mostly local staff, but it is difficult when the necessary skills are not locally available. In many other cases, NGOs have projects funded by large Inter-Governmental organisations or National aid agencies, such as the EU (European Union) or USAID (US Agency for International Development), which bear most or part of the costs, including salaries. The European Union, or better the European Commission (which is the Government of the Union) has a DG (General Directorate, the Ministries of the Commission) devoted to development cooperation: the DG VIII. In general salaries for long-term volunteers are not very high except the ones for skilled professionals when the projects are co-financed. Volunteers are helped by the fact that they have little or no expenses, that international travel is often reimbursed, and room and board are part of the benefits, or, if room and/or board are not supplied, the cost of living in general in developing countries is very low. Therefore the salary, for a long-term volunteer, is in large part saved and it can be a small sum available for when a volunteer returns home. Other benefits can be, as already mentioned: international travel, room and board, travel allowances for family members or more. Co-financing institutions usually have set contracts that clearly spell out all the benefits for the volunteers; NGOs working in co-financed projects must follow these contracts for their personnel hired within these projects. The conditions for short-term volunteers are different, particularly if they are hired with individual agreements: the benefits depend exclusively on what is stipulated. International and/or local travel, room, board, and a small stipend (or "pocket money") may be paid. The organisations do appreciate volunteers who can afford to forego any of the benefits or personally fund any of the project costs. Skilled professionals who can afford the time and expenses should not hesitate to contact the organisation they would like to volunteer for, if they think that their skills can be used. NGOs in developing countries (the Guide lists a few dozen) may only provide room and board.

Costs: The costs that a volunteer incurs are what are obviously not covered in the benefits. Long-term professional volunteers with a co-financed contract will usually only pay their personal expenses; short-term volunteers and volunteers for local NGOs, with or without individual contracts, will usually bear all the costs (travel, room, and board) that the NGO can not pay, and may have to provide a donation, whereas participants to workcamps, have usually to pay for travel and a participation fee, which usually covers the costs of room and board, and often can also be a contribution to the project itself.

Applic.: This section briefly describes the application procedures required by the organisation. Applications may or may not require a CV (curriculum vitae or resume), letters of recommendation, or whether the prospective volunteer must fill out an on-line or printed application form, etc. When communicating with organisations in developing countries it is advisable to use e-mail, if they have it, because of the low cost and the velocity. However, some projects in Africa may have problems receiving e-mails, so it is recommended to telephone these organisations if the e-mail receives no response.

Notes: This section gives relevant additional information. For example if the organisation requires participation to pre-selection meetings or training courses, if they have local groups or international branches, or if a prospective volunteer must become member of the organisation before applying, etc.

TIPS FOR CONTACTING AN ORGANISATION

Having a copy of **World Volunteers** has been the first step. Below are some suggestions to help you find the organisation most suited to your interests and be accepted on their project.

1) **Have clear in mind what you want to do, the sector you prefer, the geographical location, the duration of your volunteering period, and the costs you can afford.** This will help you select and reduce the number of organisations you need to apply to. If you have a limited amount of time, leave out from your selection the organisations that only take long-term volunteers; vice-versa, if you want to work long-term, omit the organisations that don't offer this possibility. If you are professionally qualified in a specific field, and you think that your skills may be useful, look specifically for organisations in your sector where you would best be able to use your qualifications. Conversely, do not consider organisations that do not need your skills. A good approach can be to select a list of organisations and divide them into your first and second priorities. The first priority should include the organisations that are of primary interest to you, the second should include the organisations you would volunteer for only under certain circumstances; then start contacting both groups systematically.

2) **Use the fastest possible method to contact an organisation.** Remember that interesting projects or organisations also have many applicants, and they usually fill their available positions on a first come, first serve basis. Therefore, you want to be as fast as possible in letting them know that you are interested in taking a position with them. Do not lose time by sending a letter by regular mail, unless you are required to do so, but immediately start sending e-mails, even if only as preliminary enquiries. E-mail is usually a good way to make a first contact with an organisation and get to know who they are without being too committed. It is also a good idea to verify before applying whether or not you have a good chance to be accepted. If not, do not waste time, go on to the next organisation on your list. Should you not receive a reply within 3–5 days, be prepared to send reminders or telephone them to confirm their e-mail address or verify whether or not it is worth continuing your application process with them, particularly if it requires filling out lengthy forms.

3) **Inform the organisation you would like to work for about yourself as much as possible.** With your request for information, send a description of

your skills and interests and possibly a CV—which you always have ready so it would not be a waste of time to attach it. Always enclose a cover letter and ask if in addition to the CV other information about yourself is required. Make the cover letter and the CV as professional as possible. In the cover letter in particular stress your professional capacities, and do not exceed in "emotional" or personal aspects. A letter stressing the fact that you want to run away from the consumerist world because you think that in a poor developing country you can better find your role in life will be judged very negatively. You want to volunteer to help others; not yourself! You want to share your professional experiences not your desire to escape!

4) **If an organisation is in a developing country, make it easy for them to respond to you**. Remember that organisations in poorer countries often are short of funds. Therefore, help them by enclosing self-addressed stamped envelopes should you exchange regular mail (for example you may need an original letter in their stationary paper to obtain the Visa). Always enclose one or more international postal reply coupon(s) as a form of courtesy, even if you are not required to do so. You may also offer an organisation to fax you collect (give them an appointment, because in order to receive a fax collect you should first be able to answer vocally, accept the call, then switch on the fax mode). Better still, since a fax goes both ways regardless of who calls, you can offer to call the organisation on their fax line and have them fax back the information. Remember that you should arrange this over the phone. If you interact with a large organisation, well equipped for recruiting volunteers, they will have all the means to contact you.

5) **Do exactly what is required by an organisation for being accepted.** If they require you to complete their application form, whether it is sent to you or whether you download it from their website, do fill it out, even if you have already submitted your detailed CV. Compile in a proper and clean manner both the CV and a cover letter, which you should always enclose. Should you be required to send material by regular mail, never hand write, not even the cover letter, unless you are required to do so. If you apply with an organisation where the official language is not English but another major international language that you will be expected to use if accepted by them, send at least the cover letter in this language and be prepared to translate your CV if necessary. Many organisations with workcamp programmes, often require an advanced deposit or membership to their organisation. If accepted, do not miss an opportunity by not paying a deposit on time. Inquire about the fastest method to transfer funds: by international telegraph money order, credit card, money wire from bank to

bank, etc. Finally, many organisations require preliminary meetings or training courses if you are accepted. You should obviously attend regularly.

6) **Contact many organisations.** Select an organisation, or a specific project, well in advance. Properly planning your vacation or time in advance will allow you to find the best airfares and select the best period suitable to you. Get detailed information on what to expect: the type of work, accommodation, food, climate, clothing, equipment necessary, etc. Owing to a lack of space this information can not be included in the organisations' description in the *World Volunteers* Guide. The Guide aims to give a general overview of a given organisation and give you tools to find many others. Never show up at a project location without having first applied and having been accepted and confirmed. Most projects have limited positions, lodging and personnel. Very rarely are they equipped to take on an unexpected volunteer. If you want to do so, because you were already travelling in a certain area, do not be disappointed if you are rejected.

Good luck with your "World Volunteering"!

IMPORTANT NOTE

The Editors and the Publisher of **World Volunteers** do not endorse nor support any of the organisations listed in the guide; our intention is simply to present the reader with the widest possible choice to meet his or her interests and skills. Further and more detailed information about the organisations listed should be obtained directly by the reader from the organisations they wish to join. The Editors and Publisher of **World Volunteers** have also decided, both in order to offer prospective volunteers the widest possible choice and to help these extremely needy organisations, to cite, whenever possible, small organisations, particularly in developing countries, for the following reason:

1) **To allow extremely poor organisations to receive the help from volunteers** from developed countries and thereby use their valuable skills. We think that we should help this local grassroots potential as best we can, particularly if it comes directly from local organisations without an input from large organisations in the developed world.

However, prospective volunteers should consider that:

2) **Small organisations in developing countries often allow volunteers to come without excessive screening, and this may result in a negative experience for both the volunteer and the organisation.** We therefore recommend prospective volunteers to evaluate their own personal level of experience, both in travelling and in working abroad, and their capacity to live in extremely poor, remote, disorganised, and sometimes also unsafe conditions.

3) **A volunteer joining an organisation in a developing country directly, may find an excessive level of disorganisation, if judged by Western standards, that may not be perceived by the organisation's leaders. This may result in the volunteer being unable to conduct the task for which he or she has joined the organisation.** In such cases, particularly if the volunteer judges that his or her help can not be useful to improve the situation, we highly recommend the volunteer to leave the organisation, without incurring in further costs or frustrations. In addition, we always recommend that the prospective volunteer carefully verifies the working conditions by reading the following instructions.

BEFORE JOINING PROJECTS AND ORGANISATIONS, PROSPECTIVE VOLUNTEERS SHOULD CAREFULLY READ THE FOLLOWING CONSIDERATIONS AND WARNINGS:

1) **Because of obvious cost reasons**, which would then reflect on the sale price of this book, **the Editors and the Publisher cannot personally visit every project or organisation** listed in this guide but have to trust what projects and organisations (or their websites, previous volunteers, or references cited by the organisations) declare.

2) **Small projects and organisations**, particularly in developing countries, mainly owing to a shortage of funding or qualified personnel or because of conflicts and emergency situations, **often change their programs or even interrupt their activities without informing the Editors and Publishers of this guide.**

3) **Before joining an organisation volunteers should carefully verify the validity of the information declared** in the project website (if one exists) or reported in this guide or its updates. To obtain annual updates of this guide from the Internet, readers must type the address of our webpage (see page 19), by replacing the words links.html with /updates/

4) **Prospective volunteers, before joining an organisation, should exchange frequent e-mails, or even fax or phone calls, with the organisation leaders** and ensure that communication is always prompt and clear. They should also confirm the project details, such as the living, working, and safety conditions, prior to departure.

5) **Prospective volunteers (before joining small projects or organisations directly, particularly in developing countries) should ask for names and addresses of previous volunteers and for international references to subsequently correspond with** to further verify the working and safety conditions.

6) **Volunteers should never join an organisation by going directly to the location** without previous correspondence and verification of existing conditions.

Before joining any project or organisation prospective volunteers should carefully read the Warning on page 3 and the Important Note on pages 35–36.

ORGANISATION LIST

Aang Serian 'House of Peace'

PO Box 13732
Arusha Tanzania
Tel.: ++255 (755) 744-992
E-mail: aang_serian@hotmail.com or enolengila@yahoo.co.uk
www.aangserian.org.uk

Desc.: Qualified teachers are needed to teach English, Mathematics and/or Science at Aang Serian Noonkondin Secondary School, Monduli District, Tanzania. Volunteers are also needed for other projects in rural Maasai communities, such as construction, tree planting, small business development and reproductive health education. In Arusha volunteers help with research and curriculum development on a variety of topics including appropriate technology and sustainable agriculture. For secondary school teachers a commitment of at least 6 months is preferred, starting in January or July. Other placements can start at various times of the year and can be of flexible duration. The rural posts are community based and provide a unique opportunity to participate in the local culture.

Sector: Community development, construction, education, environment, small-enterprise development.

Country: Africa (Tanzania).

Qualif.: Teaching qualifications for secondary school posts, no particular skills required for other projects, initiative and adaptability are important requisites.

Nonpro: Yes, with relevant skills to the project.

Age: Minimum 18.

Duration: 2 months to 1 year, depending on project.

Lang.: English.

Benefits: Accommodation and food, orientation, Swahili lessons.

Costs: Volunteers make a financial contribution of around GB£400 (US$700) for 3 months.

Applic.: References and CV/resume are required and a US$100 deposit is payable on application.

Abha Light Foundation

PO Box 471-00606, Nairobi, Kenya
Tel./Fax: ++254 (20) 445-0181 (or ++254 723869133)
E-mail: info@abhalight.org
www.abhalight.org

Desc.: Abha Light Foundation is concerned with improving and maintaining the health of the people primarily using homeopathy, complementary and alternative medicines and health practices through health training programs and homeopathic and natural medicine mobile and permanent health clinics to further the well being and health of Africans in an economical and safe way. Homeopathic medicine can be very cheap and easily distributed by a qualified homeopath. The immediate goal is to provide medicine for the poor through mobile clinics. The long-term goal is to introduce homeopathy and other complementary medicines into Africa as part of the health-care solution for the people.

Sector: Health.

Country: Africa (Kenya).

Qualif.: Homeopaths (3–5 years students are possible if they can hold their own in case-taking and prescribing), acupuncturists, naturopaths, and other complimentary therapists.

Nonpro: No.

Age: Over 20. Qualifications is more required.

Duration: 6-8 weeks is recommended. Long-term (3-12 months) is welcome.

Lang.: English and Swahili. Translators are available.

Benefits: Accommodation. Unusual clinical experience.

Costs: US$800. This fee covers all usual expenses in Kenya.

Applic.: On-line form (www.abhalight.org/volunteer.html)

ACDI/VOCA

50 F Street, NW, Suite 1075, Washington, DC 20001 USA
Tel.: ++1 (202) 638-4661 (or toll free in N. Am. 1-800-929-8622)
Fax: ++1 (202) 783-7204
E-mail: volunteer@acdivoca.org
www.acdivoca.org

Desc.: ACDI/VOCA is a private, non-profit organization promoting economic development and civil society in emerging democracies and developing countries. ACDI/VOCA delivers technical assistance to address the most pressing development problems. Driven by the goal of adding value to local enterprise, ACDI/VOCA works in the following areas: Community Development, Enterprise Development, Financial Services, and Agribusiness Systems. Since 1997, volunteers have donated over $27 million worth of their time to ACDI/VOCA and their overseas partners. In recent years, approximately 300 volunteers have served each year on ACDI/VOCA volunteer assignments.

Sector: Agriculture, community development, environment, small enterprise development.

Country: Africa, Asia, Europe, Latin America and the Middle East.

Qualif.: ACDI/VOCA volunteers typically are mid-career and senior professionals in their respective fields and donate 2-4 weeks of their time and talent to work side by side with farmers and entrepreneurs who are pushing for economic progress and democratic reforms around the world. Volunteer assignments require individuals with at least 10 years of experience in one or more of the following fields: Accounting, Agricultural Extension and Education, Banking and Finance, Business Management, Community Development, Cooperative and Association Development, Domestic and International Marketing, Enterprise Development, Entrepreneurship, Farm Management, Food & Meat Processing, Food Storage & Handling, Fruit, Vegetable and Plant Production and Protection, Grain & Commodity Inspection and Storage, Information Technology and E-commerce, Livestock Production and Disease Control, Manufacturing, Natural Resources Management and Ecotourism, Policy Reform, Post Harvest Handling, Rural Credit, Sustainable Agriculture, Trade Associations, and Training of Trainers.

Nonpro: No.

Age: Enough to gain the required experience.

Duration: Volunteer assignments typically range in length from two to four weeks (a few long-term assignments are also available).

Lang.:   English.

Benefits: Employment opportunities updated on website.

Costs: Inquire with the organization.

Applic.:   On-line form.

Notes: ACDI/VOCA volunteer opportunities for non-US citizens are limited. Visit website for more information.

Action Against Hunger UK

First Floor, Rear Premises, 161-163 Greenwich High Road, London, SE10 8JA UK

Tel.: ++44 (20) 8293 6190

Fax: ++44 (20) 8858 8372

E-mail: jobs@aahuk.org

www.aahuk.org

Desc.:	Action Against Hunger UK works to fight hunger in 43 of the world's poorest countries by providing for people's immediate needs when food is scarce, and just as importantly by providing families with the tools, seeds and support they need to build a sustainable future.
Sector:	Agriculture, community development, health, hunger relief, sanitation.
Country:	Action Against Hunger works in some 43 countries worldwide. See website for a list.
Qualif.:	Nutritionists, nurses, water and sanitation experts, agronomists, administration and food security officers.
Nonpro:	N/A
Age:	N/A
Duration:	One year contracts.
Lang.:	Working knowledge of English with French or Spanish.
Benefits:	Salary depending on experience, all in-field expenses paid, as well as transportation, room and board, living expenses, per diem and full insurance package, including war risk, emergency evacuation, and medical.
Costs:	No cost to the volunteers.
Applic.:	Send on-line form and a CV to the appropriate headquarter. **Action Against Hunger New York**: info@actionagainsthunger.org; **Accion Contra el Hambre Spain**: ach@achesp.org; Action Against Hunger **UK**: jobs@aahuk.org; **Action Contre la Faim France**: recrutementvolontaires@actioncontrelafaim.org.

Adarsh Community Development Trust

Door No. 6-4-504 Maruthi Nagar
Anantapur 515 001 Andhra Pradesh, India
Tel.: ++91 (8554) 274-492 or 240-122
E-mail: info@adarshcommunitydevelopment.org
www.adarshcommunitydevelopment.org

Desc.:   This Charitable Social Organisation was formed in 1982 by a group of enthusiastic and dedicated men and women who shared a deep concern and desire to serve the less fortunate and vulnerable people in and around of Anantapur District. The organisation headquarters are located in Anantapur and the District headquarters in the Rayalaseema region of Andhra Pradesh. The organisation has been working for the welfare of disadvantaged peoples for over 2 decades. Since late 1983 the organisation has been working with the assistance of the Christian Children's Fund (CCF) with 3,500 families throughout several in the Anantapur District.

Sector: Child welfare, community development, environment, sanitation, small-enterprise development, women's issues.

Country: Asia (India).

Qualif.:   Water management/irrigation professionals and small enterprise and alternative livelihood experts desired.

Nonpro.:   Yes.

Age: 18–40.

Duration: Minimum 2 weeks.

Lang.:   English.

Benefits: Accommodation, internal transportation.

Costs: Travel, insurance and living expenses.

Applic.:   Contact the organisation.

Notes: Once accepted the applicant will be put in contact with former volunteers who have been selected as Representatives in various countries. Please see Note on page 35.

AFS International

71 West 23rd Street, 17th Floor
New York, New York 10010 USA
Tel.: ++1 (212) 807-8686
Fax: ++1 (212) 807-1001
E-mail: info@afs.org
www.afs.org

Desc.: AFS is an international, voluntary, non-governmental, non-profit organisation that provides intercultural learning opportunities to help people develop the knowledge, skills, and understanding needed to create a more just and peaceful world. The worldwide network is run mostly by volunteers who connect to their community to place exchange students, community service students and teachers in host families.

AFS Community Service Program Participants volunteer with local organisations that address community needs such as environmental education and improvement, early child development or developing Human Rights programs. During the program, participants are exposed to new customs and values that challenge them to reflect on their own cultural norms. This intercultural learning process develops in participants not only a deeper understanding of another culture but, perhaps most profoundly, a richer awareness of their own background. AFS Educator Programs provide opportunities for teachers to live and work in countries around the world. Short programs allow teachers and administrators to travel abroad during their school holidays, to meet and work with other educators. Semester and year-long programs give teachers and administrators the opportunity to have in-depth cultural and pedagogical experiences. AFS Educator Programs include cultural lessons and events, family home stays, observation of local educational practices and teaching in schools in the host country.

Sector: Child welfare, community development, culture, education, environment, health, housing.

Country: AFS has partner offices in more than 50 countries around the world. Consult website for contact information.

Qualif.: All volunteers welcome. For participating in programs, see website for qualifications specific to program and country.

Nonpro: Yes.

Age: Minimum 18. School-based exchange programs offered for students aged 12—18.

Duration: 1–4 months to 1 year.

Lang.: According to country.

Benefits: Round-trip airfare, orientation, language training, health insurance. Check with nearest AFS representative for the fees for the preferred destination.

Costs: The sending country sets costs that vary with the length of program and the destination. Australia's average cost for one year program: US$ 7,500. United States average cost for one year program: US$ 7,500. Merit or need-based scholarships are available in some countries. A number of corporations offer scholarships to the children of their employees. Approximately 20% of AFS students worldwide receive partial financial assistance for their experience. Cost vary by country, please consult specific county AFS website

Applic.: Contact local AFS office (see website).

Notes: Volunteers must be sent through the AFS organisation in their country of citizenship.

AFSAI – Association for Training and Inter-Cultural Activities and Exchange

Viale dei Colli Portuensi 345, B2, 00151 Rome Italy
Tel.: ++39(06)537-0332
Fax: ++39(06)5820-1442
E-mail:info@afsai.it
www.afsai.it

Desc.: AFSAI started over 40 years ago when a group of young people decided to start an organisation with the goal of fostering intercultural exchange between young people from different countries. AFSAI is one of the Italian partners of EVS (see listing) and regularly organises workcamps.

Sectors: Community development, culture, education, environment, human rights, skill training, various.

Country: Various countries in Africa, Asia, Europe (European Union and Eastern Europe), Latin America, the Middle East.

Qualif.: No qualifications are necessary.

Nonpro: Yes. Volunteers must show flexibility, maturity and be willing to be fully engaged in a project with strong cultural, environmental, health, and/or social implications.

Age: 18–30 for Overseas Voluntary Service and EVS; minimum 18 for the workcamps.

Duration: 6–12 months for EVS. Shorter programs (3 weeks to 6 months) possible; 3–4 weeks for workcamps.

Lang.: Basic knowledge of English for the workcamps. For long-term programs volunteers receive language and cultural training upon arrival.

Benefits: Food, accommodation, travel costs and pocket money depending on the program.

Costs: None for EVS; travel plus a participation fee for Overseas Voluntary Service and for workcamps (EUR100–300).

Applic.: Form can be found on-line or requested to AFSAI.

Notes: Membership to AFSAI (approx. EUR 30 per year) necessary.

AFSC – American Friends Service Committee

Mexico Summer Project
1501 Cherry Street, Philadelphia, Pennsylvania 19102 USA
Tel.: ++1 (215) 241-7295
Fax: ++1 (215) 241-7026
E-mail: mexicosummer@afsc.org
www.afsc.org/mexicosummer.htm

Desc.: The Mexico Summer Project, now in its sixty-ninth year, brings together youth from diverse communities to live with Indigenous people in Mexico. The Mexico Summer Project offers the mind-blowing experience of witnessing and learning from different lifestyles, of experiencing community to create changes.

Sector: Community development, culture, various.

Country: Latin America (Mexico).

Qualif.: N/A.

Nonpro: Yes. Experience in service and advocacy and interest in political, social, and cultural issues in Latin America.

Age: 18–26.

Duration: Exact dates vary yearly, but runs between June and August.

Lang.: Fluent Spanish.

Benefits: Fees waived for co-facilitators. Some scholarship are available.

Costs: The project fee is US$1,350. US$150 (non-refundable) is due upon acceptance and the remainder 6 weeks prior to project start date. Participants are responsible for travel and personal expenses.

Applic.: By mid-March with notice given by early April. Waiting list until end of April.

Notes: Remote living conditions. Spanish interview and a physical exam is required.

AID India

9, Rice Shop Street, SATAKULAM - 628 704
Thoothukudi District, Tamilnadu India
Tel.:/Fax: ++91 (4639) 267519
Mob.: ++ 91 (94425) 29442
E-mail: avemariapeter@yahoo.com
www.humanistaidindia.org

Desc.: AID India supports socio-economic development programmes for women and people with disabilities, a child adoption programme, an orphanage, a "She Home" for girls, a project called "Humanize the Earth" in collaboration with Energy for Human Rights, Rome, vocational training programmes for disabled and dhalit girls, health projects in villages, a farm for agricultural development, counselling to the differently abled people, child development centres in villages, etc.

Sector: Agriculture, child welfare, community development, construction, education, environment, health, human rights, religious, skills training, small-enterprise development, women's issues.

Country: Asia (India).

Qualif.: A strong motivation to work as a volunteer with poor people/children, differently able people, etc..

Nonpro: Yes.

Age: Any age is welcome (min. 18).

Duration: Depends on the volunteer: it can be arranged according to the volunteer's needs.

Lang.: English.

Benefits: Free simple accommodation and food in a family situation, a separate accommodation is also available for free.

Costs: Volunteer has to bear all the travel costs and personal expenses a donation to AID India is appreciated but not at all compulsory.

Applic.: On-line form.

Notes: The volunteer is expected to work with enthusiasm and a friendly attitude. Volunteer can collaborate even after going back to their countries. If the volunteers are able to raise funds for the project, it will be highly appreciated.

AJUDE – Youth Association for the Development of Voluntary Service in Mozambique

Rua da Mesquita 222, Flat 11, 1st floor, Maputo, Mozambique
Tel./Fax: ++258 (1) 312-854
E-mail: ajude@tvcabo.co.mz
www.ajude.org.mz

Desc.:	AJUDE was born during the post-civil-war period in Mozambique, when the region faced deep transformations. The need of strengthening awareness, solidarity, and exchange between populations were the main motivations for the creation of the organisation. In Mozambique, the economic and social reconstruction and the reconciliation between Mozambicans constituted an important challenge, that's why young Mozambican students were the pioneers in this area, and through their actions AJUDE was created in 1995.
Sector:	Child welfare, community development, culture, construction, education, emergency, environment, health, human rights, women's issues.
Country:	Africa (Mozambique).
Qualif.:	No particular qualifications needed.
Nonpro:	Yes.
Age:	Minimum 18.
Duration:	2 weeks for workcamps and from 4 weeks to 12-months long terms volunteer placement opportunities in local institutions/organizations/ projects.
Lang.:	English, Portuguese, Spanish, etc.
Benefits:	Room and board, return transport from Maputo to the workcamp site, pick up from and to he airport/bus station. Local families host volunteers for projects of 3 months or more.
Costs:	Approx. US$210 for 2 weeks, up to US$3,000 for one-year projects. International airfare is not included.
Applic.:	On-line form or on request.
Notes:	Please see note on page 35.

AJWS – American Jewish World Service

Volunteer Corps
45 West 36th Street, 11th Floor
New York, New York 10018 USA
Tel.: ++1 (212) 792-2900 (toll free in N. Am. 1-800-889-7146)
E-mail: volunteer@ajws.org
www.ajws.org

Desc.: American Jewish World Service (AJWS) is an international development organization motivated by Judaism's imperative to pursue justice. AJWS is dedicated to alleviating poverty, hunger and disease among the people of developing world, regardless of race, religion or nationality. Through grants to grassroots organizations, volunteer service, advocacy and education, AJWS fosters civil society, sustainable development and human rights for all people, while promoting the values and responsibilities of global citizenship within the Jewish community. AJWS Volunteer Corps places professional Jewish women and men on volunteer assignments within local NGOs in developing countries. Volunteers come from a variety of backgrounds and provide skills training, technical consultancy and general support. VC volunteers range in age from young professionals to retirees, and share a passion for service and a commitment to social justice.

Sector: Agriculture, education, health, small-enterprise development.

Country: Africa (Uganda, Ghana, South Africa, Senegal), Americas (Guatemala, Nicaragua, Honduras, El Salvador, Peru, Mexico, Dominican Republic), Asia (India, Thailand, Cambodia). AJWS volunteers are occasionally sent to countries not listed above.

Qualif.: Applicants to AJWS Volunteer Corps should have at least several years of work experience; many are advanced professionals in their fields. Please visit the website for more details on qualifications and eligibility.

Nonpro: Yes.

Age: Minimum 21.

Duration: 2 months to 1 year, with the average volunteer serving 2-3 months.

Lang.: With the exception of placements in the Americas and some parts of Africa, all assignments only require English language abilities.

Benefits: Enquire with the organisation.

Costs: There is no program fee to participate in AJWS Volunteer Corps AJWS pays for volunteers' airfare and provides emergency evacuation assistance and medical referrals. Volunteers are financially responsible for health insurance and in-country cost-of-living, including housing, food and local transportation. These costs vary greatly based on location of service.

Applic.: On-line form or request application directly from the organisation. There is no application fee. After Volunteer Corps receives and reviews a completed application, an in-person or telephone interview will be arranged. Three written references will be required. Applicants will be notified in a timely fashion if a position is available.

Alive Foundation

P.O. Box Ks. 3656
Kumasi-Ghana
Tel: ++233 (51) 63199
Mob.: ++233 (244) 221876 Fax: ++233 (51) 37379/26643
E- mail: alivefoundation@yahoo.co.uk or alivefoundation@hotmail.com
www.alivefoundation.kabissa.org

Desc.: Alive Foundation offers placement to skilled volunteers/students who want to have a work placement in Ghana during a gap year under the Internship programme. This programme gives both young and old volunteers/students the opportunity to serve in their various fields of specialization. A variety of placements are offered such as teaching, healthcare delivery, orphanage work, journalism/media work, conservation work, HIV/Aids education, law practising and women empowerment.

Sector: Agriculture, child welfare, community development, education, environment, health, IT, women's issues, various.

Country: Africa (Ghana).

Qualif.: Both professional and non-professional volunteers are welcome.

Nonpro: Yes.

Age: Minimum 18.

Duration: 3–12 weeks; all year round.

Lang.: English.

Benefits: Food and accommodation, airport pick up and drop-off, incountry orientation, 24 hour staff support.

Costs: From US$650 to US$1,650 depending on programme and duration.

Applic.: On-line form to be sent in by fax mail or sent as e-mail attachment.

Notes: Yellow fever immunisation required; Hepatitis A and B, typhoid/typhus, meningitis, rabies, and diphtheria recommended. See Note on page 35.

Alliance Abroad Group

1221 South Mopac Exwy, Suite 250 Austin, Texas 78746
Tel.: ++1 (512) 457-8062 (toll free in N. Am. 1-866-6ABROAD)
Fax: ++1 (512) 457-8132
E-mail: outbound@allianceabroad.com
www.allianceabroad.com

Desc.:	The Alliance Abroad Group has been providing educational experiential travel programs for over 10 years. The Group offers a wide range of programs in countries all over the world, and can customize each program to fit the needs of the participants. The programs offer the opportunity to gain valuable experience in another country, learn about different cultures, gain work and interpersonal skills, and in some cases, earn money to support the volunteers. Volunteer projects vary, but all are committed to the conservation of the environment, fair trade and the improvement of the living standards of the communities and their members.
Sector:	Agriculture, child welfare, community development, culture, education, environment, health, small-enterprise development.
Country:	Latin America (Costa Rica, Ecuador, Peru, Argentina, Chile)
Qualif.:	Willingness to contribute and help communities.
Nonpro:	Yes.
Age:	Minimum 18.
Duration:	1 week – 1 year. Programs run throughout the year, and allow to start at any time.
Lang.:	English.
Benefits:	Accommodation, food, in-country transportation, travel insurance, guaranteed placements, staff support.
Costs:	Varies by program and length of stay.
Applic.:	Applications can be found on-line. Application should be submitted at least 2 months before the desired departure date.

Amaudo UK

Regent House, 291 Kirkdale, Sydenham
London SE26 4QD UK
Tel.: ++44 (20) 8776-7363
Fax: ++44 (20) 8776-7364
E-mail: amaudouk@btconnect.com
www.amaudouk.org

Desc.: Amaudo UK aims to support Amaudo Nigeria in achieving its goal of eradicating homelessness amongst mentally ill people by implementing systems of sustainable mental healthcare in Nigeria. Amaudo UK also supports Amaudo Nigeria in their work to care for and rehabilitate those who have become homeless through mental illness. Amaudo UK achieves this through awareness raising, assisting volunteers and visitors to visit the project, providing resources such as medical supplies, information and technology, co-managing projects, co-ordinating supporters and donors in the UK. Volunteers require the necessary experience to teach local people skills so as to increase the quality of the service provided to people with mental health problems.

Sector: Health, human rights.

Country: Africa (Nigeria).

Qualif.: Mental healthcare professionals and managers, psychiatrists, CPNs, OTs, Physioterapists, health service delivery managers, etc.

Nonpro: Possible without formal qualifications but with appropriate experience.

Age: No age restriction.

Duration: Minimum 6 months.

Lang.: English, spoken and written.

Benefits: Various different volunteer programmes.

Costs: Contact the organisation.

Applic.: Request application form available from Amaudo UK - amaudouk@btconnect.com

Amazon - Africa Aid Organization

PO Box 7776 Ann Arbor, Michigan 48107 USA
Tel.: ++1 (734) 426-1300
Fax: ++1 (734) 378-4044
E-mail: info@amazonafrica.org
www.amazonafrica.org

Desc.: Amazon-Africa Aid is a nonprofit organization with a goal "to ensure that every person in the regions we work has access to and is provided with the proper health care and education experience that will enable him/her to lead a healthy and happy lfe". They send qualified dental health professionals to the Brazilian Amazon region to provide quality treatment in support of the dental clinic to the very poor. They support the Fundaçao Esperança, a Brazilian nonprofit organiwation providing health care and education in the Amazon region for over 30 years. Volunteers are always needed, year round.

Sector: Child welfare, education, environment, health.

Country: Latin America (Brazil).

Qualif.: The dental clinic depends on volunteer dentists and physicians. The organiwation cannot accept physicians or other medical professionals while it negotiates an agreement with the Brazilian Medical Council which will allow volunteers to practice medicine under Brazilian Law.

Nonpro: See Amizade at www.amizade.org

Age: 26 or older.

Duration: 2 weeks to 3 months. Minimum 2 weeks.

Lang.: Portuguese spoken and Spanish helpful.

Benefits: Food, lodging, laundry, and airport transfers in Santarém. For Rotary volunteers, some costs may be covered by Rotary.

Costs: Volunteers arrange and pay for travel to and from Santarém and pay for their own Visa (contact the organisation for assistance and details).

Applic.: Send a brief CV, copies of professional licenses and diplomas, and a copy of the passport. In approximately 3 to 6 weeks, a status for entry to practice in Brazil will be given and volunteers can then proceed with flight and visa arrangements

Notes: Contact home country embassy and Amazon-Africa Aid for Visa, vaccinations and medical insurance information. The cost is US$25/day for room and board for non-volunteers.

AMIGOS – Amigos de las Américas

5618 Star Lane, Houston, Texas 77057 USA
Tel.: ++1 (713) 782-5290
(toll free in N. Am. 1-800-231-7796)
Fax: ++1 (713) 782-9267
E-mail: info@amigoslink.org
www.amigoslink.org

Desc.: Founded in 1965, AMIGOS is a non-profit organisation that provides young people exceptional leadership training and volunteer service opportunities in the US and Latin America, in public health, education, and community development.

Sector: Child welfare, construction, culture, education, environment, health.

Country: Latin America (Brazil, Costa Rica, Dominican Republic, Honduras, Mexico, Nicaragua, Panama, Paraguay, Uruguay).

Qualif.: No specific qualification required.

Nonpro: Yes.

Age: Minimum 16. Aimed at youth (high school and college students).

Duration: 4–8 weeks.

Lang.: Minimum of 2 years of high school Spanish or Portuguese.

Benefits: AMIGOS volunteers have the opportunity to experience cultural traditions, learn new skills and make life-long friends.

Costs: The program fee is approximately US$3,995. It includes: international airfare, training material, project supplies, food, lodging and transportation in Latin America, emergency communication services, fund raising assistance and international insurance. Volunteers are nonetheless required to carry their own health insurance. Transportation to regional workshops or the US departure city not included.

Applic.: Send the on-line registration form, CV, and a US$40 application fee by March 15. A telephone interview will follow.

Notes: A 3-day workshop prior to departure is required. Regional workshops are conducted in the spring in some US cities. Workshops may also be conducted in the US departure city immediately prior to leaving for Latin America.

Amizade, Ltd.

PO Box 110107
Pittsburgh, PA 15232, USA
Tel.: ++1 (412) 441-6655
Fax: ++1 (757) 257-8358
E-mail: volunteer@amizade.org
www.amizade.org - www.globalservicelearning.org

Desc.: Amizade empowers individuals and communities through intercultural service and learning around the world.

Sector: Community development, construction, education, environment, various.

Country: Africa (Ghana, Tanzania), Caribbean (Jamaica). Europe (Germany, Northern Ireland, Poland), Latin America (Bolivia, Brazil), North America (USA, Mexico).

Qualif.: No qualifications needed.

Nonpro: Yes.

Age: Minimum 18; need a parent or guardian to accompany if 12-17.

Duration: 1 week-1 year.

Lang.: English.

Benefits: Comprehensive programming includes long-standing community-driven service partnerships, a local site-director, room and board, recreation and local learning, project materials and on-site transportation.

Costs: Fees vary by program and begin near US$750.

Applic.: On-line.

Notes: Amizade offers programs for groups of six or more, individual field placements, individual service-learning placements for university credit and service-learning courses for university credits. Group programs include alyternative spring breaks, opportunities for high school groups, church groups, schools, families and more. Service Learning Courses confer credits through West Virginia University and involve an integrated experience of academic learning, community-driven service, intercultural immersion, consideration of global citizenship and reflective inquiry. Credits tipically transfer to other institutions.

Amnesty International

International Secretariat
1 Easton Street, London WC1X 0DW   UK
Tel.: ++44 (20) 7413-5500
Fax: ++44 (20) 7956-1157
E-mail: info@amnesty.org.uk
www.amnesty.org

Desc.:   Amnesty International is a worldwide campaigning movement promoting all the human rights enshrined in the Universal Declaration of Human Rights and other international standards. It campaigns to free all prisoners of conscience; ensure fair and prompt trials for political prisoners; abolish the death penalty, torture, and other cruel treatment of prisoners; end political killings and "disappearances"; and oppose human rights abuses by opposition groups. Activities encompass public demonstrations, letter-writing, human rights education, fundraising, individual and global appeals.

Sector: Human rights.

Country: Worldwide. Consult website for country of interest. The International Secretariat's program is only in the London office.

Qualif.:   The Health Professional Network comprises individuals, groups, and networks of doctors, nurses, mental health specialists, and other health professionals. Other professional job placements are posted on the website regularly but are mostly with the International Secretariat based in the UK.

Nonpro: Consult website for volunteer opportunities in country of interest.

Age: Restrictions may apply.

Duration: Minimum 8 weeks full time or 3 months part time in London. Other work and volunteer opportunities may vary in duration.

Lang.:   English and/or local language of placement.

Benefits: Consult the organisation directly. In the US, The Patrick Stewart Human Rights Scholarship is for students interested human rights work for summer internships or short-term projects.

Costs: Expenses vary with each country and volunteer opportunity.

Applic.:   Directions provided from the national office offering the work.

AMURT Global Network

6810 Tilden Lane, Rockville, MD 20852 USA
Tel.: ++1 (301) 984-0217
Fax: ++1 (3) 984-0218
E-Mail: info@amurt.us
www.amurt.net

Desc.:	AMURT (Ananda Marga Universal Relief Team) is one of the few private voluntary organisations of Third World origin, being founded in India in 1965. Its original objective was to help meet the needs of victims of disasters that regularly hit the Indian subcontinent. Over the years AMURT has established teams in 80 countries, to create a network that can meet development and disaster needs almost anywhere in the world. AMURT works in communities providing individuals with education and training to give them self-reliance and self-esteem. AMURTEL is a program that works with destitute women, orphans, the handicapped, addicts, and the elderly, and the victims of war, natural calamities and crippling disease.
Sector:	Child welfare, community development, education, housing, hunger relief, sanitation, small-enterprise development, women's issues.
Country:	Africa (Burkina Faso, Congo, Ghana, Kenya, Mozambique, South Africa), Asia (India, Mongolia, Philippines, Thailand), Carribean (Haiti), Europe (Albania, Kosovo, Romania).
Qualif.:	Teachers welcome, homeopaths needed for certain projects, engineers, agricultural scientists.
Nonpro:	Young graduates may be accepted.
Age:	Enquire with organisation.
Duration:	Negotiable, enquire with organisation.
Lang.:	English, other languages depend on destination.
Benefits:	None.
Costs:	US$200 for short-term (2—3 months) and US$350 for long-term. Volunteers are responsible for all expenses—food, travel, medical, etc., during their stay.
Applic.:	E-mail CV and enquiry about volunteer opportunities.
Notes:	See website for contacts in other countries.

APA-Onlus

Amici Per l'Africa - Friends for Africa
Via Lapini 1 - 50136 Firenze, Italy
Tel.: ++39 (0332) 831660
Fax: ++39 (0332) 831664
E-mail : amiciperafrica@libero.it
www.amiciperafrica.it

Desc.: APA-Onlus originates from the experience of a group of friends, medical doctors, dentists, dental technicians, hygienists, nurses, assistants, who decided to help, in their spare time, African populations with poor or lacking dental care. APA volunteers work principally in missions where a dental chair is present. Currently APA has 5 projects in Kenya, 2 in rural hospitals and 3 in religious health centers.

Sector: Health.

Country: Africa (Kenya).

Qualif.: Dentists, dental technicians, hygienists, nurses, assistants. Volunteers must have at least 2 years of professional experience after-graduation. Must be motivated, flexible and professional. Non medical volunteers are accepted only with useful skills for the missions.

Age: No age limits, depends on the experience.

Duration: At least on month. Longer periods are possible. Volunteers who can commit a short period each year are preferred.

Lang.: English.

Benefits: The organization offers room and board.

Costs: Annual membership (EUR50), travel (to Africa and one for a personal interview in Italy), personal expenses and insurance.

Applic.: Online application form. Telephone interviews. At least one personal meeting near Milan will be required. Interest applicants can call or e-mail Dr. Rodolfo Piana (chairman) at the number and e-mail address above, or Dr. Dino Azzalin (Vice President).

Notes: The Milan area can be easily reached with low cost flights from the main European towns.

ARC – American Refugee Committee

430 Oak Grove Street, Suite 204
Minneapolis, Minnesota 55403 USA
Tel.: ++1 (612) 872-7060
Fax: ++1 (612) 607-6499
E-mail: archq@archq.org
www.archq.org

Desc.:	ARC works for the survival, health, and well being of refugees, displaced persons, and those at risk, and seeks to enable them to rebuild productive lives of dignity and purpose, striving always to respect the values of those served. ARC has provided multi-sector humanitarian assistance and training to millions of international beneficiaries for over 25 years.
Sector:	Child welfare, construction, education, emergency, environment, health, refugee aid, sanitation, small-enterprise development, women's issues, various.
Country:	Africa (Liberia, Rwanda, Sierra Leone, Darfur-Sudan, Southern Sudan, Uganda), Asia (Pakistan, Thailand).
Qualif.:	Minimum 1 year professional experience in development work.
Nonpro:	No. Unpaid internships in Minneapolis Headquarters and overseas positions may be available.
Age:	Dependent upon experience.
Duration:	Most positions require a 1-year commitment with the option to extend based upon mutual agreement.
Lang.:	English.
Benefits:	Usually a small stipend, housing (group) and evacuation insurance.
Costs:	Travel, health insurance, visa costs and personal expenses.
Applic.:	All positions are online. We only accept applications at www.acrelief.org
Notes:	Recruitment is very competitive. See website for details.

Australian Volunteers International

PO Box 350
71 Argyle Street, Fitzroy Victoria 3065 Australia
Tel.: ++61 (3) 9279-1788 (toll free in Australia 1-800-331-292)
Fax: ++61 (3) 9419-4280
E-mail: info@australianvolunteers.com
www.australianvolunteers.com

Desc.: Australian Volunteers International (AVI) deploys professionals from a range of occupations to share skills and build relationships with people of developing communities around the world. AVI volunteers help to build the capacity of local organizations to deliver services to the people that need them. They work on an equal level with their local colleagues and live within their host communities.

Sector: Agriculture, community development, construction, culture, education, environment, health, human rights, IT, sanitation, skills training, small-enterprise development, various.

Country: Africa (Lesotho, Malawi, South Africa, Swaziland, Tanzania), Asia (Cambodia, China, India, Indonesia, Maldives, Philippines, Sri Lanka, Thailand, Vietnam), Middle East (Lebanon, Syria), Pacific (Cook Islands, Micronesia, Fiji Islands, Kiribati, Marshall Islands, Niiue, Palau, Papua New Guinea, Samoa, Solomon Islands, Tonga, Tuvalu, Vanuatu), Australia.

Qualif.: Profession, trade, or commercial qualification with relevant experience.

Nonpro: Yes. Short-term, team-based youth projects for 18-25.

Age: Minimum 18. No upper age limit set, and AVI welcomes applicants aged 50+.

Duration: The majority of volunteer assignments for 12 months, with some 3-12 months. Youth assignments are 6-10 weeks.

Lang.: Language training provided if needed.

Benefits: Return airfare, pre-departure briefings, and medical insurance. Volunteers receive living and accomodation allowances. Some projects roles reimbursed at market rates.

Costs: Personal expenses. Youth Program is self-funded by participants.

Applic.: All assignments available online at www.australianvolunteers.com/work. Subscribe on website to receive email notifications of new assignments.

Notes: Australian citizens and permanent residents only.

AVSO – Association of Voluntary Service Organisations

174, Rue Joseph II
1000 Bruxelles Belgium
Tel.:++32 (2) 230-6813
Fax:++32 (2) 231-1413
E-mail: info@avso.org
www.avso.org

Desc.:   AVSO forms a European platform for national and international non-profit organisations active in the field of longer term voluntary service. They lobby for the legal status of volunteers and enhanced mobility within Europe and aim to broaden participation in voluntary service among new organisations in non-profit sector and among individuals who may traditionally not have access to volunteer opportunities (disabled, socially/ economically disadvantaged, and ethnic minorities).

Sector: Community development, culture, education, environment, human rights, various.

Country: Avso members have projects worldwide.

Age: 18–25 (18-13 for the "Youth in Action" program).

Duration: 6–18 months, depending on the organisation.

Lang.:   Language and intercultural training provided.

Benefits: Accommodation, food, small stipend, appropriate insurance against illness and accidents, other benefits in accordance with the status of a volunteer.

Applic.:   Contact project organisation.

Notes: Residents of the European Union or an applicant country only. AVSO does not itself organise volunteer exchange programs, applicants should contact directly the AVSO members listed in the website.

AYAD – Australian Youth Ambassadors for Development

c/o Austraining International
Level 1, Dequetteville Terrace
Kent Town, SA 5067 Australia
Tel.: ++61 (8) 8364-8500 (toll free in Australia 1-800-225-592)
Fax: ++61 (8) 8364-8585
E-mail: info@ayad.com.au
www.ausaid.gov.au/youtham or www.ayad.com.au

Desc.: The Australian Youth Ambassadors for Development (AYAD) program is an Australian Government, AusAID initiative which supports skilled young Australians who want to live, work and make a difference in the Asia Pacific region. The aim is to strengthen mutual understanding between Australia and the countries of the Asia-PAcific region and make a positive contribution to sustainable development.

Sector: Community development, construction, education, environment, health, sanitation, women's issues.

Country: Asia Pacific region.

Qualif.: No particular skills required. Previous volunteer work, coaching a sporting team, mentoring in the workplace, travel and a demonstrated interest in working in a developing country may count.

Nonpro: Yes, with skills beneficial to the project.

Age: 18—30.

Duration: 3—12 months (departing March, June or September).

Lang.: Volunteers should learn the local language but all assignments will be with English speaking counterparts and supervisors.

Benefits: It is a fully-supported program; it includes pre-departure training, medical examinations and vaccinations, comprehensive insurance, return airfare, living and accommodation allowances, post placement medical examinations and debrief on return from assignment.

Costs: AYADs Youth Ambassadors should incur no costs.

Applic.: Application Cover sheet, CV (3 pages max.), 2 references, photographs and passport documentation, filled criminal history check form, copies of qualifications. See website for downloading and details.

Notes: Australian citizens only. Police and medical check required.

Balkan Sunflowers

Prishtina Office, Youth, Culture and Sports Hall #114
Prishtina, Kosovo/a
Tel.: ++381 (38) 246-299 or ++377 (44) 501-819
Fax: ++381 (38) 246-299
E-mail: office@balkansunflowers.org
www.balkansunflowers.org

Desc.: Balkan Sunflowers implemented hundreds of projects from day-long events and celebrations to long-term education programs, campaigns, and television series. Program emphases currently are education support in Roma communities, volunteer activism, and media as a vehicle for social changes. Balkan Sunflowers' mandate is to promote understanding, further non-violent conflict transformation, and celebrate the diversity of the lives and cultures of the Balkan region.

Sector: Child welfare, community development, culture, education, environment, human rights.

Country: Europe (Albania, Macedonia, Kosovo/a).

Qualif.: Specific skills are required for some project placements.

Nonpro: Yes.

Age: Minimum 21.

Duration: Minimum six months.

Lang.: English. Local language skills are assets.

Benefits: Accommodation, food, basic insurance, travel to the project sites, and office costs. Orientation and on-going training provided. Some SCI (see listing) branches provide training sessions.

Costs: Many volunteers come through the European Voluntary Service (EVS). If a potential volunteers is not eligible for EVS, then we will advise on raising funds to support volunteering. For more information, check the website or contact the office.

Applic.: On-line form e-mailed directly to the project or via the relevant SCI branch.

Notes: Applications can be submitted via SCI branches (see listing).

BERDSCO – Benevolent Community Education and Rural Development Society

House N° 15, Federal Quarters, P.O.Box 368, Buea, South West Province, Cameroon
Tel.: ++ (237) 9627-8884
Fax: ++ (237) 3332-2543
E-mail: berdsco_65@yahoo.com
www.berdsco.org

Desc.: Founded in 1990 as a non-governmental organisation (NGO), non-political, non-profit and non-religious society and recognised by the Government of Cameroon in Sept. 1993. Gained special consultative status with the economic and social council of the United Nations in July, 2001. BERDSCO was created to alleviate poverty and hunger among the rural poor, especially women. The aims are to improve living conditions, create awareness to help integrate women in development activities, carry out programs on environmental education and sustainable development, and sensitise the public on issues of health and drug abuse, addiction, and misuse. The NGO is also active in diagnoses of community diseases, awareness programme on HIV/AIDS pandemic and setting up of community HIV/AIDS Control Committees.

Sector: Agriculture, community development, education, environment, health, small-enterprise development, women's issues.

Country: Africa (Cameroon).

Qualif.: The following expertises are particulalrly needed: Microfinance (deep knowledge of poverty, development issues and income generating activities, finance or business studies), Consultancy and Project Proposals (skills in project conception and grant proposal development for projects of NGO and feasibility studies), Prevention (education in community health, skills in fundraising and project proposal), Training of Local People (skills in the identification of training needs, facilitation and reporting), Environmental Development (skills in environmental education of forestry and wildlife, proposal development and reporting), Teaching (professional skills and experience in teaching in primary school children from 6-12 years old), Agro-forestry (skills in forestry, agriculture or environment and project proposal skills), Research and Publishing (knowledge in research activities and development work, publishing for BERDSCO organization), Agriculture and Food Processing and Engineering (education in agriculture or food processing, skills in tropical agriculture would be advantage), Building Engineering (4 years of building experience), Agricultural Engineering (Master Degree in Agriculture, 4 years of working experience and specialized in sugar cane cultivation), Sugar Processing Engineering (processing engineers specialized in sugar processing),Industrial Consultancy (should be industrial consultant with experience in the field of agro-industrial projects and especially sugar cane into sugar projects).

Nonpro: Yes. Volunteers with strong motivation and desire to learn are welcome.

Age.: Minimum 18.

Duration: 6 – 24 months renewable if necessary.

Lang.: English.

Benefits: Volunteers gain new skills, learn new ways of life and cultures, gain experience on development issues and meet new friends.

Costs: Volunteers are responsible for rent, food, utilities and personal expenses. BERDSCO assists in finding housing. Volunteers may come in with their own equipment such as computers, vehicles and other equipment. Volunteers are accepted year round. Groups of 5 – 10 are also accepted.

Applic.: Applicants must send cover letter plus CV.

Notes: See Note on page 35.

BMS World Mission

PO Box 49, 129 Broadway
Didcot, Oxfordshire OX11 8XA UK
Tel.: ++44 (1235) 517-700 or 517-653
Fax: ++44 (1235) 517-601
E-mail: opportunities@bmsworldmission.org
www.bmsworldmission.org/opportunities

Desc.:	BMS World Mission currently supports approx 370 people serving overseas plus around 250 short-term volunteers each year. BMS teams combine high-energy people with the needs of the world and include summer teams, gap-year teams, student medical and language electives, and professional placements.
Sector:	Community development, education, emergency, health, IT, religious.
Country:	Over 40 countries across four continents (Africa, Asia , Europe, Latin America).
Qualif.:	Medical professionals, teachers, administrators, engineers and many more.
Nonpro:	Yes. Students, professionals taking unpaid leave, retirees.
Age:	Minimum 18. BMS Action Teams for ages 18-23.
Duration:	Two weeks to a lifetime. Summer and Professional teams go for between 2- 5 weeks, Action Teams (gap year) for 10 months (including 6 months overseas).
Lang.:	English.
Benefits:	Program expenses, flights, food, accommodation, insurance, Visa, training, and debriefing are in the project fee.
Costs:	Medical Teams approx. GB£1,200. Summer teams GB£850-1,600, Action teams GB£3,700. Vaccinations, travel to the airport and training centre, and spending money not included in costs. Individual volunteers are completely self-financing.
Applic.:	Download application form for different programs.
Notes:	UK residents only. Committed Christians recommended by local church. Criminal record and medical clearance required.

Brethren Volunteer Service

1451 Dundee Avenue, Elgin, Illinois 60120 USA
Tel.: ++1 (800) 323-8039 (toll free in N. Am.)
Fax: ++1 (847) 742-0278
E-mail: bvs_gb@brethren.org or dmcfadden_gb@brethren.org
www.brethrenvolunteerservice.org

Desc.:	Brethren volunteer service, a program of the Church of the Brethren, has emphasized working for peace, advocating justice and serving basic human needs since 1948. Volunteers give their time and skills to help find solutions to deep-rooted problems and to bring about an awareness and understanding of justice and peace.
Sector:	Agriculture, child welfare, community development, education, environment, health, housing, hunger relief, refugee aid, religious, various (elderly and disabled assistance).
Country:	Africa (Nigeria), Asia (Japan), Europe (Belgium, Bosnia-Herzegovina, France, Germany, Ireland, Netherlands, Serbia, Slovakia), Latin America (Dominican Republic, Guatemala, Honduras, Mexico), North America (United States).
Qualif.:	Generalists or persons willing to learn a new skill. If a volunteer wants to use their specific skill, the BVS office will try to help.
Nonpro:	Yes, with college degree or similar life experience. BVS also provides special orientation units for adults over 50 years.
Age:	Minimum 18, min. 21 for international placements.
Duration:	1 year for US placements, 2 years for overseas projects; this includes a 10-day to 3-week (depending on project) orientation.
Lang.:	English, other languages useful.
Benefits:	Accommodation (group, individual, on-site, or home-stay), monthly stipend, orientation, health insurance.
Costs:	US$500 fee for international projects. Volunteers provide their own transportation to the orientation site.
Applic.:	Deadline 6 weeks before each orientation. CV, photo and transcripts sent with application. Consult website for details.
Notes:	Overseas assignments for US and Canadian citizens only.

The Bridge Foundation

No. 8 Third Ringway, Ringway Estate
PO Box 13463
Accra, Ghana
Tel.:+233 (21) 229-933
E-mail: planet35@hotmail.com
www.thebrigefoundationghana.org

Desc.: The Foundation works in promoting human resource development. It focuses on assisting disadvantaged children or youth in deprived rural and informal peri-urban settlements, individually and collectively, to assert social values and skills required in improving their natural talents, especially in the fields of sports, literacy, and Information Communication and Technology (ICT). The organization is running a Youth Sports Development Resource Centre, comprising of a gymnasium, library, and ICT Training Unit. Also, engaged in environmental management and protection of a fishing village on the Atlantic Coast, west of Accra.

Sector: Education, environment, skills training, IT, religious.

Country: Africa (Ghana).

Qualif.: Teachers, environmentalist, volunteers with computer skills, sports coaches and like-minded organizations for partnership in projects in the above activities in Ghana.

Nonpro: Yes, with relevant skills.

Age: 18-45.

Duration: 3-6 and 12 months.

Lang.: English

Costs: Administrative costs of US$ 50. Volunteers must also budget US$10 per day for food and personal expenses. Personal expenses such as travelling for tourism, sites, entertainments are not included.

BUNAC

16 Bowling Green Lane
London, EC1R 0QH   UK
Tel.: ++44 (207) 251-3472
Fax: ++44 (207) 251-0215
E-mail: enquiries@bunac.org.uk or volunteering@bunac.org.uk
www.bunac.org

Desc.:	BUNAC is a non-profit member organisation promoting cultural exchange through work and voluntary work overseas.
Sector:	Agriculture, child welfare, community development, culture, education, environment, health, human rights, IT, small-enterprise development, women's issues, various.
Country:	Africa (Ghana, South Africa), Latin America (Costa Rica, Peru), Asia (Cambodia, China) and America.
Qualif.:	No qualifications needed.
Nonpro:	Yes.
Age:	Minimum 18.
Duration:	5 weeks—12 months.
Lang.:	English, Spanish language skills required for Peru and Costa Rica.
Benefits:	Group departures, in-country orientation, full support both in country and in the UK. Free time to travel at the end of the programmes.
Costs:	Participants must contribute towards travel, insurance and programme costs (fees range from GB£250 to GB£1500).
Notes:	Nationality requirements vary, however volunteers must be resident in the UK or Ireland. See www.bunac.org for full details of eligibility. Bunac has also an office in the USA (see website for details) and a partner organisation in Australia and New Zealand (IEP International Exchange Programs PTY Ltd (see websites: www.iep-australia.com and www.iep.co.nz).

BWCA – Bangladesh Work Camps Association

289/2, Work Camp Road, North Shajahanpur
Dhaka-1217, Bangladesh
Tel.: ++88 (2) 935-8206 or 935-6814 - Mob.: ++88 (0175) 021918
Fax: ++88 (2) 956-5506 or 956-5483 (Attn: BWCA)
E-mail: bwca@bangla.net
www.mybwca.org

Desc.: BWCA organises national and international workcamps, inter-cultural youth exchange programs, study tours, and leadership training on issues proclaimed by the UN/UNESCO towards establishing world peace. Being a member organisation of CCIVS (see listing), BWCA aims to expand and popularise workcamps around Bangladesh in collaboration with local partner NGOs. Volunteers may join local partner NGOs in on-going projects like assisting in the school/office work, motivational campaigns, and environmental/agricultural/construction activities.

Sector: Agriculture, construction, education, environment, health, IT.

Country: Asia (Bangladesh).

Qualif.: No qualification or experience. Specific project volunteers should have some practical and professional experience in physiotherapy, nursing, agriculture, teaching, computers, etc.

Nonpro: Yes.

Age: Minimum 18 - 35.

Duration: Short-term projects (workcamps) are 12–15 days; RTYP (Round the Year Program) projects are 3–12 months.

Lang.: English.

Benefits: Accommodation and internal transportation.

Costs: US$200 per camp and US$250 registration fee for the first 3 months (RTYP). US$50 per month for any additional period. The food charge is US$ 2.50 per day (additional charge for RTYP only).

Applic.: Apply through partner organisations in applicant's own country.

Individual applications are accepted only where there is no overseas partner organisation of BWCA with a payment of US$25.

Notes: Drugs and alcohol are prohibited. Couples are not accepted. BWCA also organizes special voluntary projects for groups from any overseas high school or university.

Canada World Youth (Jeunesse Canada Monde)

2330 Notre-Dame Street West, 3rd floor
Montreal, Quebec H3J 1N4 Canada
Tel.: ++1 (514) 931-3526 (toll free in Canada 1-866-786-9243)
Fax: ++1 (514) 939-2621
www.canadaworldyouth.com

Desc.: Canada World Youth (CWY) offers international educational programs to young people aged 17 to 24. With CWY, groups of 18 young people from different cultures leave their homes to spend a total of six months together—three in a Canadian community and three in a community in one of the partner countries. The participants live with host families and do volunteer work in the field. Each participant is also paired with a participant from the partner country for the duration of the program. Since 1971, close to 30,000 people from Canada and around the world have participated in CWY programs in 67 countries.

Sector: Agriculture, community development, education, environment, health.

Country: Canada and various countries in Africa, Asia, the Caribbean, Eastern Europe and Latin America.

Qualif.: No professional qualifications needed.

Nonpro: Yes.

Age: 17-24.

Duration: 6 months.

Lang.: English, French.

Benefits: Transportation, food, lodging, insurance and educational materials for the program.

Costs: A CAD$250 participation fee and pre-program expenses (passport, vaccinations, medical and dental exams). Each participant also has to raise at least CAD$2,100 (training and support for fundraising are provided).

Applic.: On-line form. For more information contact: recruitment@cwy-jcm.org or call 1(866)786-9243). See also website.

Notes: Canadian citizens or landed immigrants within age requirements, in good health, open-minded and flexible.

Canadian Crossroads International

317 Adelaide Street West, Suite 500
Toronto, Ontario M5V 1P9 Canada
Tel.: ++1 (416) 967-1611
Fax: ++1 (416) 967-9078
E-mail: info@cciorg.ca
www.cciorg.ca

Desc.:	Canadian Crossroads International (CCR) works with organizations in West Africa, Southern Africa and South America that are fighting poverty, women's inequality and HIV/AIDS. CCI brings these organizations into partnerships with Canadian organizations working on similar issues. Each year, CCI places skilled Canadian volunteers on work placements with its partners in the global South and brings staff and volunteers from its partners to Canada to work with Canadian organizations. Through these partnership projects, CCI leverages skills, expertise and resources to build the capacity of organizations to meet the needs of their communities and, in so doing, fosters solidarity internationally.
Sector:	HIV/AIDS, community economic development, women's rights.
Country:	Bolivia, Ghana, Mali, Niger, Senegal, Swaziland, Togo, Zimbabwe.
Qualif.:	Specific skill criteria are outlined in each job description.
Nonpro:	State skills on application to aid in placement.
Age:	Minimum 19 (18 in Quebec).
Duration:	Length of placements varies according to the projects, usually 4–6 months. Departure is in May, September, or December/January of the year of application.
Lang.:	English, French or Spanish.
Benefits:	Accommodation with host families, return airfare, and modest living allowance based on cost of living.
Costs:	CAD$1,000–2,000 depending on program. Fundraising support is provided by CCI.
Applic.:	Contact nearest Canadian Regional Office (see website, www.cciorg.ca).
Notes:	Canadian citizens or landed immigrants and staff and volunteers of Southern partner organizations only.

Casa de Los Amigos, A. C.

Ignacio Mariscal 132, Col. Tabacalera
Mexico DF, 06030   Mexico
Tel.: ++52 (55) 5705-0521/5705-0646
Fax: ++52 (55) 5705-0771
E-mail: amigos@casadelosamigos.org
www.casadelosamigos.org

Desc.: The Casa de Los Amigos is a 50 years old Quaker center for peace and international understanding. It also mantains a social justice oriented guest house in Mexico City. The Casa is largely run by volunteers.

Sectors: Community development, human rights, various (peace, non-violence, economic justice, hospitality).

Country: Latin America (Mexico).

Qualif.: Depends on the projects.

Nonpro: Yes.

Age: From 18 on.

Duration: Commitment of 3 months up to 1 year.

Lang.: Volunteers must speak Spanish.

Benefits: Full-time Casa volunteers receive a private room (possibly shared with one person), kitchen, laundry, internet, and use of all the facilities of the house.

Costs: Volunteers must cover their travel expenses to and from the Casa and their living expenses (about 6-10 dollars per day)..

Applic.: Send an inquiry to amigos@casadelosamigos.org.

Notes: Many people live in the Casa de Los Amigos, short and long term, while doing volunteer work with other organizations in Mexico City. Please contact the Casa for more informations.

Catholic Institute for International Relations - Progressio

Unit 3 Canonbury Yard, 190a New North Road
London N1 7BJ UK
Tel.: ++44 (20) 7354-0883
Fax: ++44 (20) 7359-0017
E-mail: enquiries@ progressio.org
www.ciir.org

Desc.: CIIR is an international development agency tackling poverty and exclusion and pursuing lasting change in policy and practice. It works with partner organisations and people of any or no faith. It offers a progressive Catholic perspective independent of church structures. Development workers might work with peasant farmers in the Caribbean to find markets for their products, set up HIV and AIDS counselling services in Africa, support local NGOs in the Middle East, or work with a women's group in East Timor.

Sector: Community development, education, environment, health, human rights, IT, skills training, small-enterprise development, women's rights, various.

Country: Africa (Somaliland, Zimbabwe), Asia (East Timor), Caribbean (Dominican Republic), Latin America (Ecuador, El Salvador, Haiti, Honduras, Nicaragua, Peru), Middle East (Yemen).

Qualif.: 2 years work experience in the above mentioned sectors, and preferably with experience in capacity building.

Nonpro: Yes.

Age: N/A with the necessary experience.

Duration: Minimum 1–2 years.

Lang.: Training in local language of host country provided.

Benefits: Local stipend plus home country and a discretionary dependants allowance, accommodation, return airfare, pre-departure grant, medical/accident insurance and national contributions for workers. Travel and lunch expenses for volunteers.

Costs: Personal expenses.

Applic.: For each post there is a job description and selection criteria. See website for openings. For volunteering at Progressio London office, send CV and covering letter explaining areas of interest and availability to: recruitment@progressio.org.uk.

Catholic Medical Mission Board

10 West 17th Street, New York, New York 10011 USA
Tel.: ++1 (212) 242-7757 (toll free in N. Am. 1-800-678-5659)
Fax: ++1 (212) 242-0930
E-mail: rdecostanzo@cmmb.org
www.cmmb.org

Desc.: The Catholic Medical Mission Board places healthcare professionals in clinical facilities in developing countries. Volunteers serve in hospitals and clinics in collaboration with the local healthcare staff.

Sector: Health.

Country: Africa (16 countries), Asia (7 countries), Eastern Europe (4 countries), Caribbean (5 countries), Latin America (12 countries).

Qualif.: All candidates should be currently licensed in the US or Canada and must present all educational and professional credentials for review.

Nonpro: No.

Age: Minimum 21, no maximum but in good health. Families accepted.

Duration: Short term: 2 weeks to several months. Long term: 1 year.

Lang.: Varies with project. Spanish necessary in Latin America.

Benefits: Room and board provided free to all volunteers. All volunteers receive coverage for medivac, malpractice, liability and life insurance and assistance with visas. Volunteers going for more years also receive full health insurance coverage, all travel expenses and a modest monthly stipend.

Costs: Immunization and prophylactic medications. Short term also need to pay for airfare.

Applic.: Request application form to be returned along with notary copies of licenses and diplomas, a physical examination form, a CV or resume, a passport-size picture and 3 letters of recommendation by regular mail.

Notes: Candidates must be licensed in the US or Canada. No opportunities for non-medical or medical students.

CCIVS – Coordinating Committee for International Volunteers

UNESCO House, 1 rue Miollis, 75015 Paris France
Tel.: ++33 (1) 4568-4936
Fax: ++33 (1) 4273-0521
E-mail: ccivs@unesco.org
www.unesco.org/ccivs

Desc.: CCIVS is an international non-governmental organisation that plays a coordinating role in the sphere of voluntary service. CCIVS has 250 members and branches in more than 100 countries. The aims of the CCIVS are to fight against the dangers of war, social and racial discrimination, underdevelopment, illiteracy, and the consequences of neo-colonialism; to promote international understanding, friendship, and solidarity as preconditions to firm and lasting peace on earth; to enable social and national development; and to establish a just international economic and social order. Volunteers from different countries live and work together on a common project to benefit the local population.

Sector: Construction, culture, education, environment, health, peacekeeping.

Country: Members are in over 100 countries in the 5 continents.

Qualif.: CCVIS members require volunteers with a broad spectrum of qualifications.

Nonpro.: Yes; many CCVIS members organise workcamps and seminars in above domains.

Age: Generally from 18 for non-professional volunteers, older for skilled volunteers.

Duration: 3–4 weeks. Projects for 1–6 months or 1–3 years are available.

Lang.: Local languages of the member organisations. Common languages are English, Spanish, French, and Portuguese.

Benefits: Contact the member organisations.

Costs: Contact the member organisations.

Applic.: Apply with member organisations directly.

Notes: No direct recruitment: volunteers have to contact organizations in their countries.

CECI – Canadian Centre for International Studies and Cooperation

3000, Omer-Lavallée, Montréal, Québec H1Y 3R8 Canada
Tel.: ++1 (514) 875-9911 Fax: ++1 (514) 875-6469
www.ceci.ca
UNITERRA Program
www.uniterra.ca
WUSC
www.wusc.ca

Desc.: Uniterra, the largest Canadian international volunteer program, is jointly operated by the Canadian Centre for International Studies and Cooperation (CECI) and the World University Service of Canada (WUSC) and is present in 13 countries. Uniterra offers Canadian citizens and organizations the possibility to make a contribution towards reaching the UN Millennium Development Goals (MDGs) and to address world poverty.

Sector: Community development, culture, education, health, small-entrprise development, various.

Country: Africa (Botswana, Burkina Faso, Guinea, Malawi, Mali, Niger, Senegal), Asia (Sri Lanka, Nepal, Vietnam), Central and South America (Bolivia, Guatemala).

Qualif.: Preference to candidates with a diploma or degree and professional experience.

Nonpro: A minimum of 2 years of professional experience in a developing country is often required. Each volunteer position is targeting specific competencies. Refer to the list of positions on the Uniterra website.

Age: Families are accepted and children may be covered if they are under 18 years of age. It is strongly recommended that dependants over 18 years of age (or who will reach this age during the assignment) do not accompany.

Duration: Positions range from 2 weeks to 2 years.

Lang.: English, French and Spanish. Multilingualism is an asset. Training in local languages may be provided.

Benefits: A monthly stipend is provided to cover basic needs, including accomodation and food. The totlal allowance is subject to changes depending on the cost of living in the host country and the numbere amount depends on the cost of living in the host country and the number of dependants. Travel expenses, vaccinations, and insurance are provided for the volunteer and the recognized dependents.

Costs: No required fees. Personal expenses only.

Applic.: Online applixcation form through the Sygesca database. The CECI and WUSC Recruiting Department will arrange a series of interviews once the potential candidate is selected. Before departure, chosen volunteers must complete a mandatory pre-departure training for 1 week. Allow for 3 months between the interview and departure date.

Notes: Canadian citizens and landed immigrants only.

CESVI – Cooperation and Development

Via Broseta 68/a
24128 Bergamo Italy
Tel.: ++39 (035) 205-8058
Fax: ++39 (035) 260-958
E-mail: cesvi@cesvi.org
www.cesvi.org

Desc.: CESVI, established in 1985, is an independent organisation working for global solidarity. CESVI believes in transforming the moral principles of human solidarity and social justice into humanitarian aid and development, reinforcing an affirmation of universal human rights. CESVI believes strongly that helping the underprivileged in developing countries, or those in difficulty due to war, natural calamities, and environmental disasters, does not only helps those who suffer, but contributes also to the wellbeing of all of us on the planet, our "common home" to be looked after for future generations.

Sector: Community development, construction, emergency, health.

Country: Over 30 countries in Africa, Asia , Europe, Latin America and The Middle East.

Qualif.: Professional qualifications necessary, e.g., engineers, medical doctors, etc.

Nonpro: No, professionally qualified personnel only.

Age: N/A with necessary experience.

Duration: 1–3 years; shorter term may be possible with private partners.

Lang.: English, French, Spanish, or Portuguese; it is expected that long-term volunteers learn the local language.

Benefits: All costs covered plus salary based on experience.

Costs: Covered by contract except personal expenses.

Applic.: On-line form.

Notes: Training is provided for all prospective volunteers.

CFHI – Child Family Health International

995 Market St. Suite 1104,
San Francisco, California 94103 USA
Tel.: ++1 (415) 957-9000
Fax: ++1 (415) 840-0486
E-mail: students@cfhi.org
www.cfhi.org

Desc.: Since 1982, Child Family Health International has run global health, service-learning electives for over 3.500 pre-medical, medical and other students of the health professions. Students travel to immerse themselves in new cultural contexts and to learn about the way healthcare is practiced and experienced worldwide. Students come from nearly 500 of the top universities in the U.S. and the world. CFHI recognizes that today's program students are tomorrow's healthcare leaders and hopes that through cultural immersion in the medical education process it might help increase awareness and understanding so that a new cadre of healthcare practitioners can bring about solutions while upholding the highest moral, legal and ethical principles.

Sector: Education, health.

Country: Africa (South Africa), Asia (India), Latin America (Ecuador, Mexico, Bolivia, Nicaragua).

Qualif.: Pre-medical, nursing, PAs, MPH and medical students.

Nonpro: Yes, with college education.

Age: Minimum 21.

Duration: 4–12 weeks.

Lang.: English and, in some cases, Spanish.

Benefits: Pre-trip orientation and materials. In-country accommodation, food, orientation, training, global health lectures, medical electives and educational program, travel insurance, alumni services, staff support, and medical supplies to carry along as a donation. Scholarships, academic credits and fundraising suggestions to cover program costs are also available.

Costs: US$1,950 on average.

Applic.: On-line form.

Chantiers Jeunesse

4545, Avenue Pierre-De Coubertin , PO Box 1000, Branch M Montreal, Quebec
H1V 3R2   Canada
Tel.: ++1 (514) 252-3015 (toll free in N. Am. 1-800-361-2055)
Fax : ++1 (514) 251-8719
E-mail : cj@cj.qc.ca
www.cj.qc.ca

Dsc.:   The goals of Chantiers Jeunesse (Mouvement Quebecois des Chantiers Jeunesse) are to support and strengthen the development of the autonomy (self-reliance) of young people, mainly by the realisation of workcamps, which encourage community involvement; to initiate social involvement and encourage the intercultural communication and understanding between people from different countries and cultures. Most exchanges are between Quebec and European volunteers.

Sector: Community development, construction, culture, environment.

Country: 30 countries in North America, Europe and Asia.

Age: 15–30 at the beginning of the project.

Duration: 3-4 weeks; occasionally projects for 2 months or longer.

Lang.:   French, English.

Benefits: Food, accommodation, transportation from home to workcamp site, recreational activities, and a minibus to explore the region.

Costs: Application fee: CAD$15. Standard participation fee: CAD$140. Extra fees for Mexico and Mongolia: CAD$175-300. Transportation fee: CAD$700-1,500 (depending on destionation). Personal expenses, medical insurance, passport and Visa costs not included.

Applic.:   On-line form.

Notes: Canadian citizens or permanent residents with permanent residence in Quebec only.

The Chol-Chol Foundation for Human Development

Casilla 45, Temuco, Chile
or 4431 Garrison Street NW Washington, DC 20013 USA
Tel./Fax: ++56 (45) 614-007 or 614-008
E-mail: info@cholchol.org
www.cholchol.org

Desc.: The Chol-Chol Foundation is a Fair Trade organisation that works in indigenous communities in the ninth region of Chile. The Mapuche people had been extirpated from their ancestral homeland since the arrival of the Spaniards, and the communities had been isolated from the current of modernity; without sufficient food, without passable roads, lacking medical facilities and secondary schools, and immersed in poverty, marginalisation, and an overwhelming lack of opportunities. The Foundation has grown from the work of an American missionary who arrived in Chol-Chol in 1953. Today the main programs are fair trade of Mapuche weaving, textile development and medicinal plants.

Sector: Culture, small-enterprise development, women's issues.

Country: Latin America (Chile).

Qualif.: Business students, fund-raisers, grant writers, and social workers are especially welcome.

Nonpro: Yes, with at least an undergraduate degree.

Age: Enquire with the organisation.

Duration: Minimum 3 months.

Lang.: Spanish fluency.

Benefits: No fee. Enquire with the organisation.

Costs: Monthly living expenses. Enquire with the organisation.

Applic.: On-line form. Volunteers should send a CV.

Christian Peacemakercorps

PO Box 6508
Chicago, Illinois 60680-6508 USA
Tel.: ++1 (773) 277-0253
Fax: ++1 (773) 277-0291
E-mail: personnel@cpt.org
www.cpt.org/corps.php

Desc.: Since 1993, Christian Peacemaker Teams (CPT) has been recruiting and training individuals for the Christian Peacemaker Corps. Corps members, trained in peacemaking skills and non-violent direct action, are available on a full-time or part-time basis to enter emergency situations of conflict and areas of militarisation at the invitation of local peacemakers, and responding to confront injustice and violent situations. The objectives are to advance the cause of lasting peace by giving skilled, courageous support to peacemakers working locally in situations of conflict; to inspire people and governments to discard violence in favour of non-violent action as a means of settling differences; to provide home communities with first-hand information and resources for responding to worldwide situations of conflict and to urge their active involvement; to interpret a non-violent perspective to the media; and to accompany individuals or communities who are threatened. CPT also sponsors short-term education/action delegations.

Sector: Human rights, peacekeeping, religious, various.

Country: Latin America (Colombia), Middle East (Palestine, Iraq), native communities in North America (United States, Mexico, Canada).

Qualif.: Experience/interest in human rights, non-violent direct action and cross-cultural work.

Nonpro: No particular professional skills are required just a strong motivation for peace and a willingness to communicate.

Age: Minimum 21 (18 for short-term delegations).

Duration: 3 years. Members are available for short-term organising, speaking, training, or other peace work within their home communities when not on project site. Part-time members commit to 2 to 12 weeks each year for 3 years. Short-term delegations are 7 to 14 days.

Lang.: English, Spanish, Arabic.

Benefits: Modest stipend for full-time corps members. All living expenses and travel on project sites.

Costs: Part-time members and delegates fund their own work. Enquire with organisation.

Applic.: On-line application or request form directly from office. The application process includes a phone interview, contact with references, and participation in a short-term CPT delegation (cost dependent on destination). The selection process continues through a period of training with final discernment about acceptance into the Corps occurring at the end of the training period. No special training required for short-term delegates.

Notes: Volunteers must be of Christian faith. The organisation has representatives in Chicago and in Toronto, Canada. See website for contacts.

CNFA – Citizens Network for Foreign Affairs

Agribusiness Volunteer Program
1828 L St, NW, Suite 710
Washington, DC 20036 USA
Tel.: ++1 (202) 296-3920 (toll free in N. Am. 1-888-872-2632)
E-mail: ewallace@cnfa.org
www.cnfa.org

Desc.: US farmers, agribusiness professionals, and other agriculturalists help build democracy and market economies by sharing their expertise with aspiring entrepreneurs across the globe. In order to achieve the greatest impact, CNFA sends multiple volunteers to long-term projects, with each volunteer assignment building upon previous ones. CNFA's long-term projects seek to develop private farmer associations, cooperatives, private agribusiness, women's and young farmer groups, and other organisations that can help people increase their incomes and wellbeing. Volunteers provide help to a wide variety of groups, including dairy processors and producers, beef cattle farmers, mushroom producers, honey producers, fruit growers, and greenhouse producers.

Sector: Agriculture, small-enterprise development.

Country: Europe (Ukraine, Moldova, Belarus).

Qualif.: Agribusiness professionals: farmers and ranchers, cooperative specialists, food processing professionals, agribusiness executives, extension agents, organisation leaders, etc.

Nonpro: No.

Age: N/A with necessary experience.

Duration: 16-19 days.

Lang.: English.

Benefits: Airfare, lodging, meals, local transportation, and other project-related costs.

Costs: Volunteers donate only their time and unique skills.

Applic.: On-line form or request form via phone or post.

Notes: US citizens and permanent residents only.

Concern America

PO Box 1790, Santa Ana, California 92702 USA
Tel.: ++1(714)953-8575
or 1 (800) 266-2376 (toll free in N.Am.)
Fax: ++1(714)953-1242
E-mail:concamerinc@earthlink.net
www.concernamerica.org

Desc.:	Concern America is a small non-profit, non-sectarian, non-governmental development and refugee aid organisation. Its philosophy enphasizes the transference of skills and thus the creation of opportunity, rather than the placement of resources into impoverished regions. Concern America does this by training community members in health, education, and income-generation, so that the villagers themselves become the health care providers, educators, cooperative members, etc. Since its establishment in 1972, Concern America has worked in 15 countries on three continents, making a measurable difference in the lives of more than 2 million people in thousands of communities.
Sector:	Agriculture, child welfare, community development, education, health, refugee aid, sanitation, small-enterprise development.
Country:	Africa (Mozambique, Sierra Leone, Liberia), Latin America (Bolivia, Colombia, El Salvador, Guatemala, Mexico).
Qualif.:	Medical doctors, public health specialists, educators, agriculturalists, engineers, and other experts. Degree or experience in public health, medicine, nutrition, nursing, agriculture, community development, education, or appropriate technology.
Nonpro:	No.
Age:	Minimum 21.
Duration:	Minimum commitment of 1 year; 2 preferred. There are no short-term internships or assignments.
Lang.:	Fluency in Spanish (Portuguese in Mozambique) or ability to learn the language at own expense.
Benefits:	Accommodation, board, round-trip transportation, annual trip home, health insurance, small monthly stipend, support services from the home office, simple repatriation allowance.
Costs:	Personal expenses.
Applic.:	Additional information on the website.
Notes:	Work experience abroad is desirable.

Concern Worldwide

52-55 Lower Camden Street, Dublin 2 Ireland
Tel.: ++353 (1) 417-7700/77
Fax: ++353 (1) 475-4649
E-mail: hrenquiries@concern.ie or info@concern.net
www.concern.net

Desc.: Concern Worldwide is a non-governmental, international, humanitarian organisation dedicated to reducing suffering and eliminating extreme poverty in the world's poorest countries. Currently, Concern works in 28 countries and has a workforce of around 4,000 people. Its headquarters are in Dublin, Ireland, and the organisation has other offices throughout the world. Concern focuses on 5 key programs: education, emergency response and preparedness, health, HIV/AIDS and livelihood. Its aim is to balance innovation and necessary risk-taking with prudent judgement and a professional approach.

Sector: Education, emergency, health, human rights, hunger relief, sanitation.

Country: Africa (Angola, Burundi, Chad, Congo, Ethiopia, Kenya, Liberia, Malawi, Mozambique, NigerRwanda, Sierra Leone, Somalia, Sudan, Tanzania, Uganda, Zambia, Zimbabwe), Asia (Afghanistan, Bangladesh, Cambodia, East Timor, India, Nepal, N.Korea, Laos, Pakistan), Caribbean (Haiti).

Qualif.: Professional job postings are listed on website.

Nonpro: No.

Age: N/A with necessary experience.

Duration: Varies with each project.

Lang.: English (Spanish, French, Portuguese helpful).

Benefits: Stipend varies with position and project.

Costs: Personal expenses.

Applic.: Vacancies are posted on the website. Apply on-line.

Notes: Concern has branches in the UK and the USA. See website.

Concordia

19 North Street, Portslade, BN41 1DH, UK
Tel.: ++44 (1273) 422-218
Fax: ++44 (1273) 421-182
E-mail: info@concordia-iye.org.uk
www.concordia-iye.org.uk

Desc.: Concordia is committed to international volunteer exchange in the hope of promoting greater international understanding, cultural awareness, and peace. The International Volunteer Programme offers volunteers aged 18+ the opportunity to join international teams of volunteers working on short-term projects in over 60 countries worldwide. A selection of projects is available for teenagers aged 16 and 17. Projects are community-based initiatives that would not be possible without volunteer action, focusing as much on the aspect of intercultural exchange – both within the group and the local community - as on the work itself. Projects are mainly short-term and last on average 2-4 weeks.

Sector: Child welfare, construction, culture, education, environment.

Country: Africa (Botswana, Ghana, Kenya, Malawi, Morocco, Tanzania, Togo, Uganda, Zambia, Zimbabwe), Asia (Bangladesh, Japan, South Korea, India, Indonesia, Mongolia, Nepal, Thailand, Vietnam), Latin America (Argentina, Ecuador, Mexico, Peru) Europe, North America.

Qualif.: No particular skills required.

Nonpro: Yes, with some previous relevant experience.

Age: 16+, minimum age of 19 for projects in Africa, Asia and Latin America.

Duration: 2–4 weeks.

Lang.: English

Benefits: Food and accommodation. Travel and insurance not included.

Costs: Approx. between GB£150 - £300 depending on the country.

COOPI – Cooperazione Internazionale

Via De Lemene 50
20151 Milano Italy
Tel.: ++39 (02) 308-5057
E-mail: coopi@coopi.org
www.coopi.org

Desc.:	COOPI is an NGO founded in 1965. Its mission is to foster international solidarity by developing multi-sector projects in order to respond to the various needs of the local communities and by working in close relationship with local partners. COOPI intervenes in emergency situations in areas affected by war or natural disaster. COOPI has 120 projects in 37 countries.
Sectors:	Agriculture, community development, construction, education, emergency, environment, refugee aid, skills training, sanitation, small-enterprise development, various.
Country:	Africa (Cameroon, Central Africa Rep., Chad, Congo, Ethiopia, Kenya, Malawi, Morocco, Mozambique, Senegal, S. Leone, Somalia, Sudan, Tunisia, Uganda), Asia (Bangladesh, Tajikistan), Europe (Albania, Serbia), Latin America (Bolivia, Colombia, Ecuador, Guatemala, Paraguay, Peru), Middle East (Palestine, Yemen).
Qualif.:	Agronomists, engineers, hydrologists, healthcare professionals, emergency relief, and social workers, etc.
Nonpro:	Yes, for workcamps only. Professionals for mid-/long-term projects.
Age:	Minimum 21, dependent upon experience.
Duration:	3 months to 3 years for professionals; 3–4 weeks for workcamps.
Lang.:	English, Spanish, French, and Arabic.
Benefits:	Long-term professionals are fully funded with the standards of the funding organisation, such as the EU and UN agencies.
Costs:	Workcamp participants pay for travel, insurance, room, and board.
Applic.:	Send application via fax or e-mail selezione@coopi.org. For the workcamps contact campiestivi@coopi.org.
Notes:	Available positions are always announced on the website.

CORD – Christian Outreach Relief and Development

1 New Street, Leamington Spa, Warwickshire CV31 1HP UK
Tel.: ++44 (1926) 315-301
Fax: ++44 (1926) 885-786
E-mail: personnel@cord.org.uk or info@cord.org.uk
www.cord.org.uk

Desc.:	CORD is a UK-based Christian relief and development agency, established in 1967 to help war-orphaned and abandoned children in Vietnam. CORD works with marginalised and vulnerable people, especially children and people displaced by conflict. CORD's overall objective is to enable communities and individuals to have greater control over situations that affect their lives, to encourage self-reliance and to provide sustainable solutions to problems. CORD emphasises an integrated approach and brings specialist expertise in areas such as health, education, water/sanitation, and agriculture.
Sector:	Agriculture, community development, education, health, sanitation, small-enterprise development.
Country:	Africa (Burundi, Chad, Mozambique, Zambia), Asia (Cambodia, India, Philippines, Thailand, Uzbekistan).
Qualif.:	Health professionals, managers, accountants, administrators, agronomists, logisticians.
Nonpro:	No.
Age:	N/A with necessary experience.
Duration:	Initial placement is 1 year, with 1-year extension desired.
Lang.:	English. French, Spanish, and Portuguese useful.
Benefits:	All expenses covered plus stipend. Group accommodation.
Costs:	Remuneration package for overseas positions covers all costs.
Applic.:	Send CV to Head of Personnel and outline Christian commitment . Apply only for specific vacancies on the website.
Notes:	Only Christians with free right of entry into the UK. Strict medical check-up before departure.

Cotravaux

11 Rue de Clichy
75009 Paris France
Tel.: ++33 (1) 4874-7920
Fax: ++33 (1) 4874-1401
E-mail: informations@cotravaux.org
www.cotravaux.org

Desc.:	Cotravaux coordinates 11 French workcamps. Its role is to promote voluntary work and community projects concerning environmental protection, monument restoration, and social projects. The organisation offers many workcamps in different regions of France. Many of the organisations members of Cotravaux work with foreign partners.
Sector:	Culture, environment, construction, various (land-clearing, restoration of ancient monuments).
Country:	Europe (France) and abroad (network of parteners).
Qualif.:	No specific skills needed.
Nonpro:	Yes.
Age.:	Minimum 14.
Dur.:	2–3 weeks. Certain projects offer 4–12 month volunteering.
Lang.:	In France, a few projects require French.
Benefits:	Room and board provided (some camps require a daily contribution).
Costs:	Volunteers must pay for their own transportation to the camps.
Applic.:	Contact Cotravaux by fax or mail to obtain the list of partner workcamps in France or other specific countries.

Council for Mayan Communication in Sololà

Barrio Jucanya
Panajachel, Sololá   Guatemala
Tel.: ++ (502) 293-5756
E-mail: padma@mayacom.org
www.mayacom.org

Desc.: The Mayan Council for Communication in Sololá is a small group of citizens and community leaders living in the 'Department' of Sololá who have a continual interest in supporting the advancement of equitable access to communications technologies in the region. The motivation of each member is to secure free access to communications technologies, most specifically the Internet, for all people, organisations, and agencies that show interest and need. The specific objective is to create a network of rural Telecenters that provide community access to regional and international information resources with satellite reception, the ability to connect 24 hours a day and support 10–40 computers on-line. The Sololá network could consist of from 10–20 independent and self-administrating Telecenters, strategically situated around the lake to provide the most practical use for the region.

Sector: Education, IT, skills training, small-enterprise development, women's issues, various.

Country: Latin America (Guatemala).

Qualif.: Each volunteer program is tailored to suit the particular interest and abilities of the volunteer.

Nonpro: Yes.

Age: Minimum 18.

Duration: Minimum 1 month. Short-term stays available by negotiation.

Lang.: Spanish, English. The population is mainly indigenous, representing 3 of the 24 official indigenous Guatemalan languages: Kaqchikel, Tsutujil, and K´iche. Spanish is a second language to the majority and basic knowledge is essential .

Benefits: The application fee covers volunteer placement, administration, marketing, program information, and arrangements with host communities. The program fee covers 3 meals a day plus lodging. The projects are rurally located, high up in the mountains or in small villages around the lake. Most places are accessible by a combination of 'chicken' bus, pick-up, and hiking. Accommodations will have a shower, a flush toilet, and a bed with a mattress. Alternatively, modern services are available in Panajachel, and a program can be created to include day visits to the project with transport by boat or bus to nearby villages.

Costs: Flights, travel/health insurance, and corresponding airport departure taxes, plus a weekly budget of up to US$20. US$275 application fee and US$350 per month participation fee (variable according to accommodation and meal requirements), both paid prior to arrival. Costs are lower for committed long-term volunteers. Additional costs for transport are US$10–100 for airport transfer, US$1-60 for local travel; accommodation ranges from US$100 per night, week, or month, according to the standard of the lodging chosen.

Applic.: On-line form. Volunteers select a participating organisation in the Mayacom Network.

Cross-Cultural Solutions

2 Clinton Place, New Rochelle, New York 10801 USA
Tel.: ++1 (914) 632-0022 (toll free in N. Am. 1-800-380-4777)
Fax: ++1 (914) 632-8494
E-mail: info@crossculturalsolutions.org
www.crossculturalsolutions.org

Desc.:	As a Cross-Cultural Solutions international volunteer, you will work side-by-side with local people and share the goals of a community that warmly welcomes you. You will have the possibility to experience another culture, really getting to know its people. It is a personally inspiring experience. The in-country staff of the organization welcomes volunteers in the CCS Home-Base and ensure them that all of their needs are met - from safety and lodging to perspectives and insight about the local culture.
Sector:	Child welfare, community development, culture, education, health, women's issues, various.
Country:	Africa (Ghana, Morocco, Tanzania, South Africa), Asia (China, India, Thailand), Europe (Russia), Latin America (Brazil, Costa Rica, Guatemala, Peru).
Qualif.:	Open to people of all nationalities and ages.
Nonpro:	Yes.
Age:	Minimum 18, without adult companionship.
Duration:	1-12 weeks; all programs begin on specified start date; end date will vary, depending on length of stay.
Lang.:	English.
Benefits:	All program-based expenses: airport transfers, daily transportation, meals, lodging, professional staff guidance and supervision, orientation, medical insurance.
Costs:	US$588 for 2 weeks (till Aug. 2008). International airfare, travel insurance, and Visa fees not included.
Applic.:	On-line form and information survey.
Notes:	CCS has an office also in the UK please see website for details.

CUSO

44 Eccles Street,
Ottawa, Ontario K1R 6S4 Canada
Tel.: ++1 (613) 829-7445 (toll free in N. Am. 1-888-434-2876)
Fax: ++1 (613) 829-7996
E-mail: info@cuso.ca
www.cuso.org

Desc.: CUSO is a Canadian organisation that supports alliances for global social justice. They work with people striving for freedom, gender, and racial equality, self-determination, and cultural survival. They achieve their goals by sharing information, human and material resources, and by promoting policies for developing global sustainability. CUSO contributes to the sustainable development of developing countries by helping to reduce poverty, by promoting democratic governance and human rights, and by supporting sustainable and equitable natural resource management practices.

Sector: Agriculture, culture, environment, health, housing, human rights, IT, small-enterprise development, women's issues, various.

Country: Africa (Burkina Faso, Ghana, Mozambique, Nigeria, South Africa, Tanzania), Asia (East Timor, Indonesia, Laos, Thailand), Caribbean (Belize, Jamaica), Latin America (Bolivia, Chile, Costa Rica, El Salvador, Guatemala, Honduras, Mexico, Nicaragua, Peru) Oceania (Fiji, Papua New Guinea, Solomon Islands, Vanuatu).

Qualif.: Skilled and experienced in professional fields with an interest in and personal commitment to social movements.

Nonpro: Enquire with organisation. University or college degree required.

Age: CUSO is obliged to respect mandatory retirement requirements in countries where cooperants are placed. In some countries the retirement age may be as low as 55..

Duration: 2 years. Durations may vary to accommodate in-field language training programs.

Lang.: English, Spanish Portuguese.

Benefits: CUSO provides a benefit package that enables cooperants to live modestly overseas. Benefits are not linked to the type, level, or value of the work cooperants do, but are intended to cover the basic living expense of providing services overseas. CUSO offers adequate terms and conditions of employment and a comprehensive benefits package. Spouses may be accepted with long-term cooperants and certain benefits may be included.

Costs: The overseas living allowance does not provide for additional personal expenses nor specialty food and consumer goods not essential to basic needs while overseas.

Applic.: Consult the website for the listing of Current CUSO Co-operant Opportunities and complete application details. Complete the on-line application form. CUSO does not accept general resumes. All applications must be submitted through the website. Please contact: cooperant@cuso.ca if you are unable to submit an application through the website or for questions not answered in the website.

Notes: Canadian citizens or landed immigrants only. For other national enquire with the organisation.

Dakshinayan

c/o Siddharth Sanyal
F-1169, Chittaranjan Park, 1st floor
New Delhi - 110019 India
Tel: +91 (9934) 572399
E-mail: sid@dakshinayan.org or info@dakshinayan.org
www.dakshinayan.org

Desc.: Dakshinayan was set up in 1991 by Siddharth Sanyal to take over a tribal development project in Bihar, which was being managed by an international voluntary service organisation. Local villagers and activists manage the Cheo Project, which now falls within the newly formed tribal state of Jharkhand. Cheo is the name of the village where the project started in 1979, but now it's an acronym for Children, Health, Education, and Organisation. The project aims to initiate small locally-managed grassroots development projects at village level with emphasis on self-reliance; gather and disseminate information regarding development efforts and issues; promote development education for a better understanding of the cause, reality, and myths of rural and urban poverty; and create linkages between small projects and possible support sources within India and abroad.

Sector: Community development, education, environment, health.

Country: Asia (India).

Qualif.: No particular skills required, just a strong motivation.

Nonpro: Yes.

Age: Minimum 18.

Duration: 30 days minimum. There are no maximum limits.

Lang.: English.

Benefits: Accommodation at the project and food (vegetarian).

Costs: US$300 per month. Volunteers must cover all expenses incurred while travelling to and from the project.

Notes: Open to all nationalities. Volunteers must arrive in Delhi before the 5th of the month.

Desteens Volunteering Services

PO Box 68130
Nairobi Kenya
Tel.: ++254 (722) 255-311(mobile)
E-mail: des_teencenter@yahoo.com or epeco99@yahoo.com

Desc.: Desteens organise workcamps for volunteers to come and help the community by teaching, working with the poor, working with local NGOs and local projects, and raising cultural understanding.

Sector: Community development, construction, education, environment, IT, small-enterprise development.

Country: Africa (Kenya).

Qualif.: Volunteers with skills are placed in relevant institutions. Mechanics, electricians, special education teachers, doctors, nurses, orthopedists, IT experts desired.

Nonpro.: Yes.

Age: 17–75.

Duration: 2 weeks to 2 years. Short-term teachers should note that schools closes for holidays in the months of April, August, and December.

Lang.: English. Swahili is the local language.

Benefits: Accommodation and food.

Costs: U$60 administration fee plus US$17 per day for living expenses. Cash donations, books, educational magazines, clothing, computers, toys, or any other donations gratefully received.

Applic.: Request application form via e-mail.

Notes: Once accepted the applicant can request to be put in contact with former volunteers. See note on page 35.

Development in Action

78 York Street
London W1H 1DP UK
Tel.: ++44 (7813) 395 9574
E-mail: recruitment@developmentinaction.org
www.developmentinaction.org

Desc.: Development in Action is a small UK-registered charity dedicated to raising awareness about global development issues amongst young people. The main volunteer scheme supports locally-based NGOs in India, with volunteers working on projects in both urban and rural locations. During their placements, candidates get hands-on experience of grassroots development, and are encouraged to engage in the wider issues of global citizenship and sustainable development. Candidates are encouraged to continue their engagement, after their placements in India, through their own development education projects designed to raise awareness back in th UK.

Sector: Child welfare, community development, education, women's issues and more (depending on needs of partner organizations in India).

Country: Asia (India).

Qualif.: No specific skills required.

Nonpro: Yes. Training provided in the UK. Required attitudes are: cultural sensitivity, enthusiasm, humility, interest in global issues and commitment to DiA's development education goals.

Age: Minimum 18.

Duration: Summer placements run from July to September and 5-month placements from September to February.

Lang.: English. Some Hindi and Tamil language training provided where necessary.

Benefits: Accommodation and training.

Costs: GB£660 for the summer placement and GB£1,210 for the 5-month placement . Volunteers pay for their flights, insurance, Visas (total cost about GB£350–550) and personal expenses.

Applic.: Download application form website.

Notes: Placements are not restricted to UK citizens but interviews and training are in the UK.

Emergency

Via Meravigli 12/14 - 20123 Milano Italy
Tel.: ++39 (02) 881-881
Fax: ++39 (02) 863-16336
E-mail: info@emergency.it
www.emergency.it

Desc.: EMERGENCY provides emergency surgical assistance and rehabilitation for the civilian victims of war and landmines, through the collaboration of medical and technical staff with specific experience in war zones. Training of the national personnel in the clinical management and rehabilitation of landmine and war injuries ensures the sustainability of the programs. The international community is moving towards a global ban of these inhuman, indiscriminate, and persistent weapons. However, more than 110 million unexploded landmines are scattered in at least 67 countries, and they will continue to maim and kill for the decades to come. New projects have been opened also in the field of paediatrics, midwifery and obstetrics.

Sector: Emergency, health.

Country: Africa (Sierra Leone, Sudan), Asia (Afghanistan, Cambodia).

Qualif.: Medical professionals: general surgeons, orthopaedic and plastic surgeons, anaesthesiologists, paediatricians, gynaecologist (female), midwives (female), nurses, physiotherapists, internal medicine doctors, radiologists, x-ray technicians. Other professionals: logistics experts, administrators, construction foremen, mechanics, thermal and a/c technicians.

Nonpro: No.

Age: N/A with the necessary experience.

Duration: 3/6 months minimum.

Lang.: English.

Benefits: Basic salary, room and board, travel expenses, insurance.

Costs: Personal expenses.

Applic.: Send CV via fax or e-mail to curriculum@emergency.it.

Notes: **For further informations on volunteering with Emergency, contact the organisation at: coordinamento.volontari@emergency.it.**

EnterpriseWorks/VITA

1825 Connecticut Avenue, Suite 630
Washington, DC 20009 USA
Tel.: ++1 (202) 293-4600
Fax: ++1 (202) 293-4598
E-mail: info@enterpriseworks.org
www.enterpriseworks.org

Desc.: For over 4 decades EnterpriseWorks/VITA (EWV) has empowered the poor in developing countries by providing access to information and knowledge, strengthening local institutions, and introducing improved technologies. Its particular focus is on support to entrepreneurs in the private, public, and community sectors and on facilitating connectivity and technical information exchange between and among individuals and organisations.

Sector: Agriculture, community development, environment, IT, sanitation, skills training, small-enterprise development, various.

Country: Various countries in Africa and worldwide.

Qualif.: Experience in the above listed sectors. Necessary skills vary between programs.

Nonpro: Only positions for expert consultants or volunteers.

Age: N/A with the necessary experience.

Duration: Both short- and long-term consultancy positions are available. Occasional internships are also available. See website for openings.

Lang.: English, French, Spanish depending on programs.

Benefits: Airfare, lodging, food, local transportation, project-related costs.

Costs: Volunteers donate only their time and unique skills.

Applic.: All resumes and cover letters should be e-mailed to jobs@enterpriseworks.org or via fax.

Notes: EWV operates primarily in Africa, but it collaborates with local organisations in need of expert volunteers all over the world.

EVS – European Voluntary Service

Education, Audiovisual & Culture Executive Agency
SOS Volunteer Helpdesk - Youth Unit
Rue Colonel Bourg 135-139, B -1140 Evere Belgium
Tel: +32 (2) 296-8724
Fax: +32 (2) 292-1330
E-mail: volunteers@ec.europa.eu
http://ec.europa.eu/youth/program/sos/index_en.html

Desc.: The European Voluntary Service (EVS) is an Action of the YOUTH programme, implemented by the European Commission and YOUTH National Agencies. It allows young people to do a voluntary service in a local host organisation in a foreign country. Each year, about 4000 volunteers participate in EVS. The annual funding is more than 30 million euro. The volunteer gains a variety of personal, professional and intercultural skills, and brings some added value and intercultural flavour to the host organisation and the local community. Within the Euro-Med Youth Programme support is available also for voluntary service activities with partners in Mediterranean countries. The SOS Volunteer Helpdesk offers support to volunteers and organisations as well as to young people interested in EVS. In 2006 EVS celebrates its 10th anniversary. Under the proposed "Youth in Action" programme (2007-2013) a considerable extension of EVS is planned, including the possibility for group EVS projects.

Sector: Community development, culture, education, environment, various.

Country: Programme countries are the EU Member States, Norway, Iceland, Liechtenstein, the 3 candidate countries Bulgaria, Romania and Turkey. A smaller number of projects take place with partners in South Eastern Europe, Eastern Europe and Caucasus, Mediterranean countries, and Latin America.

Qualif.: Participation in the European Voluntary Service does not require any professional qualification. On the contrary, it is open to all young people.

Nonpro: Programs are open with no particular expertise required.

Age: Minimum 18 - maximum 25 years (26 for young people with fewer opportunities).

Duration: There are two types of EVS projects: most of the projects are long-term with a duration between 6 and 12 months; short-term projects have a duration of 3 weeks to 6 months, aiming at young people with fewer opportunities.

Lang.: EVS volunteers do not need extended language skills. Linguistic support is available in the project.

Benefits: The projects receive grants as a contribution for preparation, travel, accommodation, food, activity costs directly related to the project plus a monthly allowance for the volunteer (pocket money).

Costs: Volunteers cannot be charged for participating in EVS. Sending and host organisations are responsible for project expenses. EU grants are supposed to cover most of the costs.

Applic.: Each EVS project is built on a partnership triangle between sending organisation, host organisation and volunteer. The organisations can be any type of non-governmental organisation, an association, a local authority or any non-profit-making local initiative. National Agencies / National Coordinators in the country of the prospective volunteer can provide contacts with existing sending organisations. Sending organisations would establish an agreement with a host organisation. For volunteers going from one Programme country to another both organisations submit grant applications to the National Agencies in their country. In other projects it is the project partner in the Programme country or Mediterranean partner country submitting one grant application.

Notes: The programme is accessible to young people with legal residence in the EU and some nearby countries (see website for details). Prospective volunteers must contact the YOUTH National Agency in their country or the SOS Volunteer Helpdesk for more information.

Foundation for Sustainable Development

870 Market Street, Suite 321
San Francisco, California, 94102 USA
Fax: ++1 (415) 283-4873
E-mail: info@fsdinternational.org
www.fsdinternational.org

Desc.: The FSD supports the efforts of grassroots development organizations in the Gloobal South that are working to better their communities, environments, and the economic opportunities around them.Also, it aims to raise international awareness of the economic chanllenges in developing countries and support cross-cultural communities in finding more effective solutions to development issues.

Sector: Community development, education, environment, health, human rights, women's issues, small-enterprise development.

Country: Africa (Kenya, Uganda), Asia (India), Latin America (Argentina, Bolivia, Ecuador, Nicaragua, Peru).

Qualif.: FSD looks for participants who have completed coursework and /or have relevant professional experience related to one of the sectors listed above.

Nonpro: Not specified.

Age: Minimum 18.

Duration: Depending on the experience and lenght of time of the volunteer, FSD offers "Internship Program", "Pro Corps Volunteering" (minimum 4 weeks), "Short-Term Volunteering".

Lang.: Not specified.

Benefits: Academic credit is available.

Costs: For a list of program contribution fees, please visit the website.

Applic.: Online (see website).

Notes: FSD's programs provide comprehensive training, including a series of tools to maximize your project work and your understanding of sustainable development principles. As a FSD participant, the volunteer is placed individually with a host family for at least the first 8 weeks. Volunteers work in a locally managed FSD partner organization that fits their skills and interests, allowing full immersion into the local language and culture.

Fundaciòn Aldeas de Paz-Peace Villages Foundation

Lomas de Piedra Canaima
Santa Elena de Uiarén, Municipio Gran Sabana, Estado Bolívar Venezuela
Tel.: ++58 (289) 416-0820
E-mail: mail@peacevillages.org
www.peacevillages.org

Desc.:	Peace Villages Foundation (PVF) is a sustainable, transparent, grassroots, NGO which supports and promotes disadvantaged communities and their members in acheiving susatinable development, social justice and peace. It is independent from political, religious and economic interests and it mantains its financial independence by funding its programs completely with financial donations of volunteers.
Sector:	Child welfare, education, environment, small-enterprise development.
Country:	Latin America (Venezuela).
Qualif.:	Necessary skills learnt on the job. Spanish lessons possible. Flexibility and motivation to be exposed to the local culture.
Nonpro:	Yes.
Age:	Minimum 16.
Duration:	1 week to 12 months.
Lang.:	English.
Benefits:	Room and board, full support from local staff.
Costs:	Between US$75 and US$ 882 per week, depending on lenght of stay and accomodation preferences.
Applic.:	Send CV and cover letter.
Notes:	Leisure time, during weekends, includes: discovering the Amazon beauty through river trips, trekking, hiking, etc.

Global Citizens Network

130 N. Howell Street
St. Paul, Minnesota 55104 USA
Tel.: ++1 (651) 644-0960 (toll free in N. Am. 1-800-644-9292)
E-mail: info@globalcitizens.org
www.globalcitizens.org

Desc.: Team members have the opportunity to immerse themselves in the daily life of a developing community, while working closely with local residents on such projects as building a health clinic, teaching in a pre-school, planting trees, or renovating a youth centre. Local hosts provide volunteers with education in the local culture, language, social structure, environment, economy, and arts. Communities are visited that offer insight into specific issues or trends, such as environmental protection, women in development, and traditional medicine. Home visits, local farm and factory tours, and hikes in surrounding areas are common. Volunteers are often invited to watch or participate in local ceremonies and holiday festivities. Teams consist of 6–10 people, and are led by a trained team leader.

Sector: Agriculture, community development, construction, education, environment, women's issues.

Country: Africa (Kenya, Tanzania), Asia (Nepal, Thailand), Latin America (Ecuador, Guatemala, Mexico, Peru, Brazil), North America (USA and Canada).

Qualif.: No special skills are required to participate.

Nonpro: Yes. Families are welcome to join the teams.

Age: Minimum 8. Must be 18 to travel without a parent or guardian.

Duration: 1–3 weeks.

Lang.: English.

Benefits: Travel, food, accommodation (group or home-stay), tourist excursions, staff support. Academic credit is available.

Costs: US$800–2,200 depending on the project plus airfare.

Applic.: Download application off the website or request via telephone or e-mail.

Global Routes

1 Short Street
Northampton, Massachusetts 01060 USA
Tel.: ++1 (413) 585-8895
Fax: ++1 (413) 585-8810
E-mail: mail@globalroutes.org
www.globalroutes.org

Desc.: Global Routes designs experiential community service projects and teaching internships that allow high school and college aged students to extend themselves by living and working with people in communities throughout the world. High school programs are 3, 4 and 5 weeks long and offered in the summer. A primary focus of the programs for high school aged students is to develop the individual student through the experience of working, travelling and living with a group of peers in new and compelling environments. Typical service projects include: constructing classrooms, laboratories and libraries for village schools, running educational workshops and day camps, and renovating community buildings. High school programs exist in Belize, China, Costa Rica, the Dominican Republic, Ecuador, Ghana, India, Kenya, Mexico, Nepal, Peru, Thailand and Vietnam. The college-level internship is 10 to 12 weeks long and is offered in the summer, fall and winter. A primary focus of this program is to develop the individual's sense of self and personal responsibility through the experience of living and volunteering in a remote community. The primary service project for our college interns is teaching, from the elementary to high school levels. College programs exist in Costa Rica, Ecuador, Ghana, India, Kenya and Thailand.

Sector: Construction, education, environment, various.

Country: Africa (Ghana, Kenya), Asia (China, India, Thailand, Vietnam), Caribbean (Dominican Republic), Latin America (Costa Rica, Belize, Ecuador, Mexico, Peru).

Qualif.: Programs are open to those students who show great enthusiasm to contribute to a developing community and a genuine desire to further their own learning and growth.

Nonpro: Yes.

Age: 13 – 17 for high school programs; 17 and older for college programs.

Duration: 4 - 12 weeks depending on project.

Lang.: English. 1 - 3 years French or Spanish for some projects.

111

Benefits: Accommodations (home-stays and group living), food, recreation, workshops and tourist excursions.

Costs: High School Programs: US$3,475–5,475. College Programs:US$4,250–4,950. Program fees do not include airfare.

Applic.: On-line application form.

Notes: Leadership Positions are available. Leading a high school program generally involves a 4–7-week commitment (late June through mid-August) as well as attending a 5-day orientation prior to departure in mid-to-late June. These are co-leadership positions: 2 leaders, 1 man and 1 woman, lead a group of up to 18 high school students. Qualifications for staff positions include: minimum age of 24 to lead high school programs and 26 to lead college programs; extensive experience working with North American high school and/or college students is necessary; travel experience in the desired region; Spanish language proficiency for programs in Costa Rica, the Dominican Republic, Ecuador, Mexico and Peru, French language proficiency for Guadeloupe program (local language proficiency highly desirable for programs in all other regions); certification in Standard First Aid and CPR (higher level certifications desirable); backgrounds in counselling, cross-cultural learning, wilderness and/or environmental education, and classroom teaching.

Global Service Corps

300 Broadway, Suite 28
San Francisco, California 94133-3312
Tel.: ++1 (415)788-3666, ext. 128
Fax: ++1 (415)788-7324
E-mail: gsc@globalservicecorps.org
www.globalservicecorps.org

Desc.: Global Service Corps (GSC) is a nonprofit international service-learning organization that provides opportunities for volunteers to live abroad in Tanzania and Thailand, doing service work in the areas of education, health, and the environment. GSC participants enjoy full cultural immersion, through working alongside local people and living with generous host families. In Tanzania, volunteers work on Sustainable Agriculture projects or HIV/AIDS Prevention. In Thailand, participants teach English to school students and Buddhist monks, work on HIV/AIDS awareness, or shadow Thai healthcare professionals to gain experience in international health.

Sector: Agriculture, education, health.

Country: Africa (Tanzania), Asia (Thailand).

Qualif.: No professional qualifications necessary.

Nonpro: Yes.

Age: Minimum 18. Volunteers with children accepted on Thai project.

Duration: 2 weeks to 6 months.

Lang.: English. Swahili lessons provided in Tanzania.

Benefits: None.

Costs: From US$2,325 to approx. US$4,600 depending on length and program. Groups discount: 10%.US$25-28/ day after 12 weeks.

Benefits: Room and board, mentorship by an in-country coordinator, local transportation, language lessons, and a safari/excursion.

Applic.: On-line form (or from a brochure) to be completed, printed, each page signed, and returned via post with deposit.

Notes: Volunteers live with local families in order to receive a full insider's prospective of the country.

Global Vision International

3 High Street
St. Albans, AL3 4ED, UK
Tel.: ++44 (0) 1727-250250
Fax: ++44 (0) 1727-840666
E-mail: info@gvi.co.uk
www.gvi.co.uk

Desc.: Global Vision International promotes sustainable development through research, education and direct financial support through a network of international partners and full-time staff. GVI matches people with environmentalists, researchers and educators in the fields of conservation and community development to assist in many of the world's most critical conservation and community projects. Volunteer opportunities are available in over 20 countries worldwide.

Sector: Community development, education, environment.

Country: Africa (South Africa, Kenya, Madagascar, Seychelles), Asia (Nepal, Thailand, Indonesia), Latin America (Belize, Bolivia, Brazil, Chile, Ecuador, Mexico, Guatemala, Honduras, Panama, Peru).

Qualif: No particular skills necessary: professionals are welcome.

Nonpro.: Yes.

Age: Minimum 18.

Duration: 2 weeks to 1 year.

Lang.: English.

Benefits: Accommodation, food, project equipment and training all included, as well as full pre-departure and in the field support. See www.gvi.co.uk for more information.

Costs: GB£250 to GB£3,000 depending on project and duration. Flights and insurance not included.

Applic.: Place in a project is secured with a non-returnable deposit of GB £250. This sum is deducted from the expedition cost. Full payment is due 3 month prior to the expedition start date.

Notes: Reasonable physical fitness and ability to swim over 200 metres is necessary. International volunteers welcome.

Global Volunteer Network

PO Box 30-968, Level 2, 105 High Street
Lower Hutt, New Zealand
Tel.: ++64 (4) 569-9080
(toll free in the UK 0800 032 5035, in N. Am. 1-800-963-1198,
in Australia 1-800-203 -012)   Fax: ++64 (4) 569-9081
E-mail: info@volunteer.org.nz
www.volunteer.org.nz

Desc.	The Global Volunteer Network's vision is to support the work of local community organizations in developing countries through the placement of international volunteers. Local communities are in the best position to determine their needs, and GVN provides volunteers to help them achieve their goals. GVN's aim is to provide challenging and affordable volunteer opportunities around the globe, and the network continues to expand with new programs being researched and assessed. GVN places every year almost 2,000 international volunteers.
Sector:	Culture, education, environment, health, sanitation.
Country:	Africa (Ghana, Kenya, South Africa, Tanzania, Uganda), Asia (Cambodia, China, Nepal, Philippines, Thailand, Vietnam), Europe (Romania, Russia), Latin America (Costa Rica, Ecuador, El Salvador, Honduras), North America (Alaska, South Dakota), Oceania (NZ).
Qualif.:	Varies from program to program, but most do not require specialised skills.
Nonpro:	Yes.
Age:	Minimum 18 unless otherwise noted.
Duration:	Programs run year round and last between 2 weeks to 1 year.
Lang.:	English.
Benefits:	Training, accommodation, food, transportation, supervision.
Costs:	Application fee of US$350. Program fees cover food and accommodation, and vary from program to program. Volunteers also need to cover return air travel, Visa, vaccinations, and corresponding airport departure taxes.
Applic.:	On-line form.
Notes:	Volunteers may come from anywhere in the world. Prices and other details are subject to change. See website for updates.

Global Volunteers

375 East Little Canada Road
St. Paul, Minnesota 55117-1628 USA
Tel.: ++1 (651) 407-6100 (toll free in N. Am. 1-800-487-1074)
Fax: ++1 (651) 482-0915
E-mail: info@globalvolunteers.org
www.globalvolunteers.org

Desc.: Global Volunteers, a private non-profit, non-sectarian development organisation, was founded in 1984 with the goal of helping to establish a foundation for peace through mutual international understanding. As a non-governmental organisation (NGO) in special consultative status with the United Nations, Global Volunteers is uniquely positioned to represent local leaders in a national and international arena, and to engage short-term volunteers in local development efforts with long-lasting results. At the request of local leaders and indigenous host organisations, Global Volunteers sends teams of volunteers to live and work with local people on human and economic development projects identified by the community as important to its long-term development. In this way, the volunteers' energy, creativity, and labour are put to use at the same time that they gain a genuine, first-hand understanding of how other people live day-to-day.

Sector: Community development, education, health.

Country: Africa (Ghana, Tanzania), Asia (China, India), Caribbean (Jamaica), Europe (Greece, Hungary, Ireland, Italy, Poland, Portugal, Romania), Latin America (Brazil, Costa Rica, Ecuador, Mexico, Peru), North America (USA-Hawaii), Oceania (Australia, Cook Islands).

Qualif.: No particular qualifications are necessary.

Nonpro: Yes.

Age: Global Volunteers welcomes individuals and groups of all ages and backgrounds.

Duration: 1, 2, or 3 weeks depending on the community and the site. Volunteers who wish to stay longer in the community may choose to sign up for additional Global Volunteers programs. Programs are often offered back-to-back, during consecutive weeks. See the program date page on the website for more specific information about the dates for each program.

Lang.: English.

Benefits: Accommodation, meals and the services of a team leader.

Costs: US$350 deposit is required with application. The service program fee for 1-, 2-, or 3-week international service programs, including non-continental US programs, ranges from US$1,470 to US$ 2,650, excluding airfare. The service program fee for 1-week continental US service programs is US$750 (or $650 with Internet processing), excluding airfare. All expenses, including airfare, are tax-deductible for US taxpayers. See each program page for specific price information. Discounts available for students, groups, and repeat volunteers.

Applic.:   On-line form with credit card for deposit, or print the text form and mail or fax the application and deposit. Volunteers select the site and program dates during which they want to volunteer. More than 90% of all applicants are accepted. Make travel arrangements as soon as placement on the service program is confirmed. The balance is due 75 days before the team is scheduled to arrive in the community, or immediately if the application is received within 75 days of the team's arrival date.

Notes: Before applying carefully read the On-line Volunteer Booklet. For further questions, phone the organisation and ask to speak to a volunteer coordinator.

Global Works Travel

2342 Broadway
Boulder, Colorado 80304 USA
Tel.: ++1 (303) 545-2202
Fax: ++1 (303) 545-2425
E-mail: info@globalworkstravel.com
www.globalworkstravel.com

Desc.:	The programs are aimed to introduce students to new cultures and countries and positively affect the communities in which they visit. Students stay in a community and contribute their labour and in exchange begin to learn about other cultures, global issues, and often another language. Global Works summer programs are located in all types of climates and cultures around the world. Students live in places such as villages in the mountains of Fiji or in small fishing villages in Ireland. Students spend roughly sixty hours of their time doing community service projects and the remaining time on travel and adventure activities.
Sector:	Community development, construction, culture, environment.
Country:	Caribbean (Martinique), Europe (Ireland, France, Spain), Latin America (Argentina, Costa Rica, Ecuador, Mexico, Panama, Peru, Puerto Rico), Oceania (Fiji, New Zealand).
Qualif.:	No qualifications needed.
Nonpro:	Yes, high school students.
Age:	14–18. High school students only.
Duration:	Summer programs, 15–35 days.
Lang.:	Some English, other "Immersion" programs require 2 years of Spanish or French. Immersion programs include homestays and focus on conversational language learning.
Benefits:	Food, accommodation, adventure activities.
Costs:	US$3,495–5,695, depending on program. Airfare and insurance not included.
Applic.:	On-line form. Health and medical insurance forms required.
Notes:	Staff must be over the age of 23 to apply.

Globe Aware

7232 Fisher Road
Dallas, Texas 75214 USA
Tel.: ++1 (877) 588-4562
www.globeaware.org
info@globeaware.org

Desc.: Globe Aware , a nonprofit 501 (c) (3) organization, develops short-term volunteer programs in international environments that encourage people to immerse themselves in a unique way of giving back. These short-term (one week) adventures in service focus on cultural-awareness and sustainability, and are often compared to a "mini peace corps". All program costs, including the cost of airfare, are tax-deductible for US Citizens and permanent residents.

Sector: Community development, education, environment, skills training, various.

Country: Africa (Ghana), Asia (Cambodia, China, Laos, Nepal, Thailand, Vietnam), Europe (Romania), Latin America (Brazil, Costa Rica, Cuba, Mexico, Peru), the Caribbean (Jamaica).

Qualif.: Volunteers need no special skills. Just the motivation to be immersed in a new culture and to enjoy befriending people in new and interesting countries and experience the reward of helping them on meaningful community projects.

Nonpro: Yes.

Age: Minimum age for an unaccompanied minor is 17. Families with children welcome.

Duration: Programs are designed to last one week, but volunteers can choose to extend for a maximum of two weeks at the cost if US$350 per additional week.

Lang.: English.

Benefits: Program fees cover community donations, program materials, accommodations, food, onsite transportation, medical insurance, emergency evacuation insurance, planned cultural activities and a bilingual Volunteer Coordinator.

Costs: Refer to program fee and date schedule on www.globeaware.org/Content/trips. Cost is between US$1090 and US$1,300. 15% discount for children and a 10% discount for repeat Globe Aware volunteers.

Applic.: Volunteers can register online, via phone, or fax.

Good Shepherd Volunteers

337 East 17th Street
New York, New York 10003 USA
Tel.: ++1 (888) 668-6GSV ext. 780
Fax: ++1 (212) 979-8604
E-mail: gsv@goodshepherds.org
www.gsvolunteers.org

Desc.: Good Shepherd Volunteers collaborates with the Sisters of the Good Shepherd to provide full-time volunteers with the opportunity to work in social service ministries and to use their God-given talents serving women, adolescents and children affected by poverty, violence and neglected in the U.S. and Latin America. Developing relationships with the marginalized of our world empowers volunteers to grow in knowledge and faith that inspire them to lead a life of seeking justice.

Sector: Child welfare, education, religious, women's issues.

Country: Latin America (Mexico, Paraguay, Peru), North America (USA).

Qualif.: Part-time volunteer experience (helpful), awareness of human and social needs, high school graduate, college-educated or have 2 years work experience, maturity, flexibility, sense of humor, commitment to working with others .

Nonpro: Yes, with some college education and work experience.

Age: Minimum 21.

Duration: 1 year (US sites) or 2 years (international sites) renewable.

Lang.: Spanish proficiency for Latin America programs.

Benefits: Room and board, small stipend, medical insurance, deferred student loans, if applicable, supervision, workshops.

Costs: Fundraising of US$4,000-5,000 only for international programs.

Applic.: On-line form. Apply by Feb.1st. for international programs, by June 1st for domestic. Positions may still be available after.

Goodwill Community Center

PO Box 645 - 00902
00902 Kikuyu, Kenya
Tel.: ++254 (733) 470-285 or (723) 82-9077
E-mail: goodwillkenya@yahoo.com
www.goodwillkenya.com

Desc.: The Centre is a rural based non-profit organization, active since 2000 in the Kanjeru slum, Kikuyu, 21km west of Nairobi. The 3 programs are: childcare and support, HIV/Aids prevention and control, and socio-economic empowerment. The Centre offers free basic education to orphans and vulnerable children, emergency relief, referral of HIV/ positive children, advocacy and public education on the rights of orphans, and supports families caring for orphans. It also educates the public on HIV/aids prevention and control, and provides IT and marketing services, for the local handicrafts, to rural comunities. A fully fledged educational centre targeting orphans and the destitute is being established. Volunteers will be supervised by a mentor and will have an opportunity to participate in the programs, also of many other affiliate organisations in Kenya, and to be exposed to local culture and values.

Sector: Child welfare, community development, education, IT, small-enterprise development..

Country: Africa (Kenya).

Qualif.: Skills in child welfare activities, NGO and project planning and management, IT, working in community based projects, fundraising, and financial management.

Nonpro.: Yes, with relevant skills.

Age: Minimum 18. No maximum age limit but must have physical ability to partake in occasional walking.

Duration: 3 months and up. Placements can start throughout the year.

Lang.: English. Free basic training in Kiswahili and Kikuyu.

Benefits: No guaranteed food and accommodation. Volunteers are helped logistically upon request.

Costs: US$15 per day to cover living expenses in a religious hostel (if chosen as lodging facility). Single-time contribution of US$150 upon arrival.

Applic.: E-mail CV. References required by accepted volunteers.

Notes: Once accepted the applicant can request to be put in contact with former volunteers. Please see note on page 35.

Habitat for Humanity International

Global Village Program and International Volunteer Program
121 Habitat Street, Americus, Georgia 31709 USA
Tel.: ++1 (229) 924-6935
(toll free in N. Am. 1-800-HABITAT)
E-mail: publicinfo@habitat.org or ivp@habitat.org or gv@habitat.org
www.habitat.org/getinv/default.aspx

Desc.: Habitat for Humanity International is a non-profit, ecumenical Christian housing ministry. It has several volunteer programs. Global Village Program organizes 1-3 week teams internationally to help construct houses with those in need. International Volunteer Program organizes individuals to volunteer for 6-12 months off the construction site. With the US Volunteer Program one can go to the organisation's HQ in Americus, GA, USA to volunteer in various capacities.

Sector: Construction, housing.

Country: Over 80 countries in Africa, Asia, Caribbean, Europe, Latin America, Middle East, Oceania.

Qualif.: Depends on the program- some require specific skills, some do not.

Nonpro: Yes.

Age: 18 for international programs. Students and school children can sometimes join 'home based' programs in their home country.

Duration: Depends on the program- Global Village trips are 1-3 weeks. International Volunteer Program assignments last from 6-12 months.

Lang.: English. Other languages need varies depending on location.

Benefits: Global Village short-term trip volunteers must bear all the costs .

Costs: Volunteers are responsible for all the costs, which depend on destination and length of program. Many volunteers seek support from friends, family, churches, schools and businesses for this humanitarian trip.

Applic.: Contact Habitat for Humanity International or visit the website.

Notes: Travel, medical and evacuation insurance is required. Participants should be in good health. Volunteer assignments may require strenuous manual labour, sometimes at high altitudes. Habitat for Humanity Ghana, for example, works in rural areas to build decent affordable housing . People build their own home and the homes of others in the community. Repayment of the no profit, no interest loan in the form of building materials goes into a revolving fund for Habitat for Humanity to build more houses. This revolving fund is maintained by the community to create a sustainable, community-based housing program.

Heifer International

55 Heifer Rd
Perryville, Arkansas 72110 USA
Tel.: ++1 (501) 889-5124
Fax: ++1 (501) 889-5407
E-mail: ranchvol@heifer.org   lcvol@heifer.org
www.heifer.org

Desc.: Heifer International provides livestock and training to small-scale farmers worldwide. Along with the gifts of livestock, Heifer helps communities develop sustainable agriculture while improving the environment and strengthening the community. Heifer International's education program increases understanding of issues related to hunger and poverty, and empowers and inspires people to take action to create a sustainable, socially just, economically viable, and environmentally sound world. Heifer International has three Learning Centers which offer a variety of experiences designed to fulfil that mission, while also serving as working examples of the type of sustainable agriculture supported around the world.

Sector: Agriculture, community development, education, environment.

Country: United States: at Learning Centers in California, Arkansas and Massachusetts.

Qualif.: Experience and education in relevant fields.

Nonpro.: No.

Age: Minimum Age 18

Duration: Minimum one month or seasonal commitment.

Lang.: English.

Benefits: Housing and stipend

Costs: All expenses including travel, insurance, etc.

Applic.: Contact the organisation directly. Or see online http://heifer.applicationharbor.com

Help2Educate

8 Hutchcombe Farm Close
Cumnor Hill
Oxford, OX2 9HG UK
Fax: ++44 (870) 705-8808
E-mail: contact@help2educate.org
www.help2educate.org

Desc.: Help2educate is a small registered charity that raises money to fund the education of child labourers in Nepal. It makes it possible to move children from dangerous working conditions and place them in a hostel where they can live and study. Most of the funds are raised by arranging for volunteers to teach in Nepal throughout the year. To teach in a Nepali school or help deprived children in a hostel can be a challenging, adventurous and worthwhile experience for people of any age and background.

Sector: Education.

Country: Asia (Nepal)

Qualif.: None.

Nonpro: Yes.

Age: Minimum 18.

Duration: 1-5 months

Lang.: English.

Benefits: Free flight over Mount Everest.

Costs: 1 month: GB£500. 3 months: GB£700. Costs include food, lodging, volunteering, donation to charity and administrative costs. Volunteers must make their own travel arrangements to and from Nepal. All volunteers are met at the airport.

Applic.: Accepted throughout the year. Application forms available on website.

IBO – International Building Organization

St. Annastraat 172
6524 GT Nijmegen The Netherlands
Tel.: ++31 (24) 322-6074
Fax: ++31 (24) 322-6076
E-mail: info@bouworde.nl
www.bouworde.nl

Desc.:	IBO aims to assist with the implementation of construction projects for people who need help, regardless of their race, nationality, or philosophy. Aid is provided by volunteers who do short-term manual work. The IBO wants to assist in creating conditions for real peace between people and nations by encouraging volunteers of different nationalities to work together and live with people in other countries. IBO's most important field of work is the improvement of the housing conditions of underprivileged people: homes for handicapped children, old people's homes, orphanages, and hostels for the homeless.
Sector:	Construction, housing, human rights.
Country:	Europe (Albania, Austria, Belgium, Bulgaria, Croatia, Czech Republic, Denmark, France, Germany, Hungary, Italy, Lithuania, Moldova, Netherlands, Poland, Portugal, Romania, Russia).
Qualif:	No specific qualifications needed.
Nonpro:	Yes.
Age:	Minimum 18.
Duration:	3 weeks.
Lang.:	English, German.
Benefits:	Available accommodation or tents. Meals are usually prepared by the volunteers. IBO pays for travel (from NL) and insurance.
Costs:	40 hours per week without pay. Partial camp costs (about EUR100–400 depending on the country). Travel to Holland.
Applic.:	Preferably via e-mail. Alternatively phone, write, or fax to request an application form.
Notes:	Volunteers must be in good physical and mental condition. See also: **IBO Austria**: www.members.eunet.at/oebo **IBO Belgium**: www.bouworde.be **IBO Germany**: www.bauorden.de **IBO Italy**: www.iboitalia.org **IBO Switzerland**: www.bauorden.ch

ICYE – International Cultural Youth Exchange

Große Hamburger Str. 30, D-10115
Berlin Germany
Tel.: ++49 (30) 2839-0550 or 2839-0551
Fax: ++49 (30) 2839-0552
E-mail : icye@icye.org
www.icye.org

Desc.: ICYE is an international non-profit youth exchange organisation promoting youth mobility, intercultural learning and international voluntary service. ICYE organises long and short term exchanges combining home stays with voluntary service in more than 34 countries around the world.

Sector: Child welfare, community development, culture, education, environment, health, human rights, IT, refugee aid, women's issues.

Country: Africa (Ghana, Kenya, Morocco, Mozambique, Nigeria, Uganda), Asia (India, Japan, Nepal, South Korea, Taiwan), Europe (Austria, Belgium, Denmark, Finland, France, Germany, Iceland, Italy, Lithuania, Sweden, Switzerland, Russian Federation, UK), Latin America (Bolivia, Brazil, Colombia, Costa Rica, Honduras, Mexico), Oceania (New Zealand).

Qualif.: N/A.

Nonpro: Yes.

Age: 16–25; 18–30 for some international projects.

Duration: 6 or 12 months; some 2–8 week projects available.

Lang.: English.

Benefits: In general no scholarship as the ICYE program is self-sustained. Possibility to join the EVS (see listing) program subsidised by the European Union.

Costs: Varies from country to country (consult each member national Committee). Average 1-year fee is approximately US$5,000–6,000.

Applic.: After registration application forms are provided by respective ICYE National Committees (see website for addresses).

ICYE-UK – Inter-Cultural Youth Exchange

Latin American House, Kingsgate Place
London NW6 4TA UK
Tel.: ++44 (207) 681-0983
Fax: ++44 (207) 681-0983
E-mail: international@icye.co.uk or info@icye.co.uk
www.icye.co.uk

Desc.: ICYE-UK promotes peace, cultural understanding, and youth empowerment through opportunities of international exchange and voluntary work overseas.

Sector: Child welfare, community development, culture, education, environment, health, human rights, women's issues.

Country: Worldwide

Qualif.: N/A.

Nonpro: Yes.

Age: 18–30 for long term programmes, 18-70 for short-term.

Duration: 6–12 months (long-term), 3 weeks-4 months (short-term)..

Lang.: Language course included during orientation in long term programme.

Benefits: International travel costs, Visa support, flights to and from host country, board and lodging, health insurance, host country orientation and language course, mid-year camp and final evaluation, support and supervision during the year, pocket money. For short-term programmes see website fro details.

Costs: 12-month participation fee is GB£3,900 and the 6-months participation fee is GB£3,300. Fundraising support offered. For short-term programmes see website fro details.

Notes: UK nationals or residents only. For non-UK residents, please refer to ICYE International (see listing). Consult the ICYE website for contact details.

IESC Geekcorps

1900 M St NW, Suite 500
Washington, DC 20036 USA
Tel.: ++1(202)326-0280 - Fax: ++1(202)380-0289
E-mail: geekcorps@iesc.org
http://geekcorps.org

Desc.: IESC Geekcorps promotes economic growth in the developing world by sending highly skilled technology volunteers to teach communities how use innovative and affordable information and communication technologies to solve development problems, creating digitally independent nations in the process. Volunteers are matched with projects based on the technical skills required.

Sector: IT, small-enterprise development.

Country: Africa (Ghana, Rwanda, Senegal, Mali, Zimbabwe), Asia (Armenia, Kyrgyzstan, Mongolia, Thailand), Europe (Romania, Bulgaria), and Middle East (Lebanon).

Qualif.: Programmers, web designers, database and software developers, network administrators, graphic artists, and business and marketing professionals have all volunteered through Geekcorps.

Nonpro: IT professionals with at least five years of industry experience.

Duration: Six weeks to six months. The average Geekcorps assignment is three to four months.

Lang.: English.

Benefits: All costs are covered: airfare, vaccinations, insurance, a living stipend, accommodations, visas, etc.

Costs: Geekcorps covers all costs but asks volunteers and/or their employers to contribute if possible.

Applic.: On-line form.

IFESH – International Foundation for Education and Self-Help

5040 E. Shea Blvd., Suite 260, Scottsdale, AZ 85250 USA
Tel.: ++1 (480) 443-1800
Fax: ++1 (480) 443-1824
E-mail: see online contact forms
www.ifesh.org

Desc.:	IFESH was established as a charitable organization under the vision and leadership of the late Reverend Leon H. Sullivan to reduce hunger and poverty, empower the local community by raising the standard of literacy, and to foster cultural, social, and economic relations between Africans and Americans particularly those of African descent.IFESH focuses on empowering individuals through the operation and support of community-based programs in the areas of literacy, education, vocational training, agriculture, nutrition and health care. The organization seeks the development and utilization of technical skills of all people, regardless of race, color, creed or sex. The primary area of concern is sub-Saharan Africa.
Sector:	Agriculture, community development, education, health, IT, small enterprise development, skills training.
Country:	Africa (various sub-Saharan countries).
Qualif.:	Various experience in a professional field depending upon program. Computers skills are very important.
Nonpro:	Yes.
Age:	Variable.
Duration:	One year; also depends upon program.
Lang.:	English. Foreign language not required but helpful.
Benefits:	Various depending upon program.
Costs:	Contact organization for more information.
Applic.:	TFA/IFP (see notes) online form, others available on request.
Notes:	The Teachers for Africa Program places experienced teachers, professors, and education administrators for one academic year. The International Fellows Program provides 9 month internships for graduate students or recent graduates.

INFO Nepal - Volunteer in Nepal

Post Box No 19531
Kathmandu, Nepal
Tel.: ++977 (1) 470-0210
Mob.: +977 (985) 105-4813
E-mail: infonepal@mail.com.np
www.infonepal.org

Desc.:	Based in Kathmandu, INFO Nepal is a non-governmental organization (NGO) registered with the Social Welfare Council of Nepal. Founded in 2000 by four Nepalese with many years of experience managing other International NGOs, INFO Nepal is the first Nepali run volunteer organization for social benefit. Info Nepal's mission is to create a global understanding by encouraging volunteers to assist with community development and youth mobilization programs. Since its inception, INFO has placed over 950 volunteers from 45 countries in villages throughout Nepal and has developed a wide variety of programs addressing environmental and development issues.
Sector:	Child welfare, community development, education, environment, health, skills training, sanitation, various.
Country:	Asia (Nepal).
Qualif.:	No formal qualification needed. However a genuine desire to help people is a must together with the willingness to experience a new culture and lifestyle.
Nonpro:	Yes.
Age:	Minimum 18.
Duration:	Two weeks to 4 months.
Lang.:	English.
Benefits:	Accommodation, which varies from project to project, food, training and supervision.
Costs:	Refer to information schedule on the website. Cost start from approx. EUR250 for two weeks to EUR900 for four months.
Applic.:	On-line application form.

Interconnection Virtual Volunteer Program

2222 N Pacific St
Seattle WA 98103 USA
Tel.: ++1 (206) 310-4547
Fax: ++1 (206) 633-1517
E-mail: info@interconnection.org
www.interconnection.org

Desc.: InterConnection works to make Internet technology accessible to underserved communities around the world by providing high quality, no cost and low cost Internet services, refurbished computers, and Internet and computer training programs. The goal is to create an international community network via the Internet that fosters a two-way flow of support, information and expertise among organizations working to make a difference. InterConnection's main international volunteer program is the Virtual Volunteer Program. This program matches web-savvy volunteers from all over the world with non-profit organization in developing countries who need websites. Volunteers work with the organizations, via the Internet, to create custom-made, professional websites. The accessibility of this innovative program is the key to its tremendous success. Since all work is done online, it provides a venue for global-minded people to help developing communities without leaving home.

Sector: IT.

Country: Worldwide.

Qualif.: Web design, technical expertise, graphic design skills, etc.

Nonpro: Yes, with relevant skills.

Age: N/A with necessary experience.

Duration: Approximately 1 month.

Lang: Varies with each organisation.

Benefits: Web design expericence.

Costs: None.

Applic.: On-line form at www.interconnection.org

International Executive Service Corps

1900 M St NW, Suite 500
Washington, DC 20036 USA
Tel.: ++1 (202) 589-2600
Fax: ++1 (202) 326-0289
E-mail: iesc@iesc.org
www.iesc.org

Desc.: Volunteer experts have worked in more than 130 countries worldwide transferring their knowledge and skills to assist entrepreneurs, small and medium-sized businesses, NGO's, trade associations, and business support organizations in the developing world and emerging democracies. Volunteers are committed to promoting free enterprise and democracy by assisting, instructing, and inspiring people, businesses and organizations around the world. IESC programs include: technical and managerial assistance; micro, small and medium sized enterprise development; institution strengthening; quality enhancement; grants management; health and human resources; public administration policy, conflict and post-conflict management, and training programs, workshps and seminars.

Sector: Agriculture, IT, skills training, small-enterprise development, various.

Country: Various countries worldwide: Africa, Asia, the Caribbean, Europe, Latin America and the Middle East.

Qualif.: At least 10 years experience in a professional field. Volunteers with expertise in tourism/hospitality, textiles/apparel, handicrafts, and agribusiness/food processing are in great demand. Computer proficiency and active email address are essential.

Nonpro: No.

Age: Variable, typically senior-level business professionals.

Duration: Both short-term and long-term ranging from 1 week to several months.

Lang.: English. Foreign language not required but highly desirable, particularly French, Spanish and Arabic.

Benefits: Airfare and specified travel related expenses, such as immunizations and Visas, are covered. Volunteers receive a per diem set by the federal government for meals and housing.

Costs: Contact organization for more information.

Applic.: On-line form through website. Electronic version of CV required.

International Medical Corps

1919 Santa Monica Blvd., Suite 400,
Santa Monica, CA 90404, USA
Tel.: ++1 (310) 826-7800
Fax: ++1 (310) 442-6622
E-mail: imc@imcworldwide.org
www.imcworldwide.org

Desc.: International Medical Corps is a global, humanitarian non-profit organization dedicated to saving lives and relieving suffering by providing health-care training and medical-relief programmes worldwide. IMC is a private, non-political, non-profit, non-sectarian organization with the organizational flexibility to respond rapidly to emergency situations. IMC's mission is to improve the quality of life through health interventions and related activities that build local capacity.

Sector: Child welfare, emergency, health, hunger relief, sanitation, women's issues.

Country: Africa (Burundi, Central African Republic, Chad, DRC, Eritrea, Ethiopia, Kenya, Liberia, Mozambique, Sierra Leone, Somalia, Sudan, Tanzania, Uganda), Asia (Afghanistan, Azerbaijan, Indonesia, Nepal, Pakistan, Sri Lanka), Europe (Georgia, Russia), Middle East (Jordan, Iraq, Lebanon, Syria).

Qualif.:: Qualifications preferred: physicians, registered nurses, psychosocial advisors, emergency medicine personnel, public health, country program directors, finance officers, nurse practitioners, logistics and administrative specialists.

Nonpro.: No. Volunteers with professional qualifications (licensed with International or Emergency Medical experience) only.

Duration: Minimum 3 months; paid positions minimum 6-months.

Lang.: English, French, Arabic.

Benefits: Medical evacuation, health insurance, shared housing.

Costs: Inquire with organisation for details.

Applic.: Submit CV on-line. No telephone calls.

Notes: Minority group members, women, and disabled individuals are actively recruited and hired as part of the commitment to equal opportunity employment. Positions are open to qualified professionals of any nationality.

International Partnership for Service Learning and Leadership

815 Second Avenue, Suite 315
New York, New York 10017-4594 USA
Tel.: ++1 (212) 986-0989
Fax: ++1 (212) 986-5039
E-mail: info@ipsl.org
www.ipsl.org

Desc.: Founded in 1982 to promote a new pedagogy for higher education based on the ideals of service-learning and to put these ideals into practice. All projects are locally based and serve the local community. Service agencies are schools, orphanages, recreation, health, or education centres, community development projects, museums, and cultural centres, etc. A typical day, in most programs, consists of some time spent with the host family, attending class, doing assignments, serving in the agency, and also having free time to participate in day to day activities. Field trips and special events are planned in weekends.

Sector: Child welfare, community development, construction, education, emergency, environment, health, housing, human rights, small-enterprise development, women's issues, various.

Country: Asia (India, Philippines, Thailand), Caribbean (Jamaica), Europe (Czech Republic, England, France, Italy, Russia, Scotland), Latin America (Ecuador, Mexico), North America (Lakota Nation, South Dakota, USA).

Qualif.: No specific skills required.

Nonpro: Yes, with high school education.

Age: Minimum 18.

Duration: 3–18 weeks, typically 15. Programs are 3 weeks, 8–10 weeks (summer), or 3–4 months (semester). Most students serve for a semester or the summer. Students in the MA program serve 1 year.

Lang.: English, Spanish, or French, depending on country. Spanish and French require at least 2 years high school or 1 year college background.

Benefits: The costs include instruction, administration fees, service placement and supervision, orientation, and accommodation (group or home-stay), most meals (except for the Scotland program), in-country travel, tourist excursions, staff support and required health insurance.

Costs: See website for cost details. Students are responsible for airfare, books, spending money, local travel, Visas, and health insurance.

Applic.: Written application, letters of reference, health records, and transcripts.

Notes: A physical exam will be required. Academic credit is available.

International Volunteer Program

678 13th Street Suite 200
Oakland, California 94612 USA
Tel.: ++1 (510) 433-0414 (Toll free: 1-866-614-3438)
Fax: ++1 (510) 433-0419
E-mail: layne@swiftusa.org
www.ivpsf.org

Desc.: The International Volunteer program (IVP) is a non-profit organization that promotes volunteering in Europe, the United States and Latin America. Programs are designed to facilitate hands-on service opportunities, with the aim of fostering cultural understanding and philanthropy at a local and global level. Participants work full-time in non-profit organizations while equipping themselves for effective citizenship. IVP volunteers work on a variety of projects in the areas of social justice, arts and culture, and the environment.

Sector: Child welfare, community development, culture, environment, health, human rights, various.

Country: Europe (UK, France, Spain), Latin America (Costa Rica) North America (USA).

Qualif.: No particular qualifications required.

Nonpro: Yes.

Age: Minimum 18. No upper age limit.

Duration: 6–12 weeks; typically 8.

Lang.: English, French, Spanish.

Benefits: In-country transportation, accommodation and meals provided from the receiving agency or a local host family. In-country and pre-departure training/orientation. Comprehensive health/accident/civic liability and repatriation insurance. Language and training (Costa Rica Program)

Costs: Varies with program. See website for details.

Applic.: IVP admits volunteers after an application process that includes a written application, letters of reference, CV, and a phone interview. IVP candidates must be flexible, open-minded and demonstrate a strong commitment to helping others.

i-to-i Meaningful Travel

Woodside House, 261 Low Lane,
Leeds LS18 5NY UK
Tel.: ++44 (870) 333 2332
Fax: +44 (113) 205 4618
E-mail: info@i-to-i.com
www.i-to-i.com

Desc.: i-to-i is an award-winning volunteer travel and TEFL training organisation. Arranging volunteer travel opportunities and paid teaching contracts for over 5,000 people every year and training a further 15,000 people worldwide to Teach English as a Foreign Language via our online and weekend training courses. With more than 500 projects available, in 38 countries the opportunities to make a difference are endless.

Sector: Child welfare, community development, construction, culture, education, environment, health, small-enterprise development, various.

Country: Africa (Egypt, Ghana, Kenya, Madagascar, Mozambique, South Africa, Swaziland, Tanzania, Uganda, Zambia), Asia (Cambodia, China, India, Indonesia, Malaysia, Nepal, Philippines, Sri Lanka, Thailand, Vietnam), Latin America (Argentina, Brazil, Costa Rica, Dominica, Dominican Republic, Ecuador, Honduras, Peru, Trinidad & Tobago), Europe (Czech Republic, Greece, Hungary, Slovakia, Spain) Oceania (New Zealand).

Qualif.: Volunteer Travel - No formal qualifications are required to join i-to-i volunteer placements or TEFL courses, just fluent English. Business/media/health placements may require a CV/resume in advance - www.i-to-i.com/projects/volunteer.Paid Teaching (Professional) - Some destinations require participants to be educated to degree level - www.i-to-i.com/paid-jobs-abroad

Nonpro: Yes. See above.

Age: 18-80. Special trips are also available for families, school groups ad those under 18.

Duration: Volunteer Travel - 1 to 12 weeks.Paid Teaching - 3 to 12 months.

Lang.: English. Spanish useful fro South American destinations.

Benefits: Full pre-departure information and TEFL training (Teaching & Community Development) included as standard. Detailed information on project and country, fundraising advice and support, visa instructions and forms, vaccination and recommendations, DVD with advice on health & safety & culture shock, contact details to pass along to those at home, pick-up from the airport on the designated arrival date, welcome orientation, regularly-inspected accommodation, meals provided or self-catering accommodation, a well-researched placement, access to an emergency support team 24/7, assistance of the global i-to-i staff, guidance and advice from experienced i-to-i travellers.

Costs: Volunteers projects cost GB£495-1,895 depending on the destination and length of placement. Paid Teaching placements come with a salary of GB£250 -1,000 pcm.

Applic.:   Contact nearest office or view project opportunities online at www.i-to-i.com

Notes: i-to-i has five main offices worldwide:

UK (0870 333-2332, uk@i-to-i.com)

USA (800 985 4852, usa@i-to-i.com)

Canada (800 985 4864, canada@i-to-i.com)

Ireland (058 400 50, ireland@i-to-i.com)

Australia (1300 556 997, australia@i-to-i.com)

IVDN – Interactive Voluntary Development Service

Interactive Voluntary Development Network-Africa
PO Box 40195-80100
Mombasa, Kenya
Tel.: ++254 (41) 470-147
Mob: ++254 (721) 393 347
E-mail: info@ivdn-africa.org or volunteerkenya@yahoo.com
www.ivdn-africa.org

Desc.:	IVDN's mission is to provide opportunities for both locals and international volunteers to interact in both educational and development programmes thus enabling them to gain experience and build their capacities. Volunteers are able to work in both rural and urban areas especially in marginalised areas. Other places of work include orphanages, community health centres, hospitals, research centres and community based organisations projects. A variety of skills are also needed to help build the organisations. Volunteer positions provide a unique opportunity for visitors to participate in the local culture and better understand the values of the people of the region. Volunteers are supervised by a mentor during their stay. IVDN-Africa also recruites medical students for two purposes: 1.Elective programs for medical students 2.Pre-medical programs for non-medical students who want to join medical colleges later. Students are placed in big public, mission and private hospitals and health centers accross Kenya.
Sector:	Child Welfare, community development, culture, education, health, skills training, various.
Country:	Africa (Kenya).
Qualif.:	No particular skills required other than initiative and adaptability.
Nonpro:	Yes.
Age:	Minimum 17.
Duration:	Minimum 2 weeks to 6 months.
Lang.:	English.
Benefits:	Accommodation and food, orientation on arrival, all airport transfers and 3 days safari Camping to Maasai Mara National park.
Costs:	Cost varies according to the duration and location of the programme but the average cost is EUR650 for 4 weeks to cover living expenses. Cost of the medical program: US$1850
Applic.:	E-mail CV or Resume.
Notes:	Once accepted the applicant can request to be put in contact with former volunteers. Please see note on page 35.

IVS – International Voluntary Service

IVS - GB
Oxford Place Centre, Oxford Place, Leeds, LS1 3AX
Tel.: ++44 (113) 246 9900
Fax: ++44 (113) 246 9910
E-mail: england@ivs-gb.org.uk
www.ivs-gb.org.uk

Desc.:	IVS-GB is the British branch of SCI (see listing), a peace movement that was founded in the aftermath of the first world war. IVS is a voluntary NGO that aims to promote peace and international co-operation and understanding. IVS organises volunteer projects both in Britain and in some 45 countries throughout the world. Volunteers work for the sustainable development of local and global community organisations.
Sector:	Child welfare, construction, culture, education, environment, peacekeeping.
Country:	Over 45 countries in Africa, Asia, Europe, Latin America, Middle East..
Qualif.:	No particular qualifications needed.
Nonpro:	Yes.
Age:	Minimum 18; max. 70, for some countries volunteers must be 21.
Duration:	2–4 weeks; some longer term posts available.
Lang.:	Generally English. Some projects have a language requirement.
Benefits:	Accommodation and food are provided by the project. IVS provides basic insurance.
Cost:	Volunteer project registration fee which includes IVS membership from GB£50/95 for GB to £185/£145 abroad, volunteers pay travel costs.
Applic.:	See website for nearest office.
Notes:	**IVS England**: england@ivs-gb.org.uk
	IVS Scotland: scotland@ivs-gb.org.uk
	IVS Ireland and Northern Ireland: info@ivsni.org

Jesuit Refugee Service

Borgo S. Spirito 4, 00193 Rome Italy
Tel.: ++39 (06) 6897-7386
Fax: ++39 (06) 6897-7380
E-mail: international@jrs.net
www.jrs.net

Desc.:	The Jesuit Refugee Service is an international Catholic organisation, active in more than 60 countries. Its mission is to accompany, serve, and defend the rights of refugees and displaced people. The mission includes all those who have been displaced form their homes because of conflicts or persecution, tragedy, and violations of human rights. The services include educational programs for children, teenagers, and adults, pastoral guidance, small economic activities, advocacy, social services, and health counselling and assistance.
Sector:	Education, emergency, human rights, refugee aid, skills training.
Country:	Over 50 countries; on every continent.
Qualif.:	Social workers, skills trainers, lawyers, educators, medical doctors, administrators, and project coordinators are desired. Occasionally other skilled staff is recruited.
Nonpro:	No. Skilled personnel only and preferably with experience in emergency and/or conflict situations.
Age:	Generally not under 25; exceptions based upon experience.
Duration:	2-year standard contract.
Lang.:	English, plus the official language of country of placement.
Benefits:	Round-trip travel, food, accommodation, insurance, contribution towards personal expenses (varies with country of placement).
Costs:	None.
Applic.:	Send CV via post, fax, or e-mail to humanresources. international@jrs.net Apply only to a specific placement posted on the website. An e-mail newsletter posts available positions.
Notes:	Volunteers must share and respect the mission and vision that underlies the organisation's philosophy.

Joint Assistance Centre, Inc.

PO Box 6082
San Pablo, California 94806 USA
Fax: ++1 (510) 217-6671
E-mail: jacusa@juno.com
www.jacusa.org

Desc.: Joint Assistance Centre is a voluntary group based in the USA. It works with various non-governmental organizations in India, Nepal and Bangladesh.. Most programs involve working with villagers in cooperation with non-governmental and community based organisations devoted to their welfare.

Sector: Agriculture, child welfare, community development, construction, education, environment, health, sanitation, women's issues.

Country: Asia (India, Nepal and Bangadlesh).

Qualif.: No particular qualifications needed.

Nonpro: Yes.

Age: Minimum 18.

Duration: Short-term projects are 1–4 weeks; long-term projects are from 3 months.

Lang.: English. Long-term volunteers should be prepared to learn some basic Hindi or Nepali languages, preferably before arriving or can take a quick refresher course on arrival.

Benefits: Accommodation, food, staff support, airport pick-up.

Costs: Application registration fee of US$50, short-term work camp programs are US$300 for 1 month, additional costs per month are US$150. Long-term placements cost US$500 for 3 months and US$150 per additional month.

Applic.: On-line form, letters of reference, telephone interview. Processing time from 3-6 weeks.

Notes: Individual medical insurance coverage should be obtained before departure. Processing time may be longer if physically handicapped.

Kibbutz Program Center – Takam-Artzi

Hashomer Hatzair
18 Frishman Street/cr.
Ben Yehuda, Tel-Aviv 61030 Israel
Tel.: ++972 (3) 527-8874 or 524-6156
Fax: ++972 (3) 523-9966
E-mail: kpc@volunteer.co.il
www.kibbutz.org.il

Desc.: Although Israel can not be considered a developing country the kibbutz movement has been an example of the success of volunteering and communal life. After the Six-Day War in 1967, a wave of volunteers from all over the world began arriving in Israel. Their intentions were to show their goodwill towards the State of Israel and the Israeli People by becoming kibbutz volunteers. The notion of a kibbutz community carrying out the true principles of a socialistic society, having all work, property, and profit equally shared by its members, intrigued the volunteers. The volunteers work 8 hours a day, 6 days a week. The agricultural work branches in the kibbutz are very varied. The work includes fruit picking, working in greenhouses, with irrigation systems, in fisheries, in chicken and turkey houses and egg incubators, and with cows and diaries. The work in tourism includes helping out in guest houses, restaurants, nature sights, health spas, and tourist shops. The services include work in the kitchen, the dinning room, and in the laundry. Sometimes the volunteers work in the metal workshop, the children's zoo, the children's houses, or help in the kibbutz industry and in any other service related work branch in the kibbutz. The Kibbutz Program Center of the United Kibbutz Movement and the Kibbutz Haartzi is the office officially representing all the approximately 250 kibbutzes spread throughout the country of Israel. Since 1967, more than 100,000 kibbutz volunteers have arrived in Israel to participate in this experience.

Sector: Agriculture, various.

Country: Middle East (Israel).

Qualif.: None. Volunteers with specific professions or trades can be placed where their skills can be used.

Nonpro: Yes.

Age: 18-35.

Duration: 2-6 months.

Lang.: English, Hebrew.

Benefits: Accommodations (rooms with between 2-4 people in each room), food, laundry service, pocket money each month (approx. US$80), tourist expeditions. The volunteers are free to use the sports facilities of the kibbutz and the swimming pool. In most kibbutzes, a pub and even a disco is arranged for the volunteers and the younger population. Each month the volunteers are given 3 free days.

Costs: International travel, Visas ($17 for 3 months), insurance (US$55), registration fee (US$100, valid for 1 year; there is no extra charge for transferring between kibbutzes), a US$50-100 security deposit that is returned to the volunteers after 2 months in the kibbutz, minimum US$250 personal funds.

Applic.: Contact a kibbutz representative in country of residence (see website for contacts) or register directly through the Kibbutz Program Center via e-mail or fax including name, a short bio, age, passport number and nationality, date of birth, and date of arrival. Volunteers with specific requests must apply at least 6 weeks in advance stating their job, education, and experience. Volunteers must bring a valid passport, a medical certificate, a return ticket, and at least US$250 (not to be paid to the kibbutz, but the volunteer must prove they have some personal funds).

Note: Upon arrival (especially in the busy seasons) there is no guaranty of being placed on a kibbutz immediately. Volunteers may have to wait a few days in a hostel for a free place in a kibbutz. Volunteers from Sweden can read more on www.svekiv.se

Kids Worldwide

Administration HQ
40 Shrewsbury Street
Christchurch, New Zealand
Tel.: ++64 (3) 3669015
E-mail: kwwinfo@kidsworldwide.org
www.kidsworldwide.org

Desc.: Kids Worldwide is an international volunteer organisation run by volunteers for volunteers. It deals with local grassroots organisations in Africa, Asia and South America. Most of the projects are either schools, orphanages or programmes for street children. There is the option for volunteers to take on leadership roles in the organisation through becoming volunteer coordinators for new projects or existing projects after volunteering on site. Prospective volunteers are assisted with information and booking. Many of the projects also maintain close links between old and new volunteers through discussion groups and mailing lists. Volunteers arrange their travel and dates. More specific orientation on site is provided upon arrival at the project. A donation is only requested upon arrival at the project to assist with covering food and accommodation. Fundraising prior to arriving is encouraged and welcomed by the project directors.

Sector: Child welfare, education, environment, health, women's issues.

Country: Africa (Ghana, Cameroon, Liberia, Ethiopia, Sierra Leone, Tanzania, Uganda), Asia (India, Indonesia, Nepal), Latin America, (Peru, Brazil).

Qualif.: No particular qualifications needed. Certain volunteer positions require teaching experience, PR, or medical qualifications.

Nonpro: Yes.

Age: Minimum 18.

Duration: Projects in South America request a minimum of 3 months. Projects in Africa and Asia are open to volunteers' time commitments (usually 1-12 months).

Lang.: English for African and Asian projects, Spanish for Peru, Portuguese for Brazil. South American projects do offer some assistance in learning the local language but stress that volunteers start to learn the language before arrival.

Benefits: Accommodation, food, training, project-related transportation in some cases, living expenses such as electricity, linen, etc.

Costs: Approx. US$200/month. Travel expenses to and from the project, medical insurance, and personal expenses (US$100 per month is adequate). US$ 30 non refundable application fee.

Applic.: On-line form or via e-mail. Response will be given in 2 weeks. Apply at least 2 months in advance.

Notes: The following projects are currently available (see website for further information and for specific webpages). **Ghana**: *Ejura Primary school* (Ejura) caters for approximately 200 primary age children. *Lotus Children Centre* (Accra) a home for 10 girls from disadvantaged backgrounds. Children library and KG. *Tafo and Tintinto street kids project* (Nkawkaw) a cultural and drama programme for primary aged children and a teaching and sports programme for boys from at-risk families. *Christ Our Hope school* (Kumasi) caters for primary aged children with a focus on foreign languages. Five kindergartens / primary schools in Accra accommodate volunteers in homestays with local staff. **Sierra Leone**: *Rhema Preparatory School* (Freetwon) caters to 300 primary aged children. **Liberia**: *F-SHAM of Faith Girls Academy* (Monrovia) provides education to girls from 1-18 years of age. **Cameroon**: *United Action for Children* (see listing). **Ethopia**: *Tsige Tadesse Orphanage Centre* (near Addis Ababba). **Uganda**: *Kinship House* (Kampala) orphanage for boys and girls. **Tanzania**:*Hands for Mercy* (Mwanza) orphanage. **India**: *Daya Orphanage* (Orissa) caters for 35 boys and girls.*Uma Nivas* (West Bengal) orphanage, KG and Primary school. **Nepal**: *Harka Orphanage* (near Chitwan National Park) home to 16 orphans. **Indonesia** (Bali): *Narayan Seva* girls orphanage and KG **Peru**: *Incawasi* (Cajamarca).

LA-NO-CHE Orphanage

La No Che Orphans & Youth Camp - Kibaha
PO Box 30828, Kwa Matias Nyumbu Road
Kibaha Coast Regional, Tanzania
Tel.: +255 (755) 044-448 or +255 (753) 220-312
E-mail: lanochecamp@yahoo.com or workcamptz@hotmail.com
www.go-mad.org/projlanoche.php

Desc.:	The Organisaton, founded in 2003, has the aim to provide a safe and secure home for Tanzanian children orphaned by AIDS, Malaria and Tuberculosis. It provides orphans with food, accommodation, clothing and education, while ensuring that they receive the physical and emotional care a child requires. The organisation is establishing a new center for youth and HIV/AIDS orphans at Mkuza village, Kibaha coastal district. Volunteers help in construction, and in all the activities that take place: education, play, sports, cooking, cleaning, etc. A small replanting project also takes place nearby. Volunteers are expected to work 4 to 5 hours a day, 5 days a week.
Sector:	Child welfare, community development, construction, education, environment.
Country:	Africa (Tanzania).
Qualif.:	Strong motivation and particulsr love for children.
Nonpro:	Yes. Anyone, with or without skills is welcome.
Age:	Minimum 16 with no maximum age limit.
Duration:	From 1 week or longer.
Lang.:	English, volunteers will be exposed to Kiswahili.
Benefits:	Food and accommodation in the Youth center, schools, public halls and some times (very seldom) in tents. Volunteers attend cultural activities, visit schools and villages, practice sports.
Costs:	US$100 per week for short term volunteers (from 1 to 12 weeks) plus personal expenses. For long term volunteers enquire with the organisation.
Applic.:	Application formvia e-mail. Volunteers must specify their interest and intended length of stay. A Tourist Visa is valid for 3 months. For longer stays the organisation helps to appky for the proper Visa.
Notes:	Volunteers can apply through other workcamp organizations such as: Involvement Volunteers Association-Australia www.volunteering.org.au, Go MaD Organization www.go-mad.org, or others, see website. Also direct applications are accepted.

MADRE – International Women's Human Rights Organization

121 West 27th Street, Room 301, New York, New York 10001 USA
Tel.: ++1 (212) 627-0444
Fax: ++1 (212) 675-3704
E-mail: volunteers@madre.org
www.madre.org

Desc.:	MADRE is an international women's human rights organization that works in partnership with community-based women's groups worldwide. Programs reflect a human-rights-based and people-centered approach to the UN Millennium Development Goals, which aim to: eradicate extreme poverty and hunger; achieve universal primary education; promote gender equality and empower women; reduce child mortality; improve maternal health; combat HIV/AIDS, malaria and other diseases; ensure environmental sustainability; and develop a global partnership for development. MADRE provides resources and training to enable sister organizations to address immediate needs in their communities and develop long-term solutions. Since its foundation, in 1983, MADRE has given over US$21 million worth of support to women's groups throughout the world.
Sector:	Child welfare, community dev., education, health, human rights, hunger relief, IT, small-enterprise dev. women's issues.
Country:	Africa (Kenya), Latin America (Guatemala, Nicaragua, Peru).
Qualif.:	Credentials and experience in the relevant field of work.
Nonpro:	Yes, with skills relevant to the project.
Age:	N/A with necessary experience.
Duration:	Minimum 3 mo. (exceptionally 1 month or less for advanced professionals with language skills and experience abroad).
Lang.:	Spanish (except for Kenya), English.
Benefits:	Enquire with organisation.
Costs:	Volunteers cover all costs, including travel, housing, and food.
Applic.:	Contact the organisation directly.
Notes:	MADRE leads "Voyages with a Vision" to some programs, with experienced bilingual guides. Contact MADRE for details.

Makindu Children's Center

PO Box 51556, Eugene, Oregon 97405 USA
Tel./Fax: ++1 (541) 729-3707
E-mail: makindu@peak.org
www.makindu.org

Desc.: The Makindu Children's Center is an international non-profit organisation in Makindu town, eastern province of Kenya. It serves the basic needs (nutrition, affection, basic medical care and access to housing) of approximately 300 destitute orphans within the region. The children and their families served are amongst the most in need in this impoverished area—those with no other source of aid. Typically the orphans live with elderly grandparents or distant relatives, within 1–8 km walk to the Center. The program is a day resource facility, where the children come for food, washing and laundering facilities, and emotional support and crisis intervention. Their medical concerns are attended to and access to the local educational system is provided. Members of the community can come to the resource center and receive training in survival and vocational skills, guidance on various health (e.g., HIV/AIDS) and nutritional and agricultural concerns (solar cooking and vocational education). Other projects include a shamba (farm), which provides a good portion of the food as well as produce for sale, bee-keeping for the production and sale of honey, and multiple craft items such as hand-made baskets for marketing and income generation. In 2002-2003 the program has built a water system which allows potable water from a nearby spring to be delivered and distributed to the Center and a large portion of Makindu residents. Recently, the Makindu Children's Program assisted in starting a voluntary counseling and testing center for HIV, where youth and adults can come and receive free counseling, testing, and referral services.

Sector: Agriculture, child welfare, community development, education, environment, health, human rights, sanitation, small-enterprise development, women's issues, various.

Country: Africa (Kenya).

Qualif.: Special Project Volunteers to develop products and marketing for increased self sufficiency of older youth, elderly guardians, and community women. Well-qualified medical volunteers can sometimes be placed at the Makindu-town Medical Clinic.

Nonpro: Not at the present time.

Age: Minimum 21.

Duration: Special Volunteers' duration is negotiable.

Lang.: Kiswahili, English, and Kikamba

Benefits: None.

Costs: There is no fee for volunteering, but volunteers bear virtually all of their own costs, including immunizations, travel, a required Kenyan work permit and bond (US$275–450 depending on length of stay), room and board (about US$20 per week).

Applic.: After contacts via e-mail and telephone, volunteers are required to come to Eugene, Oregon, or to Kenya, at their own expense, for a personal interview prior to final selection.

Notes: A health clearance and a criminal record check are required. Prior third world volunteer or work experience is highly desirable.

Medair

Chemin du Croset 9, Entrance B, 3rd floor
CH-1024 Ecublens Switzerland
Tel.: ++41 (0) 21 694-3535
Fax: ++41 (0) 21 694-3540
E-mail : info@medair.org
www.medair.org

Desc.:   Medair is an international humanitarian aid agency based in Switzerland (with national offices in France, the Netherlands, and the UK). It provides emergency relief in underprivileged developing countries affected by war or natural disaster where crisis situations threaten to further undermine their future development and stability.

Sector: Child welfare, community development, construction, emergency, health, housing, hunger relief, sanitation.

Country: Africa (Congo, Madagascar, Sudan, Uganda), Asia (Afghanistan, Indonesia, Pakistan).

Qualif.:   Manager, administrator, health professional, water technician, logistician, shelter coordinator.

Nonpro: Occasionally recruits work alongside experienced field staff to become trained as professional relief workers.

Age: Not specified.

Duration: 1 year minimum.

Lang.:   English, some positions need French.

Benefits: Medical insurance, food, lodging, transport, US$100 per month and other project related costs. After the first year the pay increases, starting from US$1,000 per month.

Costs: For the first assignment volunteers have to pay for return flights and for seminar costs.

Applic.:   Online application form.

Notes: Christians in good health, married or single without children. All candidates must attend a 7-day introduction course including a personal interview (held 3 times per year).

Mercy Orphanage Primary and High School

PO Box 2350
Kisii 40200, Kenya
Tel.: ++254 (733) 416-782/(725) 826-822
E-mail: mercyorphanagehighschool@yahoo.com or
stcharlesorphanageschool@yahoo.com or henryomreo@yahoo.com

Desc.: Mercy Orphanage primary and high school is an orphanage home that was setup in Makara, Nyanza province in Kenya in January 1993 by the Church members .The aim is to provide a safe and secure home for the children of Kenya who have been orphaned by AIDS, malaria and tuberculosis. The Church and the community provides the orphans with food, accommodation, clothing and education while ensuring that they receive the physical and emotional care a child requires. There is a small clinic within the home, which desperately needs to be expanded and improved to serve the needs of approxametly 720 orphans. The Church and the Community are also establishing a new center for youth and HIV/AIDS orphans at Embonga Baptist Church in Nyamira. Volunteers will help in construction, and in all the daily activities that take place: education, play, sports, cooking, cleaning, etc. Volunteers are needed in both sites.

Sector: Child welfare, community development, construction, education, health, housing, hunger relief, sanitation.

Country: Africa (Kenya).

Qualif.: Strong motivation and particular love for children.

Nonpro: Yes. Anyone, with or without skills is welcome.

Age: Minimum 20, no maximum.

Duration: From 1 week or longer.

Lang.: English, volunteers will be exposed to Kiswahili.

Benefits: Friendship and partnership, wildlife watching, child and community interaction, learning local culture, visiting other orphanage homes. Volunteers will attend cultural activities, visit and sometime teach students to other Local schools and villages, practice sports.

Costs: Contribution starting from US$ 100 per person per week for short-term programme (from 1 week to 3 months) plus personal expenses. But the anmount of the contribution can be negotitated on a case by case basis. For long term volunteers, enquire with the organization.

Applic.: Application form via e-mail with CV and letter of intent enclosed. Volunteers must specify their interest and intended length of stay. A Tourist Visa is valid for 3 months. For longer stays, the proper Visa must be obtained; the organization provides volunteers with all the immigration documents. All information about the project, meeting point, what to bring, and much more will be given in due time before departure.

Notes: At the date of publication of this guide (January 2008) the Mercy Orphanage has never taken international volunteers, but the strength of the appeal: "...the Church and the community is overwhelmed in taking care of these children, so we are praying in seeking volunteers to come and help. This is why we decided to seek for partnership of volunteers..." made us decide to include the Orphange in the Guide regardless of the lack of experience. We therefore consider this project extremely challenging for strong, mature, motivated, and experienced "pioneer" volunteers. We recommend, however, to read carefully the note on Page 35 and to consider all the logistical, health and safety aspects that a remote location, with no other international volunteer, can present.

Mission Discovery

1509 Hunt Club Blvd., Suite 1200
Gallatin, Tennessee 37066 USA
Tel.: ++1 (615) 206-0555 (toll free in N. Am. 1-800-767-8720)
Fax: ++1 (615) 452-8001
E-mail: projects@missiondiscovery.org
www.missiondiscovery.org

Desc.: Mission Discovery began in 1991 as an effort to combine the mission resources of churches around the United States to meet the physical and spiritual needs of the world's poor through short-term team mission projects. Since its inception, over 20,000 volunteers from multiple continents have participated in Mission Discovery projects in the United States, Mexico, Central America, the Caribbean adn Africa.

Sector: Child welfare, construction, housing, religious.

Country: Africa (Kenya), Caribbean (Bahamas, Dominican Republic, Jamaica, Haiti), Latin America (Guatemala, Honduras, Mexico), North America (USA).

Qualif.: Nurses, doctors, Spanish translators, bus-drivers, anyone with a desire to serve.

Nonpro: Yes.

Age: Youth, adult and family programs are available.

Duration: 1 week to 2 months.

Lang.: English, Spanish.

Benefits: Enquire with organisation.

Costs: US$175–1,400, depending on country and duration.

Applic.: US$75 registration fee due 30 days after sign-up.

Mission Doctors/Lay Mission Helpers Associations

3435 Wilshire Blvd., Suite 1035 Los Angeles, CA 90010 USA
Tel.: ++1 (213) 368-1875 (MDA)
     ++1 (213) 368-1870 (LMH)
Fax: ++1 (213) 368-1871
E-mail: missiondrs@earthlink.net or info@laymissionhelpers.org
www.missiondoctors.org or www.laymissionhelpers.org

Desc.:	Lay Mission Helpers and Mission Doctors Association are lay Catholic organisations. LMH and MDA recruit, train send and support lay Catholics who serve the poor of the world in the fields of medicine, education, administration and ministry. The formation program of the candidates includes theology, mission culture, and Catholic social doctrine. The diocesan Bishop and religious orders administer the hospitals, schools and other facilities served.
Sector:	Community development, construction, education, health, sanitation.
Country:	Africa (Cameroon, Ghana, Kenya, Zimbabwe), Asia (Taiwan, Thailand), Latin America (Ecuador, Guatemala), Oceania (Micronesia, Samoa).
Qualif.:	Physicians, dentists, teachers, nurses, accountants, administrators, social workers or people with technical, mechanical or construction skills.
Nonpro:	Yes, with college degree or needed skills.
Age:	Minimum 21; maximum 65 (can be extended if self-insured).
Duration:	Two programs for physicians - 3 years, or 1 – 3 months. LMH 3-year program.
Lang.:	On site language training provided for long term.
Benefits:	Long-term and short term room and board provided by site. Long-term lay missionaries are also provided travel, living expenses, and small stipend.
Costs:	Personal expenses.
Applic.:	On-line form or contact for application by mail or fax. Long-term candiates attend discernment weekend and a 4-month training program in Los Angeles. Application process includes letters of recommendation, psychological tests and interview, and a medical exam. For short term Doctors attend weekend retreat/seminar also held in Los Angeles.
Notes:	Practicing Catholics and US citizens only.

Mondo Challenge

Malsor House, Milton Malsor, Northampton NN7 3AB UK
Tel.: ++44 (1604) 858-225
Fax: ++44 (1604) 859-323
E-mail: info@mondochallenge.org
www.mondochallenge.org

Desc.: MondoChallenge is a not for profit organisation which sends volunteers (students, professionals, early retired, etc.) to help with development programmes in Africa, Asia, South America and Eastern Europe. The programs are community based, providing volunteers with a unique insight into the local culture and giving them the ability to understand and learn from the values of the community they are working with. The normal stay is from 2-6 months and start dates are flexible.

Sector: Child welfare, community development, education, health, small-enterprise development, women's issues.

Country: Africa (Tanzania, Kenya, The Gambia, Senegal), Asia (India, Nepal, Sri Lanka), Latin America (Chile, Ecuador) and Eastern Europe (Romania).

Qualif: For many programs, no specific qualifications are needed. Business development projects require specific skills which can be discussed. Enthusiasm, adaptability, initiative and cultural awareness are all important requisites.

Age: 19-75. The average age of volunteers is 32.

Duration: 3-6 months.

Lang.: English.

Benefits: Pre-Departure briefing, in-country management support, accommodation, organised events, post-placement debriefing, evaluation, alumni network.

Costs: GB£1,200 contribution for a 3-month placement.

Applic.: Written application, references, interview (also by phone).

Notes: Couples and families are welcome and receive a 15% discount (this also applies to friends travelling together). Approximately 50% of volunteers are non-UK based, with a large number of volunteers from North America, Europe and Australia.

MS – Mellemfolkeligt Samvirke

Danish Association for International Co-operation
Borgergade 14, 1300 Copenhagen Denmark
Tel.: ++(45) 7731-0000
Fax: ++(45) 7731-0101 or 7731-0111 or 7731-0121
E-mail: ms@ms.dk
www.ms.dk

Desc.: MS is a Danish members' organisation combining development assistance with both political and grass-root action. Their goal is to fight poverty by means of practical development assistance as well as political efforts, mostly by posting Danish development workers with local partners.

Sector: Agriculture, community development, environment, health, human rights, various.

Country: Africa (Kenya, Mozambique, Tanzania, Uganda, Zambia, Zimbabwe), Asia (Nepal), Latin America (Guatemala, Honduras, Nicaragua).

Qualif.: Social scientists, teachers, journalists, social workers, accountants, etc.

Nonpro: Long-term development workers require a relevant education and some years of working experience. Yes for Medium Trem and Senior Volunteers (see Notes).

Age: Minimum 22 for long-term development workers.

Duration: Long-term (1-5 years); short-term(3-9 months).

Lang.: Danish, good knowledge of English. If applying for a job in Mozambique or Central America knowledge of Portuguese and/or Spanish is an advantage.

Benefits: Travel expenses, free transportation, and regular living expenses such as housing, insurance, resettlement allowances, etc. Development workers receive a fee to ensure living conditions as in Denmark.

Costs: Personal expenses.

Applic.: Contact the organisation to verify eligibility.

Notes: MS Travels runs study-work trips and workcamps as well as an extensive Medium Term and Senior Program: see www.globalcontact.dk These programs are self-financed and open to anyone without particular experience or qualifications.

MSF – Médecins Sans Frontières

MSF International Office
Rue de Lausanne 78 - CP 116, 1211 Geneva Switzerland
Tel.: ++41 (22) 849-8400
Fax: ++41 (22) 849-8404
www.msf.org
(See e-mail contacts of national offices on www.msf.org)

Desc.: MSF provides emergency medical assistance to populations in danger in countries where health structures are insufficient or nonexistent. MSF collaborates with authorities such as the Ministry of Health to rebuild health structures to acceptable levels. MSF works in rehabilitation of hospitals and dispensaries, vaccination programs, and water and sanitation projects. MSF also works in remote healthcare centres and slum areas and provides training of local personnel. More than 2,500 volunteers of 45 nationalities have volunteered for MSF projects. MSF was awarded the Nobel Price for Peace in 1999.

Sector: Emergency, health, refugee aid.

Country: Over 70 countries in 5 continents.

Qualif.: Health professionals (general practice doctors, nurses, surgeons, anaesthetists, and other specialists in such areas as tropical medicine, public health, and epidemiology, midwives, laboratory technicians, and paramedics). Non-medical volunteers look after the administration and logistics.

Nonpro: MSF recruits exclusively professionally qualified staff.

Age: N/A with at least 2 years of professional experience.

Duration: 6 months. Some 3-month missions in acute emergencies.

Benefits: MSF covers all costs associated with a volunteer's mission plus medical/ emergency insurance. Return airfare, travel costs, living expenses while on mission, a small indemnity .

Costs: Volunteers are responsible for personal expenses

Applic.: On-line form. MSF national offices are responsible for recruitment and coordination of volunteers. A contact form is on the website. Successfull candidates are normally invited to take part in an introductory course then go on stand-by, awaiting the first suitable mission.

Notes: Volunteers must live in or be able to travel to one of the countries where MSF has an office for interview and departure. No positions available for students.

NAVTI Foundation

PO Box 151 Kumbo, NWP Cameroon
Tel./Fax.: ++(237) 3348-1590
E-mail: info@navtifoundation.org
http://navtifoundation.org

Desc.: The NAVTI Foundation NGO is a non-profit, apolitical, charity and development organization, founded in 2004. The main work of the Foundation is to improve the welfare of the underprivileged in their community, and improve the capacity of the NGOs working in the area. Foreign partners audit regularly the activities of the organisation.

Sector: Community development, education, health, IT, skills training, women's issues.

Country: Africa (Cameroon).

Qualif.: Required for some positions.

Nonpro: Yes. Students also welcome.

Age: Minimum 18. Families with children accepted.

Duration: Minimum 3 months.

Lang.: English. French is useful.

Benefits: Lodging provided. Stipend not provided.

Costs: Return airfare from country of origin, US$30 application fee, personal expenses.

Applic.: Application forms provided upon request. Some volunteer positions require a cover letter and CV. Applications may be sent via e-mail, fax, or regular mail.

Notes: See Note on page 35.

NET AID Online Volunteering

267 Fifth Avenue, 11th Floor
New York, New York 10016 USA
Tel.: ++1 (212) 537-0500
Fax: ++1 (212) 537-0501
E-mail: volunteers@netaid.org
www.netaid.org or www.onlinevolunteering.org

Desc.: Since early 2000, NetAid, through a service managed by the UN-Volunteers programme, has brought Online Volunteers and organizations in developing countries together through the largest database of online volunteering opportunities anywhere in the world. Through this service, Online Volunteers translate documents, research information, create brochures and web sites, write articles, offer professional advice, moderate online discussion groups, mentor young people, and engage in various other activities for organizations working in or for developing countries. Each Spring, NetAid and UN Volunteers programme select 10 "top Online Volunteers", each of whom are profiled on the NetAid web site.

Sector: Education, IT.

Country: Worldwide.

Qualif.: Excellent written English skills, experience communicating with others online, and some area of expertise that can benefit NGOs (legal expertise, teaching experience, web design, technical expertise, computer skills, etc.).

Nonpro: Yes, with relevant skills.

Age: People beyond the age of legal majority according to the law in their respective country.

Duration: Variable.

Lang: English. Some assignments are also in Spanish and French.

Benefits: Volunteers contribute time and skills from home.

Costs: None.

Applic.: On-line form.

Oikos

Via Paolo Renzi 55, 00128 Rome Italy
Tel.: ++39 (06) 508-0280
Fax: ++39 (06) 507-3233
E-mail: oikos@oikos.org or volontariato@oikos.org
www.oikos.org or www.volontariato.org

Desc.: Oikos is an association engaged in the protection of the environment and the promotion of voluntary service. Since 1979 it has organised workcamps in many countries to work towards habitat protection, forest fire prevention, or the defence of the cultural and natural heritage. Since a few years Oikos has extended its scope of action towards humanitarian activities. Young volunteers are recruited from around the world. The projects are carried out in collaboration with the local authorities, the communities, and other non-governmental organisations.

Sector: Agriculture, education, environment, health, human rights.

Country: Africa (Benin, Burkina Faso, Cameroon, Ghana, Kenya, Lesotho, Morocco, Mozambique, Tanzania, Togo, Uganda), Asia (Bangladesh, China, India, Korea, Nepal, Sri Lanka), Europe (Austria, Bielorussia, Czech Republic, Cyprus, England, France, Georgia, Germany, Greece, Iceland, Italy, Poland, Portugal, Russia, Serbia, Switzerland, Uckraine), Latin America (Argentina, Ecuador, Guatemala, Haiti, Mexico, Peru), Middle East (Azerbaijan, Jordan, Palestine, Turkey).

Qualif.: No specific qualifications necessary.

Nonpro: Open to people of any social or economic status, race, religion, or ethnicity. Flexibility is necessary.

Age: Minimum 18.

Duration: 1–3 weeks.

Lang.: English.

Benefits: Food and accommodation included in the costs.

Costs: Association cost of EUR80. Travel. Workcamp fees, paid to the partner organisation upon arrival, vary with project.

Applic.: On-line application form.

Notes: The projects are carried out in collaboration with local NGOs and host volunteers from around the world.

Olomayani Kindergarten, Eluwai

PO Box 19
Monduli, Tanzania
Tel.: +255 (755) 744-992
E-mail: enolengila@yahoo.co.uk

Desc.: Volunteers are needed to help with curriculum development, resource production and class teaching in this newly established kindergarten (pre-primary school) in a remote Maasai village in northern Tanzania, which serves children aged 4-7. The kindergarten aims to integrate elements of Maasai culture and indigenous knowledge with internationally recognized pre-primary teaching strategies and the requirements of the Tanzanian national curriculum. There is a particular need for illustrators who can help in producing books and posters, and English language support for the kindergarten teachers is also appreciated.

Sector: Child welfare, community development, education.

Country: Africa (Tanzania).

Qualif.: Not essential, but experience of teaching young children preferred.

Nonpro: Yes, with relevant skills to the project.

Age: Minimum 18.

Duration: 2 months to 1 year.

Lang.: English, although volunteers should try to acquire at least a basic working knowledge of useful Swahili vocabulary before starting the placement (numbers, colours, shapes, animals, etc).

Benefits: Accommodation and food, orientation, Swahili lessons.

Costs: Volunteers make a financial contribution of around GB£450 (US$900) for 3 months.

Applic.: References and a CV/resume are required and a deposit is payable on application.

Notes: See Note on page 35.

Operation Crossroads Africa, Inc.

34 Mount Morris Park
New York, New York 10027 USA
Tel.: ++1 (212) 289-1949
Fax: ++1 (212) 289-2526
E-mail: oca@igc.org
www.operationcrossroadsafrica.org

Desc.:	This organization offers many opportunities for concerned persons with interest in areas such as ecology and environment, traditional medicine, archaeology, reforestation, agriculture/farming and teaching.
Sector:	Agriculture, community development, culture, education, environment.
Country:	Africa (Gambia, Ghana, Kenya, Uganda, Senegal, South Africa, Tanzania, Malawi)
Qualif.:	Group leaders must be 25 years of age. Volunteers should have an interest in Africa and a desire to live and work in a local community in Africa.
Nonpro:	Yes
Age:	Minimum age for volunteers is 18.
Duration:	7 weeks (mid June to mid August).
Lang.:	English. No language requirement
Benefits:	See website for details.
Costs:	US$3,500, including airfare.
Applic.:	Available on-line for volunteers and group leaders.
Notes:	Students who want to get academic credit can arrange an independent study program with their school.

Original Volunteers

5 Lovelstaithe
Norwich NR1 1LW UK
Tel.: ++ 44 (1603) 305 926 (toll free in the UK 0800 345 75 82)
E-mail: contact@originalvolunteers.co.uk
www.originalvolunteers.co.uk

Desc.: Places volunteers with grassroots organizations around the world. Includes supported live-in placements and more independent experiences away from the tourist trail. Original Volunteers was formed by a number of former volunteers who wanted other volunteers to be enabled by flexible opportunities and financially accessible projects.

Sector: Community development, education, environment, health, various.

Country: Africa (Ghana, Kenya), Asia (India, Nepal), Latina America (Argentina, Brazil, Costa Rica, Ecuador, Mexico, Peru).

Qualif.: Professionals, students, career breakers and those seeking an alternative to a 2 week beach holiday.

Nonpro: Yes.

Age: Most projects minimum age 18 (younger applicants and mixed aged groups should enquire for details of opportunities).

Duration: Minimum 1 week usual stay 2-4 weeks, long stays possible on some projects.

Lang.: English. Spanish and Portuguese useful for Latin America projects.

Benefits: Pick-up provided and accommodation arranged for volunteers in shared volunteer houses or with local families along with volunteering placement at established local charity/organization. Meals may be provided depending on project.

Costs: Refer to www.originalvolunteers.co.uk Costs start from approx. GB£12 per week (plus annual registration fee to join scheme)

Applic.: On-line form or by telephone. Proof of insurance, photocopy of passport and visas are required prior to travel.

Oxfam International

Suite 20, 266 Banbury Road
Oxford OX2 7DL UK
Tel.: ++44 (1865) 339-100
Fax: ++44 (1865) 339-101
E-mail: information@oxfaminternational.org
www.oxfam.org

Desc.: Oxfam International is a confederation of thirteen organizations working together in more than 100 countries to find lasting solutions to poverty and injustice. With many of the causes of poverty global in nature, the 13 affiliate members of Oxfam International believe they can achieve greater impact through their collective efforts: Oxfam America, Oxfam Australia, Oxfam-in-Belgium, Oxfam Canada, Oxfam France - Agir ici, Oxfam Germany, Oxfam Great Britain, Oxfam Hong Kong, IntermÛn Oxfam (Spain), Oxfam Ireland, Oxfam New Zealand, Oxfam Novib (Netherlands) and Oxfam Québec.

Sector: Community development, education, emergency, health, human rights, hunger relief, sanitation, women's issues, various.

Country: Various countries in Africa, Asia, Europe, Latin America, Middle East, Oceania.

Qualif.: Inquire with the local affiliate directly.

Nonpro: Local non-professional volunteers are accepted.

Age: Minimum 18.

Duration: Negotiable.

Lang.: English and/or language of partner organisation.

Benefits: None.

Costs: Volunteers are responsible for their expenses.

Applic.: Consult website for local affiliate.

Notes: Volunteers play a key role in helping Oxfam achieve its mission to reduce poverty and injustice around the world, from office work to helping in shops or stewarding at events and concerts. While Oxfam does not place volunteers overseas, the Oxfam affiliates around the world rely on volunteers in a wide variety of capacities. Prospective volunteers should review the website of the nearest Oxfam affiliate, for further information on volunteering. As the Oxfam International (OI) Secretariat is a small office based in the UK, when a volunteer is needed, is recruited through Oxfam GB, which has an extensive volunteer recruitment system.

Pamoja International Voluntary Services

PO Box 58093 - 00200 Nairobi Kenya
Buruburu Phase 3 Hse 648 Olosolani Court Off Rabai Road
Tel.: ++254 (20) 785-813 or 355-5380
Mob.: ++254 (722) 592-655 or (728)774-553
E-mail: info@pamoja.co.ke or internationalworkcamps@pamoja.co.ke
or midlongterm@pamoja.co.ke
www.pamoja-international.org

Desc: Pamoja international voluntary services (PIVS) organizes international workcamps and mid and long term volunteer programs, where both local and international volunteers offer their services, collaborating with community groups or institutions in need of voluntary labour. PIVS objective is to co-ordinate socio-cultural interaction between people of diverse background by creating opportunities for both local and international volunteers to exchange their experience and skills. Volunteers may be working in schools, teaching primary school students, working in hospitals as counsellors/nurses, facilitating leadership camps with school groups, working in Children's or Disabled homes, leading classes and working in environmental projects, arts and culture, or with the community in projects such as construction of water tanks, bridges, roads, etc.

Sector: Agriculture, community development, construction, culture, education, environment, health, human rights, IT, small enterprise development, women's issues.

Country: Africa (Kenya).

Qualif: No particular qualifications needed. Some positions require fundraising, IT, PR and administration/management skills.

Nonpro: Yes.

Age: Minimum 18.

Duration: 2-3 weeks (short-term) 1–6 months (mid and long-term).

Lang: English.

Benefits: Accommodation, food and certificate of participation.

Costs: Approx. EUR 250 - 350 for short-term, EUR 600 - 1800 for mid and long-term, travel, spending money (approx. US$50-100 per month) and medical insurance. Application fee EUR 50.

Applic: On-line form. E-mail or fax CV plus 2 letters of reference and a recent photograph. Apply at least 1 month in advance.

Notes: Orientations are held throughout the year for short, mid and long- term programs. Volunteers must come 1–2 days before. See Note on page 35.

Peace Brigades International

89-93 Fonthill Road London N4 3HT UK
Tel.: +44 (20) 7561-9141
Fax: +44 (20) 7281-3181
E-mail: info@peacebrigades.org
www.peacebrigades.org

Desc.: Peace Brigades International (PBI) is a non-governmental organisation that protects human rights by sending teams of volunteers into areas of repression and conflict. Volunteers accompany "at risk" human rights workers, their organisations, and others under threat . The presence of volunteers backed by an emergency response network helps deter potential human rights abuses as international volunteers serve as witnesses. In this way, space is created for local people to work for social justice and human rights within their own communities. The presence of PBI volunteers assists to ensure their safety and the continuation of this important work.

Sector: Human rights, peacekeeping.

Country: Asia (Indonesia, Nepal), Latin America (Colombia, Guatemala, Mexico).

Qualif: Strong motivation for justice and peace issues. The success of PBI work relies on recruiting committed individuals to volunteer on its missions who have previous experience of working with human rights, peace or development NGOs, or with organisations involved cooperative or community work.

Nonpro: Yes, with previous experience stated above.

Age: Minimum 25.

Duration: 1 year.

Lang.: Spanish fluency in Latin America. English and Bahasa Indonesian for Indonesia (volunteers are required to learn Bahasa Indonesian before joining the team).

Benefits: Accommodation, travel to the country, food, local travel, health insurance and a small monthly stipend of about US$50—200.

Costs: All costs mentioned above are met by the project.

Applic.: Request an application form and 3 reference forms.

Notes: Due to security reasons and the nature of the work involved citizens from Colombia, Guatemala, Indonesia, Nepal and Mexico cannot volunteer for PBI within their own country. An exception will be made for persons contracted to work administratively or domestically within Colombia. Potential volunteers first attend an orientation weekend training in their home country (where such trainings exist). There is then a 1-week intensive project specific training, held at regular intervals according to the project. The trainings cover practical aspects of team work; safety procedures; nonviolence; consensus decision-making; dealing with stress and fear; conflict resolution; cultural sensitivity; country-specific information and political analysis. There may also be ongoing "course-work" to be done by correspondence and completed before the intensive training.

Peace Corps

1111 20th Street NW
Washington, DC 20526 USA
Tel.: ++1 (800) 424-8580 (toll free in N. Am.)
E-mail: See Regional Contacts on website
www.peacecorps.gov

Desc.: Since 1961 over 170,00 Peace Corps volunteers have served in136 countries, working to bring clean water to communities, teach children, help start new small businesses, and stop the spread of AIDS. Volunteers receive intensive language and cross-cultural training in order to become part of the communities where they live. They speak the local language and adapt to the cultures and customs of the people with whom they work. Volunteers work with teachers and parents to improve the quality of, and access to, education for children. They work with communities to protect the local environment and to create economic opportunities. They work on basic projects to keep families healthy and to help them grow more food. Their larger purpose, however, is to work with people in developing countries to help them take charge of their own futures. At the same time, volunteers learn as much, if not more, from the people in their host countries. When they complete their service in the Peace Corps, volunteers work to strengthen America's understanding of different countries and cultures.

Sector: Agriculture, community development, education, environment, health, peacekeeping, sanitation, small-enterprise development.

Country: Over 70 countries in Africa, Asia, Caribbean, Europe, Latin America, Middle East, Oceania.

Qualif.: Certain education and work experience requirements. In most cases, applicants with a BA in any discipline, strong motivation and a commitment to Peace Corps service will be competitive.

Nonpro: Yes.

Age: Minimum 18.

Duration: 2 years plus 3 months of training in country of service.

Lang.: English. Intensive instruction in local language is provided.

Benefits: A stipend to cover basic necessities—food, housing expenses, and local transportation. The amount of the stipend varies from country to country, but will be an amount that provides a living at the same level as the people in the community served. The Peace Corps pays for transportation to and from country of service and provides complete medical and dental care. At the conclusion of volunteer service a re-adjustment allowance will be received.

Costs: Personal expenses above basic needs (covered by the monthly stipend).

Applic.: On-line form or contact the Peace Corps directly. An interview may then be scheduled. It is recommended to apply as early as 1 year in advance.

Notes: US citizens only. It is best to apply early. Student loan deferment can be obtained.

Peacework

209 Otey Street
Blacksburg, Virginia 24060-7426 USA
Tel.: ++1 (540) 953-1376 (toll free in N. Am. 1 (800) 272-5519)
Fax: ++1 (540) 953-0300
E-mail: mail@peacework.org
www.peacework.org

Desc.: Peacework arranges international volunteer service projects for groups from colleges, universities, and service organisations to provide the opportunity to learn about different cultures and customs and gain insight into the interrelationship of the needs and problems of people around the world. Volunteers help meet the critical needs of marginalised communities in developing areas by working with host organizations on existing self-development projects. The work is both challenging and rewarding. Peacework promotes peaceful cooperation, understanding, and service through volunteerism.

Sector: Child welfare, community development, education, health, religious, small-enterprise development.

Country: Africa (Cameroon, Ghana, Kenya, South Africa), Asia (China, India, Nepal, Vietnam), Latin America (Belize, Guatemala, Honduras, Dominican Republic), Europe (Czech Rep., Russia).

Qualif.: Enquire with organization.

Nonpro: Yes.

Age: Enquire with organization.

Duration: Varies with project from one week to three months.

Lang.: No language skills required.

Benefits: All required in-country expenses are included in the cost.

Costs: Based on location, project and duration.

Applic.: See website.

Notes: Volunteers with disabilities are accepted depending on project and special projects can be arranged. European office: Na Rybnì 269, ku 16, 120 00 Prague, Czech Republic; Tel.: ++ 42 (60) 3733-748, E-mail: jmagno@peacework.org.

Pitaya Suwan Foundation/Greenway Thailand

PO Box 21, Had Yai Airport, Had Yai, Songkhla 90115 Thailand
Tel.: ++66 (74) 473-506
Fax: ++66 (74) 473-508
E-mail: info@pitayasuwan.org
www.pitayasuwan.org

Desc.:	All projects Pitaya Suwan Foundation/Greenway engages in are geared to alternative ways of thinking about environmental care, small-scale economical development, and sustainable growth. Pitaya Suwan Foundation is an example of a local member organisation of CCIVS (see listing). The local member organisations are not branches of CCIVS, but the creators of the network of cooperation. The national organisations work mainly in their own countries and cooperate with each other by exchanging volunteers and meeting regularly so as to exchange experiences and new ideas, etc. In each workcamp, the national organisation cooperates with a local partner organisation.
Sector:	Agriculture, construction, culture, education, environment, small-enterprise development.
Country:	Asia (Thailand, China).
Qualif.:	No particular skills required.
Nonpro:	Yes.
Age:	Minimum 18.
Duration:	14 days, and the participant stays for 1 or a few camps. Medium- to long-term positions are for those who prefer to stay 2 months or longer; sometimes a minimum period is requested for project reasons.
Lang.:	English.
Benefits:	Contact the organisation for details.
Costs:	US$150 plus airfare.
Applic.:	Send applications via a sending workcamp organisation in country of residence (see CCIVS for a complete list).
Notes:	The organisation suggests places to stay in Bangkok upon arrival before proceeding to the workcamp.

Projects Abroad

Aldsworth Parade, Goring, West Sussex BN12 4TX UK
Tel.: +44 (1903)708-300
Fax: +44 (1903)501-026
E-mail: info@projects-abroad.co.uk
www.projects-abroad.co.uk

Desc.:   Founded in 1992, a founding member of the Year Out Group. Projects Abroad arranges voluntary projects in 22 countries worldwide. Projects Abroad sends over 3,000 volunteers a year around the world to work on a wide range of different projects. They are supported by 250 full time staff that work for Projects Abroad around the world.

Sector: Agriculture, child welfare, community development, culture, education, health, human rights, small enterprise development, various.

Country: Africa (Ethiopia, Ghana, Morocco, Senegal, South Africa) Asia (Cambodia, China, India, Mongolia, Nepal, Sri Lanka, Thailand) Eastern Europe (Moldova, Romania) Latin America (Argentina, Bolivia, Brazil, Chile, Costa Rica, Jamaica, Mexico, Peru).

Qualif.:   No specific qualification required.

Nonpro: Yes.

Age: Minimum age 16. A mix of gap year students, university students, recent graduates, career breakers, retired volunteers.

Duration: 2 weeks - 1 year. Volunteers choose length of program.

Lang.:   English. No language skills necessary.

Benefits: Projects Abroad volunteers are able to gain valuable work and cultural experiences in a supported environment. They get to meet a wide range of other volunteers as well as local people. A good opportunity to live with a local family, learn a language, help out and learn or develop a skill in a different part of the world.

Costs: Placements range in cost from £995 (approx. US$2,000) for a month program. This includes insurance, food, accommodation and overseas support. It excludes travel costs.

Applic.:   Application can be online, on the application form in the brochure or over the telephone.

Notes: Volunteers can meet Projects Abroad at an Open Day or at their office prior to application if they want to.

Project Trust

The Hebridean Centre
Isle of Coll, Argyll PA78 6TE   UK
Tel.: ++44 (1879) 230444
Fax: ++44 (1879) 230357
E-mail: info@projecttrust.org.uk
www.projecttrust.org.uk

Desc.:   The main philosophy behind Project Trust is to provide young people with an opportunity to understand a community overseas by immersing themselves in it by living and working there. All the projects are vetted for their suitability for volunteers, and none deprive local people of work.

Sector: Culture, education.

Country: Africa (Botswana, Lesotho, Malawi, Mauritania, Namibia, South Africa, Uganda, Morocco), Asia (Cambodia, China, Japan, Malaysia, Thailand, Vietnam), Latin America (Chile, Dominican Republic, Guyana, Honduras, Peru).

Qualif.:   No specific qualification needed.

Nonpro: Yes.

Age: 17–19.5 at the time of going overseas.

Duration: One year (from August or September).

Lang.:   English.

Benefits: Airfare, board, lodging, insurance, support, training and pocket money.

Costs: GB£ 4,480, which covers nearly all costs of a year overseas.

Applic.:   Contact organisation directly or consult website.

Notes: British or EU passport holders only. Currently in full-time secondary education or taking a gap year upon finishing; university entry qualifications; able to leave from the UK in August/September of gap year and spend 1 year overseas; 1-week selection course at Project Trust headquarters on the Isle of Coll in Scotland and a summer training course in July.

Quest Overseas

The North-West Stables, Borde Hill Estate
Balcombe Road, Haywards Heath
West Sussex RH16 1XP UK
Tel.: ++44 (1444) 474-744 Fax: +44 (1444) 474-799
E-mail: info@experiencequest.com
www.experiencequest.com

Desc.: Quest Overseas offers 3 month experiences in Latin America and Africa combining ethical and worthwhile voluntary work on carefully selected and grass root projects, with adventure expeditions, all with a team of other 18-25 year olds. Quest Sabbaticals gives participants some time out, find space to think - review their career, take a break from routine, change direction, help those less-fortunate, experience new culture or simply change their surroundings. Quest Sabbaticals can help arrange 2wks - 1yr overseas, either on a team trip with others aged 25 and over or on an individual placement. Use existing career skills, learn new ones or just travel.

Sector: Community development, environment, skills training, various.

Country: Latin America and Africa.

Qualif.: Skilled professionals and students seeking experience are needed to help maintain Quest's long-term projects and share in a cultural exchange with local people.

Nonpro: Yes

Age: Minimum 18.

Duration: Minimum 2 weeks placements; 3 months Gap combined trips; 6 weeks summer projects or expeditions.

Lang: English.

Benefits: Accommodation, food, airport transfer and on the ground transport, all activities, pre-departure training, in-country orientation, project donation on average approx GB£700.

Costs: Cost start from approx. GB£700 for 4 weeks plus compulsory project donation of approx £600. Approx £3,500 for 3 months plus compulsory project donation of approx £700. Refer to website for details on costs.

Applic.: On-line form or written application followed by informal interview either in person or via telephone and internet.

Notes: Quest Overseas has also an environmental and marine conservation programme called Quest Underseas that takes place in pristine dive locations worldwide.

Raleigh International

207 Waterloo Road, London SE1 8XD UK
Tel.: ++44 (20) 7183-1283
Fax: ++44 (20) 7504-8094
E-mail: info@raleigh.org.uk
www.raleighinternational.org

Desc.: Raleigh International is an educational charity that provides adventurous and challenging expeditions for people from all backgrounds, nationalities and age, especially young people. The unique expeditions are open to young participants aged 17-24 and volunteer managers aged 25 and over and combine community and/or environmental projects with adventure.

Sector: Community development, environment, various.

Country: Latin America (Costa Rica, Nicaragua), Asia (India, Malaysia).

Qualif.: Volunteers must have average fitness, be able to swim 200 metres and speak basic English.

Nonpro: Yes.

Age: 17-24 for participants, 25 and over for volunteer managers.

Duration: 10, 7, 5 or 4 weeks for participants, 13 or 8 weeks for volunteer managers.

Lang.: English.

Benefits: Experience new cultures, work with a diverse mix of nationalities and backgrounds, help local communities , make lifelong friends, see remote destinations and ecosystems, develop new skills.

Costs: Fundraising target of GB£1,500-2,995 for participants and £1,350 -1,950 for volunteer managers depending on length of programme. This includes all food, accommodation, travel and medical insurance, training and preparation, specialist equipment, in-country transport. International flights are excluded.

Applic.: Application forms can be obtained from the website, by emailing or by calling the Recruitment Team.

RCDP-Nepal – Rural Community Development Program

Himalayan Volunteers = Kathmandu Municipality, PO Box 8957, Tashindol Marga
95/48, Kalanki, Ward-14 Kathmandu, Nepal
Tel.: ++977 (1) 4278-305
Fax: ++977 (1) 4282-994
E-mail: rcdpn@mail.com.np or rcdpnepal@hotmail.com
www.rcdpnepal.com or www.rcdpnepal.org

Desc.: RCDP-Nepal has a permanent office and staff in Kathmandu, Nepal, and International Contact office in USA to co-ordinate the international volunteer program for Europe, USA, and Asia-Pacific respectively. RCDP-Nepal maintains 1 field office in Chitwan, Nepal to promote local level cultural exchange between international volunteers and local people. The mainstay of the Himalayan Volunteers is voluntary service in urban and rural projects located in the different parts of Nepal through international workcamps, home-stay programs, internship, and language programs.

Sector: Child welfare, community development, education, environment, health, various.

Country: Asia (India, Nepal, Srilanka, Tibet).

Qualif.: Experience is needed to join the health projects. No experience needed for other sectoral projects. Professionals welcome.

Nonpro: Yes.

Age: Minimum18.

Duration: 1–3 weeks; long term 1–5 months.

Lang.: 2-week language program recommended for volunteers joining for more than 1 month.

Benefits: Accommodation (with a host family near their project), Nepali food (3 meals a day) that includes rice, lentil soup, vegetable curry, meats (occasionally), and pickles.

Costs: Enquire with the national coordinator for costs and Visas. Airport tax (US$15–25) is paid upon departure from Nepal.

Applic.: On-line form.

Notes: Many placements are in collaboration with local partners. Project, job, and host family confirmed prior to departure.

Recife Voluntario Brazil (Volunteer Centre of Recife)

Av. Barao de Souza Leao, 221/Sala 33
Recife PE 51030-300 Brazil
Tel./Fax: ++55 (81) 3342-5011
E-mail: recife@voluntario.org.br
www.voluntario.org.br

Desc.: The Volunteer Centre of Recife is a non-profit organisation working to increase the volunteering culture in the Metropolitan Area of Recife, in Brazilian Northeast, providing many NGOs and community organisations with volunteers for their social, cultural, and environmental projects. Recife has a population of 1,300,000 inhabitants on its municipal area and 3,300,000 on its metropolitan area. It also has many social problems, like any other big city in Brazil, and it has a low volunteering culture among the majority of the members of its civil society.

Sector: Community development.

Country: Latin America (Brazil).

Qualif.: The Centre is in contact with many NGOs, therefore a wide variety of qualifications can be needed.

Nonpro: Some organisations can take volunteers at their first experience. Contact the Centre for further details.

Age: In general the minimum age is 18, some organisation may accept only older qualified volunteers.

Duration: Negotiable with individual NGOs.

Lang.: Portuguese, French, English.

Benefits: Negotiable with the chosen NGO. Room and board may be possible, not a stipend.

Costs: Travel, personal expenses. Room and board when not provided.

Applic.: Contact the Centre for further information and assistance for choosing the organisation.

Notes: The website is very useful for finding other volunteering contacts in Brazil.

Red Cross – International Federation of Red Cross and Red Crescent Societies

PO Box 372, CH-1211 Geneva 19   Switzerland
Tel.: ++41 (22) 730 4222
Fax: ++41 (22) 733 0395
E-mail: secretariat@ifrc.org
www.ifrc.org

Desc.: The International Federation of Red Cross and Red Crescent Societies is the world's largest humanitarian organisation, providing assistance without discrimination as to nationality, race, religious beliefs, class or political opinions. Founded in 1919, the International Federation comprises 178 member Red Cross and Red Crescent societies, a Secretariat in Geneva and more than 60 delegations strategically located to support activities around the world. There are more societies in formation. The Red Crescent is used in place of the Red Cross in many Islamic countries. The Federation's mission is to improve the lives of vulnerable people by mobilising the power of humanity. Vulnerable people are those who are at greatest risk from situations that threaten their survival, or their capacity to live with an acceptable level of social and economic security and human dignity. Often, these are victims of natural disasters, poverty brought about by socio-economic crises, refugees, and victims of health emergencies. The Federation carries out relief operations to assist victims of disasters, and combines this with development work to strengthen the capacities of its member National Societies. The Federation's work focuses on four core areas: promoting humanitarian values, disaster response, disaster preparedness, and health and community care.

Sector: Emergency, health, hunger relief.

Country: The Red Cross works in 181 countries in the 5 continents.

Qualif.: Medical and paramedical personnel are the major qualifications needed. However some national branches may need also administrative or technical personnel. For example, lawyers, fundraisers, and public relations professionals are among those who help the national society as expert volunteers at local, regional or national level. Contact the appropriate national branch for details.

Nonpro: Generally no, but contact the national branches for details.

Age: Minimum 18.

Duration: Contact the national organisation for details.

Benefits: Local volunteers usually do not receive specific benefits. For international volunteers, contact the appropriate national branch.

Costs: Contact the national organisation for details.

Applic.:   Contact the appropriate national branch.

Notes: National Societies recruit volunteers to carry out tasks that directly or indirectly help vulnerable people. Each National Society has different volunteer programs and requires different skills to make these programs effective. To become a volunteer with the Red Cross or Red Crescent, contact the nearest branch of the National Society for details on the programs offered and the current needs for volunteers. Go to: www.ifrc.org/address/directory.asp to find details on all the National Red Cross and Red Crescent Societies. It is possible that individual National Societies may run exchange programs for people wishing to volunteer to work in another country.

American Red Cross: www.redcross.org

Australian Red Cross: www.redcross.org.au

British Red Cross: www.redcross.org.uk

Canadian Red Cross: www.redcross.ca

RedR UK

1 Great George Street, London
SW1P 3AA UK
Tel.: ++44 (20) 7233-3116
Fax: ++44 (20) 7222-0564
E-mail: info@redr.org
www.redr.org.uk

Desc.: RedR is an NGO which helps to rebuild lives in times of disaster by providing aid workers with the skills they need to make a difference. The organisation delivers UK and international training programmes and maintains a register of skilled aid workers for field assignments. RedR also runs a Technical Support Service and members' network.

Sector: Community development, construction, emergency, environment, health, housing, hunger relief, human rights, sanitation, various

Country: Worldwide.

Qualif.: In general a minimum of 2 years professional experience in any of the above specified sectors.

Nonpro: No.

Age: The only criteria is that the person must be within the minimum and maximum legal working ages for the relevant country.

Duration: From 1 month to 3 years

Lang.: English. French, Spanish, Portuguese are desired but not essential.

Benefits: Salary, terms, and conditions widely vary between agencies ranging from volunteer status to daily consultancy rates.

Costs: Membership of RedR's register is free but candidates are expected to pay their own interview costs if selected for interview. There is a fee for training courses, which are available for both members and non-members to attend. They may also choose to subscribe to the organisation's magazines and publications.

Applic.: Request via e-mail and application form. E-mail: membership@redr.org.

Religious Youth Service

481 8th Ave, 30th floor
New York, NY 10001 USA
Tel.: ++1 (212) 239-1421 (toll free in N. America: +1 (800) 880 2987)
Fax: ++1 (914) 206-4615
E-mail: info@religiousyouthservice.org
www.religiousyouthservice.org

Desc.:	This interfaith service learning program networks with NGO's, individuals and government agencies training youth to become "global citizens of good character". Participants work in and with communities that have requested their help and through mutual effort provide substantial service. The Service tries to include a mixture of religions, cultures, races, and nationalities in making up each group. RYS welcomes people of all faiths and cultures. The organisation accepts people who are not actively practicing a religious tradition, but it is expected that all participants show respect and tolerance of other spiritual traditions.
Sector:	Community development, construction, culture, education, environment, health, sanitation.
Country:	Africa (Ghana, Kenya, Nigeria, Uganda, Zambia), Asia (India, Indonesia, Malaysia, Philippines, Sri Lanka, Thailand), Caribbean (Guyana, Jamaica, Trinidad and Tobago), Europe (Estonia, Netherlands, UK), Latin America (Guatemala), Oceania (Australia, New Zealand, Papua New Guinea, Salomon Islands), North America (USA).
Qualif.:	Strong motivation and openness to different cultures.
Nonpro:	No previous skills necessary. Specify skills on application.
Age:	18-30. Exceptions for those 17 or over 30 possible.
Duration:	1-4 weeks, normally 12-14 days. Internships may be possible for longer periods of work.
Lang.:	English, some projects are bilingual.
Benefits:	In-country accommodation, three meals per day, health care and transportation during the program schedule.
Costs:	Enquire with the organisation. RYS participants will be responsible to set up their own transportation to and from their service country.
Applic.:	On-line form plus a letter of recommendation.
Notes:	International contacts available on the website.

Right To Play International

65 Queen Street West, Thomson Building Suite 1900
Toronto, Ontario M5H 2M5 Canada
Tel. +1 (416) 498-1922
Fax +1 (416) 498-1942
E-mail: recruitment@righttoplay.com
www.righttoplay.com

Desc.: Right To Play is an international athlete-driven humanitarian organization using sport and play to strengthen communities and encourage the healthy physical, social and emotional development of children in the world's most disadvantaged areas. Volunteer-driven programs teach critical life skills and values, promote vital health education and empower individuals and communities. volunteer opportunities exist for Project Coordinators and Communications Coordinators with Right To Play projects in Africa, the Middle East and Asia.

Sector: Child welfare, community development, refugee aid.

Country: Africa (Benin, Chad, Ethiopia, Ghana, Guinea, Kenya, Liberia, Mali, Mozambique, Rwanda, Sierra Leone, Sudan, Tanzania, Uganda, Zambia), Asia (Azerbaijan, Indonesia, Pakistan, Sri Lanka, Thailand), the Middle East (Palestine, Jordan, Lebanon, United Arab Emirates).

Qualif.: Volunteers are passionate about sport, available for 12 months to live and work as part of a project team, have intercultural and community-development experience, and have a background in program implementation, adult education and workshop facilitation, networking and partnership building, monitoring and evaluation and event coordination.

Nonpro: No need to be a professional coach or elite athlete but should have a background and interest in coaching, training and management or communications skills.

Age: N/A with necessary experience.

Duration: One year, as well as a ten to twelve day training period.

Lang.: English. Bilingualism in local language useful, especially French and Portuguese.

Benefits: Training expenses including transportation, accommodation and food. In-field accommodations, transportation to and from the field and as needed to perform duties in-field, honorarium (US$6,000 per 12 month period plus US$2,000 upon completion of contract), Visa applications for country of placement, health Insurance costs, vaccinations (as approved by RTP up to CAD$500 reimbursed upon completion of contract), medications (as approved by RTP Health Insurance), translation/ notarization of criminal record check and other documents required for work permits, holidays.

Costs: Participant pays for own passport, in-field food and social expenses, police criminal record check, all photos, medical check-up/ consultation prior to departure.

Applic.:   On-line form on web-site with all instructions, current deadlines, etc.

Notes: No criminal record, good physical health, cultural/racial acceptance. International Headquarters based in Toronto, Canada and National Offices in Canada, Norway, Netherlands, Switzerland, United Kingdom and United States (see website).

Rokpa UK Overseas Projects

Kagyu Samye Ling, Eskdalemuir, Langholm DG13 OQL UK
Tel.: ++44 (1387) 373-232 (ext.230)
Fax: ++44 (1387) 373-223
E-mail: charity@rokpauk.org or diana108@btopenworld.com
www.rokpauk.org

Desc.: Volunteers are able to work at a Tibetan-medium school in East Tibet in the Chinese province of Qinghai. The organisation is active in funding over 100 orphanages, schools, clinics and environmental projects. Volunteers will be largely self-financing, self-supporting and will have full TEFL qualifications or teaching registration and experience. Accommodation and subsistence is provided.

Sector: Education.

Country: Asia (Tibet-China).

Qualif.: Minimum TEFL and/or primary teaching qualification and experience.

Nonpro: Yes, with relevant skills and qualifications.

Age: Minimum 25, no maximum. Elderly volunteers may find altitude affects poor respiratory health.

Duration: Volunteer placements can start at various times of the year. Minimum of six months requested.

Lang.: English.

Benefits: Accommodation and food.

Costs: Volunteers are expected to pay for their own day-to-day expenses beyond accommodation and food. These are most likely to be taxis, e-mail, telephone calls and visa extensions.

Applic.: Send detailed CV with a brief message explaining interest. References are required and interviews are usually arranged.

Notes: Once accepted the applicant will be given the contact of former volunteers for additional information, and all pre-departure relevant information will be provided. Volunteers are required to sign an agreement complying with the protocols.

RRN – Rural Reconstruction Nepal

PO Box 8130, Lazimpat, Kathmandu, Nepal
Tel.: ++977 (1) 4415-418 or 4422-153
Fax: ++977 (1) 4418-296
E-mail: rrn@rrn.org.np
www.rrn.org.np

Desc.: Rural Reconstruction Nepal is a non-profit, non-governmental development organisation established in 1989. Initially, it was established with an aim of helping the flood-affected people in east Chitwan. It started its activities with rehabilitation work. It then expanded its work on rural development and research in the various districts of Nepal. Currently, it has been working with people in the 18 districts of Nepal to encourage and strengthen them to take their own initiatives in improving their socio-economic life. It is headquartered in Kathmandu having its regional offices covering 5 development regions and district offices in the 18 working districts. Currently, it has over 500 staff and volunteers.

Sector: Agriculture, child welfare, community development, education, health, human rights, sanitation, small-enterprise development, women's issues, various.

Country: Asia (Nepal).

Qualif.: Agronomists, foresters, educators, medical and paramedical personnel and many more.

Nonpro.: No.

Age: Minimum 18, depending on experience.

Duration: Negotiable.

Lang.: English.

Benefits: Accommodation can be arranged.

Costs: Travel and living expenses.

Applic.: Contact the head office.

Notes: RRN accepts international volunteers on a one to one basis. See note on page 35.

Safety Helping Hand Organisation

P.O. Box A 515
LA- Accra Ghana
Tel. : +233 (243) 076-316
E-mail : info@helpinghandghana.org
www.helpinghandghana.org

Desc.: Teachers are needed to teach in schools, ranging from pre-schools to secondary school. Volunteers are needed to help in orphanages, hospitals and clinics, to help teach the communities in the Ghanaian societies about HIV/AIDS. Volunteers are also needed to help in Rehabilitation Centers, and to help the less privileged in the society. Volunteers have the opportunity to learn a new culture by staying with a local host family.

Sector: Child welfare, community development, construction, culture, education, health.

Country: Africa (Ghana).

Qualif.: Professional qualfication needed for teachers and health related positions. For other volunteer positions no qualifications are needed.

Nonpro: Yes, with relevant skills to the project.

Age: Minimum 18.

Duration: From 1 month to one year.

Language: English.

Benefits: Accommodation, food, a week-long orientation, twi lessons, african drumming and dancing.

Costs: EUR950 fro 3 months.

Applic.: References, a CV/Resume and 2 passport photos are required.

Notes: See note on page 35.

Save The Children

International Save the Children Alliance
2nd Floor, Cambridge House
Cambridge Grove, London W6 0LE UK
Tel.: ++44 (20) 8748-2554
Fax: ++44 (20) 8237-8000
E-mail: info@save-children-alliance.org
www.savethechildren.net

Desc.: Save the Children is the largest international and independent movement for the promotion and protection of children's rights. Since 1932, it has worked to make real and lasting change in the lives of children in need. Today it is a network of 29 member organisations coordinated by an international office—the International Save the Children Alliance. Save the Children brings immediate relief to children in emergency situations such as wars and natural disasters and develops projects to guarantee a long-term benefit for future generations.

Sector: Child welfare, education, emergency, health, human rights, women's issues.

Country: Nearly 110 countries, including Africa, Asia, Caribbean, Europe, Latin America, Middle East, and North America.

Qualif.: Job vacancies are posted on the website; they often include postings for lawyers, doctors, nurses, paediatricians, educators, social workers, psychologists, economists, etc.

Nonpro: Some national offices offer internships and most will accept willing volunteers who are able to support themselves.

Age: N/A with necessary experience and/or qualifications.

Duration: International professional positions always last a few months. Internships vary in length. Enquire with the branch of interest.

Lang: English and/or the local language.

Benefits: International professionals receive a comprehensive benefits package and have their travel expenses covered.

Costs: Interns and non-professional volunteers must cover their costs including airfare. Some benefits may be negotiable.

Applic.: The application must be addressed to the national office of interest. Consult website for contacts and positions available.

Save the Earth Network

PO Box CT 3635
Cantonments, Accra, Ghana
Tel.: ++233 (21) 667-791
Fax: ++233 (21) 669-625
E-mail: eben_sten@hotmail.com or ebensten@yahoo.com
www.gonomad.com/helps/0301/saveearthnetwork.html or
www.worldvoices.no/nyhet/sen.asp

Desc.:	Volunteer opportunities in Ghana are offered to work in areas that include renovation and construction of school buildings for poor rural communities; child education (English, math, and Christian religion) at schools for under-privileged communities; care and education for orphans and destitute and abandoned children in foster homes and orphanages; HIV/AIDS education; and re-forestation (environmental conservation), agro-forestry and rejuvenation of degraded farmlands through tree planting.
Sector:	Community development, construction, education, environment, health.
Country:	Africa (Ghana).
Qualif.:	Special skills, professional qualifications or previous experience are not required of volunteers in most of the programs, however some of the volunteers may undergo a short (1 week) training in Ghana prior to volunteering.
Nonpro.:	Yes.
Age:	Minimum 18.
Duration:	2 weeks to 1 year, dependent upon project and interest of the volunteer. Start date is flexible.
Lang.:	English.
Benefits:	Accommodation and food.
Costs:	US$475 for 4 weeks, US$775 for 8 weeks, US$1,075 for 12 weeks. Payment due upon arrival.
Applic.:	Request registration form.
Notes:	Once accepted the applicant can request to be put in contact with former volunteers. See note on page 35.

SCI – Service Civil International

International Secretariat
St-Jacobsmarkt 82, B-2000 Antwerpen, Belgium
Tel.: ++32 (3) 226-5727 - Fax: ++32 (3) 232-0344
E-mail: info@sciint.org
www.sciint.org

Desc.:	SCI is a voluntary NGO founded in 1920 that aims to promote international understanding and peace. It provides volunteers for projects worldwide for communities that cannot afford labour. Every year more than 20,000 volunteers of all nationalities work in over 100 camps. There are presently 33 international branches organised in national working groups, local groups, and one national committee. Depending on their size branches may employ paid staff to support its activities.
Sector.:	Child welfare, construction, education, environment, refugee aid, various.
Country:	Africa, Asia, Europe, North America, Oceania.
Qualif.:	Ability to work as part of a team and live simply.
Nonpro:	Yes, with workcamp experience.
Age:	Minimum 18 for Europe; 16 for North America.
Duration:	2–3 weeks. Year round, mainly June to September. Volunteers with workcamp experience can join projects for 3–6 months.
Lang.:	English. For other languages, inquire with local SCI office.
Benefits:	Accommodation, food and insurance are provided.
Costs:	See local branches websites for detailed costs.
Applic.:	Standard application; no need to be a member. Contact the nearest national branch for information.
Notes:	Only 2 volunteers from the same country per project (both workcamps and long-term volunteering).

SCI Germany: www.sci-d.de

SCI USA: www.sci-ivs.org

IVP Australia: www.ivp.org.au

IVS UK: see listing

SENEVOLU – Association Sénégalaise des Volontaires Unis

Golfe Atlantique
PO Box 26 557 P.A./Dakar
Cité Nations Unies Nno °175, Dakar – Sénégal
Tel.: ++ (221) 559-6735 Fax: ++ (221) 892-0123
E-mail: senevolu@hotmail.com
www.senevolu.mypage.org

Desc.: The Senegalese Association of United Volunteers was founded in 2002 in Dakar by Mr Magueye SY, a former SYTO (Student Youth and Travel Organisation) collaborator, to promote Community Tourism and Volunteer Work in Senegal so that Senegalese people also benefit from the proceeds of tourism in their country. Therefore, SENEVOLU cooperates with numerous Senegalese NGO's, schools, host families, artists, and musicians.

Sector: Community development, education, small-enterprise development, various.

Country: Africa (Senegal).

Qualif.: No specific qualifications necessary; each project requires different skills and appropriate placement will be determined.

Nonpro: Yes, with relevant skills to the project.

Age: Minimum 18 years.

Duration: Minimum 1 month, no maximum duration.

Lang.: French.

Benefits: Accommodation, food, 5-day orientation, and support assistance.

Costs: EUR525 per month. EUR90 for supplementary week; EUR250 for subsequent month or EUR375 for 2 subsequent months, EUR100 for each additional month.

Applic.: On-line form. E-mail, fax, or post application together with a CV and passport photo.

Notes: Once accepted, applicants may request to be put in contact with former volunteers. For a stay longer than 3 months a visa is required. See note on page 35.

Shekinah Care Centre

PO Box 11693, Dorpspruit
KwaZulu Natal, 3206 South Africa
Tel.: ++27 (33) 396-3333
Fax: ++27 (33) 396-1249
E-mail: snellr@iafrica.com or milo@mjvn.co.za
www.scf.co.za

Desc.:	Shekinah Care Centre is a Christian Care Centre that provides residential counselling and rehabilitation programs for sufferers of substance addiction. The Centre was formed in 1976. It is based in New Hanover, 40 kilometres from Pietermaritzburg, South Africa. This quiet country setting is the ideal residential base for those who are battling to come to terms with their addiction. Shekinah Care Centre is highly respected in its chosen field of operation, both nationally and internationally. It is also unique in South Africa in that it has had the same Director since its formation.
Sector:	Health.
Country:	Africa (South Africa).
Qualif.:	Nurses, social workers, counsellors. All volunteers need to be registered members of their respective professional bodies (e.g., a nurse has to be a registered nurse in own country).
Nonpro:	No.
Duration:	3–4 months or longer.
Lang.:	English.
Benefits:	Accommodation, food, allowance.
Costs:	Volunteers need to pay for their own return airfare to South Africa. No other costs will accrue to the volunteer.
Applic.:	Send a CV with references and proof of professional affiliation.

Skillshare International

126 New Walk
Leicester LE1 7JA UK
Tel.: ++44 (116) 254-1862
Fax: ++44 (116) 254-2614
E-mail: info@skillshare.org
www.skillshare.org

Desc.: Skillshare International works to reduce poverty, injustice and inequality and to further economic and social development in partnership with people and communities throughout the world. It accomplishes this by sharing and developing skills and ideas, facilitating organisational and social change and building awareness of development issues.

Sector: Community development, education, environment, health, skills training, small-enterprise development.

Country: Various countries in Africa and Asia.

Qualif.: Diverse skills covering a wide variety of occupations.

Nonpro: No. A combination of a relevant professional qualification and relevant work experience (about 2 years) is required.

Age: Minimum 21.

Duration: Many placements are for 2 years, but also short-term placements are offered.

Lang.: English. Language training is provided in country.

Benefits: Local salary or allowance; pre and post placement grants; travel to and from the country of placement; medical insurance cover and payment of the NI contributions or equivalent. In addition, development workers receive accommodation with basic furnishings.

Costs: Usually include utility bills and personal expenses.

Applic.: On-line form, completed and returned either by e-mail or post. Do not send a CV—only fully completed application forms will be accepted.

Notes: Applicants will need to attend a selection day at one of the country offices or in the UK office in Leicester.

SMILE Society

Situational Managment & Inter-Learning Establishment Society
Udayrajpur, Madhyamgram, 9 no.railgate,
Kolkata, 700129, West Bengal   India
Tel.: ++ (91) 9339-731462 - Fax: ++ (91) 33-253-76621
E-mail: info@smilengo.org
www.smilengo.org

Desc.:	SMILE Society is a Volunteer Organization working for the slum and street kids' welfare activities (i.e.: build and run different non formal schools, night shelters, health units, community houses, income generating projects) and organizes workcamps for groups or individuals, long/mid/short term, internship programs, tour & volunteering programs for international students/volunteers or groups throughout the year.
Sector:	Child welfare, community development, construction, education, environment, health, small enterprise development.
Country:	Asia (India).
Qualif.:	No experience necessary. Professionals welcome.
Nonpro:	Yes.
Age:	16 and above.
Duration:	2 weeks work camps; 1-12 weeks Internship; 2-4 weeks tour & volunteering; long term 1–12 months.
Lang.:	Interested volunteers can contact for language programs .
Benefits:	Shared accommodation (with the host family or hotel/guest houses, depending on the type of program), Indian food (3 meals a day).
Costs:	Enquire with the organisation or see website for details.
Applic.:	On-line form.
Notes:	Most of the placements are in the organization's own projects. Volunteers must confirm the project of interest, and enquire for responsibilities, working hours, holidays, etc. See Note on page 35.

Sport Skills For Life Skills Foundation

Institute for Social Development,
University of the Western Cape, Bellville South, 7135 South Africa
Tel: ++27 (21) 959 3858 - Mob.: ++27 (083) 246 25 29
E-Mail: nkock@uwc.ac.za
www.ss4ls.org.za

Desc.: The programme was established in 1998 to provide overseas volunteers the opportunity to work with University students who come from all areas and cultures within South Africa and Cape Town. Volunteers are given the opportunity to partake in Sports marketing, education and also youth development. The programme gives talented sportsmen (cricketers) the opportunity to complete a Tertiary degree by providing them with the necessary scholarship and life skills development. The volunteers will become a pivotal part of this programme by also helping in it's management. Volunteers will be doing a variety of activities within the programme, but even more so they will get an opportunity to experience South Africa's different cultures first hand.

Sector: Culture, education, IT, various (sport and youth development).

Country: Africa (South Africa)

Qualif.: No particular qualifications needed. Certain volunteer position require marketing, IT, PR, or computer skills.

Nonpro: Yes

Age: Minimum 18.

Duration: 6-12 months.

Lang.: English.

Benefits: An opportunity to experience South Africa in helping within the Cape Town community and more.

Costs: For more information see Volunteers section on the website.

Applic.: Send via e-mail CV, 2 reference letters and a current photograph . Response will be given within 2 weeks. Apply 2 months in advance.

SPW – Students Partnership Worldwide

Davina House
137-149 Goswell Road,
London, EC1V 7ET UK
Tel.: ++44 (20) 74900-100
Fax: ++44 (20) 7233-0008
E-mail: info@spw.org
www.spw.org

Desc.:	SPW is a youth led development charity which runs health, education and environment programmes in developing countries. Volunteers are recruited from the UK and abroad to partner volunteers of a similar age recruited in Africa and Asia. Volunteers live and work in mixed nationality groups in a rural community. Through a non-formal, peer-led approach, volunteers help others to gain knowledge and understanding of the health, social and environmental issues that affect their lives- and to take action. Comprehensive 4 weeks training in-country includes language learning, development theory, team building skills and cross-cultural awareness. SPW works with local NGOs to ensure the sustainability of programmes.
Sector:	Community development, education, environment, health.
Country:	Africa (South Africa, Tanzania, Uganda, Zambia), Asia (India, Nepal).
Qualif.:	No particular skills needed.
Nonpro:	Yes.
Age:	18–28. Students with A-level or equivalent qualifications.
Duration:	5–12 months.
Lang.:	English.
Benefits:	The total cost of the program covers airfare, insurance, Visa, training, in-country living allowance and local support.
Costs:	All inclusive: GB£3,600. Personal expenses are in addition.
Applic.:	On-line form or request via e-mail. Application procedures differ for international, UK, and Australian volunteers.
Notes:	Candidates must attend a selection day. SPW Australia: spw@spw.org.au; SPW USA: info@spw-usa.org

STAESA – Students Travel and Exposure South Africa

P.O. Box 15016
Dalpark 11Brakpan 1552 South Africa
Tel./Fax: ++27 (11) 910-4095
Mob.: +27 73 729-2944
E-mail:info@staesa.org
www.staesa.org

Desc.:	STAESA works, since 1995, with groups, individual, schools, colleges, universities, communities and NGOs in capacity building, development and sustainability. Currently it sends over 100 volunteers to more than 60 communities in more than 15 countries in Africa. STAESA supports global friendship through culture, work exchange, education and friendly tourism, and supports the advancement of quality of life of the African communities socially, economically and spiritually. STAESA programs provide volunteers/Interns with unique and exciting work placements in community projects, small scale industries, private and public institutions, and NGOs).
Sector:	Child welfare, culture, construction, education, environment, health, human rights, IT, skills training, women's issues.
Country:	Africa (South Africa and various other countries).
Qualif.:	No particular qualifications needed: volunteers must be passionate, ready to share, open-minded, flexible, motivated.
Nonpro:	Yes.
Age:	Minimum 18.
Duration:	From 2 weeks to 12 months and above.
Lang.:	English and French are acceptable.
Benefits:	Room and board, orientation, bicycles and mobile phones.
Costs:	Start from US$395, plus travel and insurance (US$ 120).
Applic.:	On-line form. Resume and essay in the working language(s) of country of destination. Applications accepted year round.
Notes:	USA office: america@staesa.org. UK office: Daisy Higginson - 9(1F2) Marchmont Street Edimburgh EH9 1EL, Scotland, UK; e-mail: daisy.higginson@googlemail.com. Germany office: Timo Holthoff - Kreuzbergring 56c/133 - 37075 Goettingen - +49 551 2506699; e-mail: info@afrikapraktika.org. Please see note on page 35.

Tearfund

100 Church Road, Teddington
Middlesex TW11 8QE UK
Tel.: ++44 (20) 8977-9144
Fax: ++44 (20) 8943-3594
E-mail: enquiry@tearfund.org
www.tearfund.org

Desc: Tearfund is an evangelical Christian relief and development charity working in partnership with local churches and Christian groups to tackle the causes and effects of global poverty. Tearfund recruits skilled relief staff to respond to humanitarian emergencies - and has a Disaster Management Team (DMT) Internship programme: a 6-month overseas placement for managers interested in beginning a career in relief work. Tearfund also has a Transform short term missions program for volunteers of all ages. Transform teams focus on practical tasks like building and painting, while others work in the community: teaching, working with children, or supporting churches working with the poor.

Sector: Agriculture, community development, education, environment, health, refugee aid, sanitation.

Conts: Various countries in Africa, Asia, Latin America, Europe.

Qualif: Nutritionists, public health educators, logisticians, accountants, water/sanitation engineers, shelter/rehabilitation specialists, programme managers etc, are required to apply for salaried international vacancies. See website for details.

Nonpro: Yes. For Transform, no specific skills are required, other than the ability to work as part of a team.

Age: Min.18(Transform); 5 years professional experience for DMT.

Duration: 6 months (DMT Internship); 2-16 weeks (Transform).

Lang: English, French, Spanish (desirable).

Benefits: Transform and DMT Internship posts are not salaried.

Costs: Transform: GB£1,600 - £3,000 approx., depending on length and destination. DMT Internship: expenses covered in most cases.

Applic.: Online application package.

Notes: Applicants should be committed Christians.

Terre des Hommes

International Federation Terre des Hommes
31, chemin Frank-Thomas, 1223 Cologny/Geneva, Switzerland
Tel.: ++41 (22) 736-3372
Fax: ++41 (22) 736-1510
E-mail: info@terredeshommes.org
www.terredeshommes.org

Desc.:	The International Federation Terre des Hommes is a network of 11 organisations (in Canada, Denmark, France, Germany, Italy, Luxembourg, Netherlands, Spain, Syria, and Switzerland) which works for children's rights and equitable development without racial, religious, cultural, or gender-based discrimination. The organisation was founded in 1960 in Lausanne (Switzerland), and subsequently, groups were created in various countries. In 1966, they joined together to form the International Federation Terre des Hommes. Over the years, the activities of the Terre des Hommes movements evolved from an initial concept of assisting individual children towards a community based approach to address the causes of the problems that affect children, whilst respecting local cultures.
Country:	Approximately 1200 development and humanitarian aid projects in some 70 countries in Africa, Asia, Europe, Latin America and the Middle-East.
Sector:	Child welfare, culture, human rights, women's issues, various.
Qualif.:	Agronomists, architects, engineers, administrators, surveyors, doctors, nurses, logistical coordinators, jurists.
Nonpro:	No. Local branches select professionals exclusively.
Age:	N/A with the necessary experience.
Duration:	Up to 3 years for long-term positions, with exceptions.
Lang.:	English French, Spanish, or Portuguese.
Benefit:	Long-term personnel receive a salary and all expenses paid
Costs:	Only personal expenses.
Applic:	Send CV to the national branches offering the positions.
Notes:	It is recommended to periodically consult the websites for new position openings.

Ugunja Community Resource Centre

PO Box 330, Ugunja, Kenya
Tel.: ++254 (33) 434-330
Fax: ++254 (33) 434-131
E-mail: ucrckenya@gmail.com
www.ugunja.org

Desc: The Ugunja Community Resource Centre's mission statement is to facilitate sustainable development by providing access to information and training and through communication and cooperation between various development actors (government, NGO's, and community groups).

Sector: Agriculture, child welfare, community development, construction, education, environment, health, human rights, IT, peacekeeping, skills training, small-enterprise development, women's issues, various.

Country: Africa (Kenya).

Qualif.: High school teachers especially in sciences; environmentalists working in afforestation, GIS, biodiversity, and sustainable agriculture; social workers, IT experts.

Nonpro: Yes. Tutoring, fundraising, internships, thesis opportunities.

Age: Minimum 18.

Duration: From a few days to 2 years; no time limits.

Lang.: English and Kiswahili.

Benefits: The Centre cannot offer any monetary support.

Costs: A weekly donation of US$35 is suggested. Volunteers can live either with a local family or rent their own accommodation in Ugunja town (approx. US$100 per month). Airfares, local travel costs, Visa, and insurance not included.

Applic.: On-line form plus 2 references. Applications via fax are not accepted. Successful applicants will be notified within 2 months and be sent more detailed information. A small application fee will then be required to confirm placement.

Notes: Contact the organisation regarding Visas and vaccinations. See note on page 35.

UNA Exchange

Temple of Peace, Cathays Park
Cardiff, Wales CF10 3AP UK
Tel.: ++44 (29) 2022-3088
Fax: ++44 (29) 2022-2540
E-mail: exchanges@unaexchange.org or volunteer@unaexchange.org
www.unaexchange.org

Desc.: UNA Exchange evolved from UNA (United Nations Association) Wales and was established in 1973, to organise and promoting international youth work in local communities. International Volunteer Projects (IVP) provide services to local communities to carry out tasks that would not otherwise be possible. Projects are organised on a local basis by the community that have recognised and identified a specific need. Communities then contact an IVP organiser such as UNA Exchange or another partner organisation. The aims of the program are to promote cultural understanding between the local community and the volunteer, while at the same time providing the volunteers with a unique experience. The principle emphasis is often the breaking down of cultural barriers rather than the outcomes of the work itself. IVPs provide opportunities for people of different nationalities, ages, abilities, social, cultural, and religious backgrounds to live, work, and cooperate together. MTVs (Medium-Term Volunteers) are volunteers with previous international volunteering experience, office skills and a good working knowledge of the relevant language. European Voluntary Service (EVS) gives young people the chance to gain work experience in Europe.

Sector: Agriculture, community development, construction, culture, education, environment, various.

Country: Over 75 countries in Africa, Asia, Europe and Latin America. Cultural exchanges in Europe, Latin and North America, and Asia.

Qualif.: No particular skills required, but experience should include independent travel, living or working overseas, previous residential voluntary work or participation on IVPs, experience in community or voluntary work. Some destinations require training (see website for a complete listing).

Nonpro: Yes, with previous relevant experience.

Age: Minimum 18, though projects in some countries take 14–17-year-olds.

Duration: 1 week- 3 months fro short-term volunteering in Wales; 2 weeks–1 year for volunteering overseas (with EVS or MTV).

Lang.: English, with knowledge in local language of the project an asset.

Benefits: Food and accommodation for the duration of the project (unless it states otherwise); volunteer support/preparation. As a group, volunteers are usually self-catering and sufficient money will be provided to buy food and cook together. Accommodation will vary from project to project, ranging from the basic tent to comfortable hostels.

Costs: Membership fee: GB£10-15. Placement: GB£50—140 (approx. US$100—280) depending on destination and length of stay. Volunteers organise and pay for their own travel, insurance etc.

Applic.: Applicants must also have attended a compulsory UNA Exchange North / South Preparation weekend in Cardiff.

UNAREC – Union Nationale des Associations Régionales Etudes & Chantiers

33, rue Campagne Première, 75014 Paris France

Tel.: ++33 (1) 4538-9626

E-mail: unarec@wanadoo.fr

www.unarec.org

Desc.:	UNAREC organises international workcamps for adults, and teenagers; it also has a program working with people facing social or economical difficulties. In 1997 UNAREC became involved with EVS and since 1962 has been working with many partners all over the world. Volunteers participate in projects such as: restoring a village bread oven, cleaning riverbanks, organising festivals and cultural activities.
Sector:	Community development, construction, culture, environment.
Country:	Africa, Asia, Europe, Middle East, Latin and North America.
Qualif.:	No specific qualifications needed .
Nonpro:	Yes.
Age:	Minimum 18; 14–17 for youth workcamps.
Duration:	2–3 weeks. Mid and long term volunteering also available.
Lang.:	French; English is often used on adult workcamps since there may be many nationalities.
Benefits:	Food and accommodation.
Costs:	Registration fee: EUR135-150. Placement fee: EUR250-360, including insurance. Travel costs are not included.
Applic.:	Outside France, contact the partner organisation in country of citizenship (consult website). Volunteers from a country without a partner organisation can contact directly the UNAREC international office: D.I. UNAREC, 3 rue des Petits Gras - F-63000 Clermont-Ferrand, tel.: ++33 (4) 7331-9804; fax: ++33 (4) 7331-9809; e-mail: unarec.di@wanadoo.fr

UNICEF – United Nations International Children's Emergency Fund

UNICEF House
3 United Nations Plaza, New York, New York 10017 USA
Tel.: ++1 (212) 326-7000
Fax: ++1 (212) 887-7465 or 887-7454
www.unicef.org

Desc.:	For more than 60 years UNICEF has been helping governments and communities by finding solutions to the problems plaguing poor children and their families. Programs work to protect children's and women's rights, crisis response, reopening schools and establishing safe spaces for children when armed conflict and war, flood, and other disruptions occur.
Sector:	Child welfare, education, emergency, health, hunger relief, sanitation, women's issues, various.
Country:	190 countries in the 5 continents.
Qualif.:	Qualifications or education relevant to the above sectors.
Nonpro:	Yes, with Bachelor Degree and 2–5 years relevant experience.
Age:	Minimum 21.
Duration:	A few months to 1–2 years. UNV does not offer short-term overseas summer camps or internships for students.
Lang.:	English fluency and 1 other UNICEF working language i.e., French or Spanish.
Benefits:	Settling-in grant; Volunteer Living Allowance intended to cover basic needs including housing and utilities; international travel; insurance; annual leave; resettlement allowance.
Costs:	Personal expenses.
Applic.:	UNICEF does not recruit volunteers directly. International volunteer opportunities are offered through UNV – United Nations Volunteers (see listing). US citizens must send their CV to: United Nations Volunteers, c/o The Peace Corps (see listing).
Notes:	UNICEF National Committees in industrialised countries provide information on national volunteer activities for their respective citizens. See website for national contacts and links.

UNICEF Internship Programme

Internship Co-ordinator, Recruitment Programmes Section

No. 3 United Nation Plaza, Room 2500

Office of Personnel Services, United Nations, New York, New York 10017 USA

Tel.: ++1 (212) 326-7000

Fax: ++1 (212) 887-7465 or 7454

E-mail: internships@unicef.org

www.unicef.org

Desc.:	UNICEF's Internship Programme is independent of the United Nations. Interns work in a UNICEF office on a project or several projects, such as limited research or studies and creating or improving databases or websites.
Sector:	Human rights.
Country:	Offices worldwide.
Qualif.:	Currently-enrolled graduate or post-graduate students in a field related to UNICEF's interests only. Applicants must be enrolled during the proposed internship period.
Nonpro:	Undergraduates are not accepted. Excellent academic performance demonstrated by recent university or institution records. University or related institution support—minimum requirement is a letter from a professor. Additional consideration is given for past work experience.
Age:	Minimum 23.
Duration:	6–16 weeks.
Lang.:	English fluency and another UNICEF working language (French, Spanish, Arabic, Chinese or Russian).
Benefits:	UNICEF does not provide financial support for interns.
Costs:	Travel, lodging, and living expenses.
Applic.:	On-line form plus letter from university certifying enrolment, course of study, and expected date of graduation; a copy of an up-to-date university transcript; 2 references (1 from a college professor); personal insurance information.
Notes:	See list of addresses of UNICEF National Committees on website. For internships not in the New York office, applications should be sent directly to the head of the office concerned.

United Action for Children

Balong PO Box 177
Muyuka, SWP, Cameroon
Tel.: ++(237) 772-0418
E-mail: unitedactionforc@yahoo.com
www.interconnection.org/unitedaction
www.unitedactionforchildren.org

Desc.: United Action for Children works to create and develop a caring society for children, in particular by fighting against child neglect, labour and all other forms of child abuse. Disabled children are the most affected by child neglect or abandonment, particularly in rural areas with no adequate health facilities. The organisation provides counselling to both children and parents. It is also planning to build a multipurpose centre called "The Star Centre". The objective is to permit parents to assist in the upbringing of their children, by identifying parents of at-risk children and providing them with adequate training.

Sector: Child welfare, community development, education, health.

Country: Africa (Cameroon).

Qualif.: Nursery or primary schoolteacher, project administrator or program officer, paediatrician, orthopaedic surgeon, and general surgeon, computer trainer and wood working teacher.

Nonpro: Yes, with tutoring, fundraising, computer training, or computer installation skills, depending upon position.

Age Minimum 18 for non-professional volunteers.

Duration: Negotiable.

Lang.: English.

Benefits: Help in finding room and board will be provided.

Costs: The volunteer will have to bear all the costs: international airfare plus living costs, which in Cameroon are very affordable.

Applic.: Contact the organisation for further details.

Notes: See note on page 35.

United Children's Fund, Inc.

PO Box 20341
Boulder, Colorado 80308-3341 USA
Tel./Fax: ++1 (888) 343-3199 (toll free in North America)
E-mail: unchildren@aol.com or united@unchildren.org
www.unchildren.org

Desc.:	The United Children's Fund has been in East Africa since 1994 and is committed to helping the people of rural areas realize a decent standard of living, adequate healthcare, unlimited education opportunities for their children, and proper care for the aged and the terminally ill. This organisation works on the premise that it is the responsibility and duty of all people to ensure that every child in the world has the right to live and grow in a stable environment, in an atmosphere of happiness, love, understanding and security, with the basic human right of education, healthcare, adequate shelter, food, and clothing.
Sector:	Agriculture, child welfare, construction, education, housing, sanitation, small-enterprise development, women's issues.
Country:	Africa (Kenya, Uganda).
Qualif.:	Teachers, doctor, nurses, or any talented person willing to make a difference in someone's life..
Nonpro:	Yes. Experience is appreciated but not required.
Age:	Special conditions apply to minors.
Duration:	1–2 months.
Lang.:	English, however in Uganda Luganda is the local and first language.
Benefits:	Accommodation (dormitory), food, ground transportation, administrative costs, local government fees, and all other incidental costs associated with the program.
Costs:	See website for program costs. Transportation costs to and from East Africa are not included. A nominal non-refundable deposit is required.
Applic.:	On-line form plus deposit.
Notes:	Volunteers program can be temporarily suspended, verify the website to see latest programs and opportunities available. International volunteers are welcome.

United Planet

11 Arlington Street Boston , MA 02116 USA
Tel.: ++1 (617) 267-7763 or (toll free in N. America 1-800-292-2316)
Fax: ++1 (617) 267-7764
E-mail: quest@unitedplanet.org
www.unitedplanet.org

Desc.:	United Planet (UP) is a leading international, educational, humanitarian, and peace-building, non-profit organization with members and volunteers in over 150 countries devoted to fostering cross-cultural understanding and friendship and supporting communities in need in order to bring the world together in a community beyond borders. United Planet utilizes a wide range of local, online, and international programs to achieve this essential mission. The underlying principle of its programs is the concept of Relational Diplomacy, in which UP recognizes that the relationship between two people of diverse backgrounds is the basic building block for uniting the world in a community beyond borders.
Sector:	Community development, culture, education.
Country:	Projects in 50 countries worldwide in Africa, Asia, Europe, Middle East, and Latin America
Qualif.:	Both skilled and unskilled volunteers of all ages and nationalities. Short-term quests are open to anybody from any country. However, for long-term, UP is the American and Canadian partner of ICYE and not responsible for volunteers from other regions.
Nonpro:	Yes.
Age:	16 years old with parental permission. Younger than 16 are accepted if accompanied by an adult at least 21 years old. A few programs require volunteers to be at least 18 years of age.
Duration:	Short-term 1-12 weeks; long-term 6 months and 1 year.
Lang.:	English. Some programs require language skills, especially in Latin America.
Benefits:	Language classes, cultural activities, excursions, pre-departure training and support, alumni network and e-newsletter.
Costs:	Fees start at $1200 for a 2 week Quest and increase by $200 for each additional week.
Applic.:	On-line form and interview.
Notes:	Non-American or Canadian citizens should contact the nearest ICYE office. See website: www.icye.org

UNV – United Nations Volunteers

Postfach 260 111, D-53153 Bonn Germany
Tel.: ++49 (228) 815-2000
Fax: ++49 (228) 815-2001
E-mail: roster@unvolunteers.org
www.unvolunteers.org

Desc.: Administered by the United Nations Development Programme (UNDP), the United Nations Volunteers (UNV) programme is the United Nations organization that supports sustainable human development globally through the promotion of volunteerism, including the mobilization of volunteers. Since starting its operations in 1971, the Bonn-based UNV programme has mobilized tens of thousands of UN Volunteers to serve the causes of peace and development. Every year, more than 7,000 UN Volunteers representing some 160 nationalities serve in more than 140 countries. Possessing a university education or advanced technical training as well as several years of work experience, they support the activities of UN agencies, governments, non-governmental organizations (NGOs), civil society groups and communities in such diverse areas as humanitarian relief, peace-building, human rights, electoral supervision, HIV/AIDS, education, Information and Communications Technology (ICT), gender mainstreaming, environmental management and urban development.

Sector: Agriculture, child welfare, community development, education, environment, health, housing, human rights, hunger relief, IT, peacekeeping, refugee aid, sanitation, skills training, small-enterprise development, women's issues, various.

Country: The UNV programme recruits globally. Assignments only take place in developing or transition countries.

Qualif.: Minimum, a university degree or higher technical diploma, several years of relevant work experience, and an interest in long-term volunteer opportunities in developing countries.

Nonpro: Yes. With academic or technical credentials (secondary school and/or vocational certificate); several years of relevant work experience, practical experience working with communities, and participation among different community groups.

Age: Minimum 25.

Duration: Varies from a few months to 1–2 years. No short-term overseas summer camps or internships are available for students.

Lang.: Good working knowledge of English, French or Spanish is essential. Additional language skills are an asset, in particular Arabic, Chinese, Portuguese, or Russian but are not necessary.

Benefits: UN Volunteers are professionals who do not receive a salary but in return for their services receive some or all of the following benefits: settling-in grant at the beginning of the assignment; Volunteer Living Allowance (VLA) intended to cover basic needs including housing and utilities. Travel expenses on appointment and if applicable at the end of assignment; insurances, (life, health, and permanent disability); annual leave (30 days annually); a resettlement allowance upon satisfactory completion of the assignment.

Costs: Personal expenses.

Applic.: Application on-line at www.unvolunteers.org/volunteers

Notes: Main partners recruiting UN Volunteers are: the United Nations System, UNDP/Government, UNHCR, UNOPS, WFP, UNICEF, UNFPA, NGOs and others.

VIA

PO Box 20266
Stanford, California 94309 USA
Tel.: ++1 (650) 723-3228
Fax: ++1 (650) 725-1805
E-mail: info@viaprograms.org
www.viaprograms.org

Desc.: VIA (formerly Volunteers in Asia) provides a variety of US-Asia public service and educational exchange opportunities. Continuing undergraduates from American universities may spend a summer volunteering in Asia through service or teaching. Graduates have the opportunity to spend 1-2 years living in China, Vietnam or Indonesia. Additional short-term programs for adults are being discussed. See website for the most up to date information. VIA is an independent, non-profit organization working towards peaceful trans-Pacific relationships since 1963.

Sector: Education, environment, health.

Country: Asia (Burma, China, Indonesia, Laos, Thailand, Vietnam).

Qualif.: Generally, long-term volunteers must be college graduates or graduating seniors; exceptions are occasionally made. Summer volunteers currently must be college undergraduates. See website for additional short-term programs.

Nonpro: Long-term programs: 1–2 years; short-term programs: 6-8 weeks.

Age: Minimum 18.

Duration: 1–2 years; 6 weeks for summer programs for undergraduates.

Lang.: English.

Benefits: Cross-cultural and post specific training (5-6 weeks for long-term volunteers, 1-2 weeks for short-term volunteers); some international travel (see website for details); visa expenses; accommodation, basic health and emergency evacuation insurance, in-country and home office staff support. Long-term volunteers receive a living stipend. Limited need-based scholarships are available.

Costs: Max. fee is approx. US$2,000 for the 2 years program. See website for the current participation fee. Additional costs include: immunizations, outside language study, and additional insurance. See the application package on the website for further details.

Applic.: Applications are available on the website beginning in the fall each year. Applications are due no later than February for a summer departure. Interviews will take place in early March and applicants will be notified within two weeks of their acceptance. See the website for additional details including dates an interview locations.

Notes: Undergraduate positions are open to all continuing college undergraduates. Graduate positions are open to all graduating seniors. VIA offers scholarships and fundraising support to applicants who cannot afford the entire participation fee.

VIA Netherlands: vianl@xs4all.nl.

VIP – Volunteers for International Partnership

Offered by the Participating Members of Federation EIL
PO Box 6141
Brattleboro, Vermont 05302 USA
Tel.:/Fax: ++1 (802) 258-3467
Email: info@partnershipvolunteers.org
www.partnershipvolunteers.org

Desc.: Through Volunteers for International Partnership (VIP), enthusiastic, committed individuals are matched with volunteer service opportunities in communities around the world. Experienced program directors in each country arrange for VIP's unique blend of language training, homestay and community-based host projects. Through one to three-month immersion experiences, volunteers learn about the county and the people in real, life-changing and mutually satisfying ways.

Sector: Community development, education, environment, health.

Country: Africa (Ghana, Morocco, Nigeria, South Africa), Asia (India, Nepal, Thailand), Europe (Ireland, Great Britain, Turkey), Latin America (Argentina, Brazil, Chile, Ecuador, Guatemala) and the US.

Qualif.: Host projects are selected according to participant's experience, skills and physical condition. Volunteers include students, recent graduates, professionals and retirees.

Nonpro.: Yes.

Age: Minimum 18 (21 for US participants). No maximum unless dictated by circumstances.

Duration: Average 3 months (longer and shorter programs may also be arranged)

Lang.: Depends on the country (language training is often included).

Benefits: Cultural orientation, language training, housing, most meals, in-country travel and one-to-one support.

Costs: Fees vary by country and length of program. Financial assistance may be available. A 20% deposit is required. International travel is not included.

Applic.: Through any VIP sending country offices (see website).

Notes: Sample projects in each VIP host country, an Inquiry Form (for the proper office) can be found at the VIP website.

Visions in Action

2710 Ontario Road NW
Washington DC 20009 USA
Tel.: ++1 (202) 625-7402
Fax: ++1 (202) 588-9344
E-mail: visions@visionsinaction.org
www.visionsinaction.org

Desc.: Visions in Action provides hands-on educational experiences while offering opportunities for participants to assist in efforts to make a difference in the lives of individuals in the developing world. Visions in Action programs are funded by program fees, private contributions, and in-kind donations.

Sector: Agriculture, child welfare, community development, education, environment, health, housing, human rights, hunger relief, IT, refugee aid, small-enterprise development, women's issues, various.

Country: Africa (South Africa, Tanzania, Uganda), Latin America (Mexico).

Qualif.: Individuals with equivalent experience, building, mechanical or trade skills, as well as college graduates are encouraged to apply.

Nonpro: Professional qualifications are only necessary for specific placements, but always appreciated on any project.

Age: Minimum 20.

Duration: 6–12 months. A 6-week summer program and minimum 3-month internships are also available.

Lang.: English, Spanish, depending on country.

Benefits: Accommodation (group, independent, or home-stays), stipend, medical and emergency insurance, 3-week orientation, language instruction, in-country and US staff support.

Costs: US$4,700—5,900, depending on country and duration.

Applic.: On-line and written applications, letters of recommendation, phone interview.

Notes: The program is open to international volunteers.

VOICA – Canossian International Voluntary Service

Via Aurelia Antica, 180
00165 Rome Italy
Mob.: ++39 339-1160529
Fax: ++39 (06) 6385-885
E-mail: voica@fdcc.org
www.voica.org

Desc.:	VOICA is a Canossian mission sending volunteers to live as active participants in the worldwide Catholic Church and in the global society to share their talents with the poor overseas. Volunteers join groups or centres for voluntary service.
Sector:	Community development, education, health, religious.
Country:	Africa (Egypt, Malawi, Tanzania, Togo, Sao Tomé, Uganda), Asia (East Timor), Latin America (Argentina, Brazil), Europe (Albania, Italy, Poland).
Qualif.:	Professional volunteers preferred, generic on condition.
Nonpro:	Yes. Contact the organisation for details.
Age:	Minimum 21 for long-term volunteers; 19–30 for short-term.
Duration:	1–3 years for long term volunteering. 1 month for short term volunteering (summer programs).
Benefits:	Accommodation (group). Long-term volunteers also receive training (3–months in Rome) stipend, medical insurance, travel between Rome and the overseas mission site.
Cost:	No cost for long-term; travel, room and board for short-term. All volunteers are encouraged to raise funds for the projects.
Applic.:	No deadline for long-term service. Starting date varies depending on the country and ministry. International summer program deadline is late February/early March.
Notes:	Catholics only, married couples only for long-term placements. Volunteers must be in good health and able to adapt to the poverty and simplicity of the mission and community life. Willingness to take part in community prayer and undertake a formation itinerary before, during, and after the experience.

VOLU – Voluntary Workcamps Association of Ghana

PO Box GP 1540, Accra, Ghana
Tel.: ++233 (21) 663-486 / (244) 202-294
Fax.: ++233 (2) 665-960
E-mail: info@voluntaryworkcamps.org or voluntaryworkcamp@yahoo.com
www.voluntaryworkcamps.org

Desc.:	VOLU aims to organise and run voluntary workcamps in Ghana, either independently or in collaboration with other voluntary organisations or government ministries. VOLU encourages intercultural and interracial understanding by inviting people from abroad to workcamps in Ghana and by sponsoring Ghanaians to go to workcamps abroad. VOLU organises a variety of projects, including the construction of primary or secondary schools, roads, and hospitals, as well as reforestation, cocoa plantation, literacy projects, community development, oil palm production, and AIDS awareness campaigns. Volunteers work about 7 hours per day, Monday to Friday and occasionally Saturday.
Sector:	Agriculture, child welfare, community development, construction, education, health, various.
Country:	Africa (Ghana).
Qualif.:	No particular qualifications needed, other than good health and strong motivation to work hard at manual unskilled jobs and adaptability to live with others in simple living conditions.
Nonpro:	Yes.
Age:	Minimum 16.
Duration:	3–4 weeks; summer June–October; winter December–end of January.
Lang.:	English.
Benefits:	Food and accommodation, airport pick up, camp expenses.
Costs:	A EUR200 non-refundable fee for 1 workcamp (EUR300 2 camps). All travel to Ghana and within Ghana.
Applic.:	Print the on-line form to mail or fax (e-mail is often problematic).
Notes:	Yellow fever immunisation required; Hepatitis A and B, typhoid/typhus, meningitis, rabies, and diphtheria recommended.

Volunteer Africa

PO Box 24
Bakwell DE45 1YP UK
E-mail: support@volunteerafrica.org
www.volunteerafrica.org

Desc.:	Volunteer Africa has been established to give people from around the world the opportunity to work on community initiated projects in developing countries working with partner NGOs. Health Action Promotion Association (HAPA) in Singida region, HAPO in Tambora region and Hisani in Mwanza. Projects include teaching at an orphanage, working at a HIV/AIDS resource centre or working in rural villages building schools and health clinics.
Sector:	Community development, culture.
Country:	Africa (Tanzania).
Qualif.:	N/A.
Nonpro:	Yes.
Age:	Minimum 18.
Duration:	4-12 weeks (first week training and rest working).
Lang.:	English. Kiswahili language training is provided in Tanzania during the first week.
Benefits:	Accommodation, food, camp kit, visas, pre-departure support.
Costs:	US$1,980-3,670, depending on lenght of stay. Return flight and compulsory medical insurance not included. See cost page of the website for fees and a breakdown of where the money goes. Volunteers are responsible for spending money, all personal supplies (i.e., sleeping bag, boots, backpack), vaccinations, and anti-malaria tablets.
Applic.:	On-line form.
Notes:	Volunteers from USA, Canada, UK, Australia, Hong Kong, Ireland, Europe or New Zealand. Specific medical requirements apply.

Volunteer in Africa

Box OS 602
Osu-Accra Ghana
Tel.: +233 (20) 8731745
E-mail: ghana@volunteeringinafrica.org or ebensten73@yahoo.com
www.volunteeringinafrica.org

Desc.: Volunteers are needed to assist to teach English, Mathematics and/or Science at primary and junior secondary schools in the Eastern and Central regions of Ghana. Volunteers are also needed to assist in general work at orphanages in these regions. The general work includes teaching the kids English and assisting in cooking for them. Placements can start at various times of the year and can be of flexible duration, usually 1 week to 12 weeks duration. The rural posts are community based and provide a unique opportunity to participate in the local culture.

Sector: Community development, education.

Country: Africa (Ghana).

Qualif.: No particular skills required for projects, initiative and adaptability are important requisites.

Nonpro: Yes, with relevant skills to the project.

Age: Minimum 18.

Duration: 1 week to 1 year, depending on project.

Lang.: English.

Benefits: Accommodation and food, orientation, Twi lessons.

Costs: Volunteers make a financial contribution of around GB£400 (US$800) for 1 month.

Applic.: CV/resume are required and no deposit is payable on application.

Notes: See note on page 35.

Volunteer Latin America

PO Box 585
Rochester
ME1 9EJ UK
Tel.: ++44 (20) 7193-9163
E-mail: info@volunteerlatinamerica.com
www.volunteerlatinamerica.com

Desc.: Volunteer Latin America is a comprehensive source of free and low cost volunteering opportunities in Central and South America. It offers a customized information service for people of all ages and nationalities on voluntary work opportunities in the environmental and humanitarian sectors. The organisation also provides information on recommended Spanish language schools in Central and South America and offers advice on how to set up an individually customised volunteer placement.

Sector: Child welfare, community development, construction, education, environment, various.

Country: Latin America.

Qualif.: Generally, most projects do not require any special qualification.

Nonpro: Yes.

Age: Most organizations seek volunteers aged 18 or over.

Duration: Each project will stipulate a fixed term contract or require a minimum commitment. This might be a number of weeks or months.

Lang.: English and/or Spanish.

Benefits: Volunteer Latin America has the opportunity to put in touch volunteers with very affordable volunteering opportunities . All participants have the assurance that all their fees (if any) go to the host organization rather an intermediary organization.

Costs: Dependent on project. Some require a small financial contribution whereas others provide free board and lodging.

Applic.: Details on how to apply should be acquired from the organization a prospective volunteer wish to work for.

Volunteer Missionary Movement

5980 West Loomis Road
Greendale Wisconsin 53129 USA
Tel.: ++1 (414) 423-8660
Fax: ++1 (414) 423-8964
E-mail: vnm@vmmusa.org
www.vmmusa.org

Desc.: The Volunteer Missionary Movement is an international community of Christians, with its origins in the Catholic tradition. The US office sends Christian lay volunteers, from the United States or Canada, to service-oriented ministries in Central America. The European office sends volunteers to Africa. Volunteers share their lives, resources and skills, and thus challenge oppressive and unjust structures and promote equality, respect, and dignity for all. They are committed to international justice and peace.

Sector: Agriculture, community development, construction, education, human rights, religious, sanitation.

Country: Africa (Kenya, Uganda), Latin America (El Salvador, Guatemala, Nicaragua).

Qualif.: Work experience and skills. A college degree is preferred.

Nonpro: Yes, with 1–2 years work experience.

Age: Minimum 23 is preferred but will consider 22 on individual basis.

Duration: 2 years.

Lang.: Language instruction provided if needed.

Benefits: Inquire with organisation, some positions have a stipend. Medical insurance provided.

Costs: Only personal expenses and transportation to Discernment weekend.

Applic: On-line form. Attend a 3-day introduction/discernment weekend, usually held near the US headquarters in Milwaukee, Wisconsin.

Notes: Citizens of the United States or Canada primarily, non-US Citizens are considered on individual basis. Two-week mission orientation training required and provided.

Volunteer Nepal - National Group

Jhaukhel 4, Bhaktapur 977, Nepal
Tel.: ++977 (166)13724
E-mail: info@volnepal.np.org or volunteer_nepal2002@yahoo.com
www.volnepal.np.org
www.nabinschool.np.org

Desc.: Volunteer Nepal co-ordinates local and international work camps with community groups or institutions to empower community self-help initiatives. The mission is to mobilize and sensitize women and youth on the issues affecting them in order to promote and support sustainable self-help projects focusing on advancement of women and youth initiatives, income generating activities, human development and environmental conservation efforts. Interaction between people of diverse cultures creates opportunities fo local and international volunteers to exchange their experience and skills.

Sector: Child welfare, community development, construction, education, environment, health, IT, religious.

Country: Asia (Nepal).

Qualif.: No formal qualifications needed.

Nonpro: Students or young people recently graduated from college with some experience in relevant field for internship.

Age: Minimum 18.

Duration: Minimum 2 weeks to maximum 1 year, depending on project. Volunteer placements can start at various times of the year and can be of flexible duration.

Lang.: English.

Benefits: Accommodation and food.

Costs: Application and registration fee depends upon the program type. Visit the web pages for details.

Applic.: Send a detailed CV to info@volnepal.np.org or volunteer@volnepal.np.org; references will be required to complete the application process.

Notes: Volunteer Nepal collaborates with 15 other schools as well as 3 health posts, and 5 community based, social development organisations working on projects in the Kathmandu Valley, Chitwan and other places in Nepal.

Volunteers for Peace International

1034 Tiffany Road
Belmont, Vermont 05730 USA
Tel.: ++1 (802) 259-2759
Fax: ++1 (802) 259-2922
E-mail: vfp@vfp.org
www.vfp.org

Desc.: Volunteers For Peace is a non-profit membership organisation that has been coordinating international workcamps since 1982 and is a member of CCIVS (see listing) at UNESCO and works in cooperation with SCI (see listing), EVS (see listing), and YAP (see listing). The office staff, board and thousands of volunteers in the field help facilitate this program.

Sector: Agriculture, child welfare, construction, culture, education, environment, health, housing, human rights, refugee aid, various.

Country: Many countries in Africa, Asia, Europe, Latin America, Middle East, North America, Oceania.

Qualif.: No particular skills required.

Nonpro: Yes.

Age: Minimum 18. Teen camps for volunteers under age 18.

Duration: 95% of workcamps occur June through September. There are about 80 programs between October and May; 2–3 weeks per workcamp; 25% of the volunteers register for multiple workcamps in the same or different countries.

Lang.: English is generally the language of most workcamps.

Benefits: Food and accommodation. Workcamps vary greatly in living conditions. Limited funding is occasionally available for under-represented groups (generally African, Latin, or Native Americans) in domestic (USA) programs only. Volunteers are kindly asked not to request a scholarship for a program outside of the United States. The scholarship would only cover the registration fee but not any travel expenses.

Costs: Registration fee of US$250 per workcamp (US$300 for volunteers under age 18) plus mandatory VFP membership of US$20. The registration fee covers all expenses including meals and accommodation for 1 camp. Russian, African, Asian and Latin American programs may cost US$300–500. All transportation is arranged and paid for by the volunteer.

Applic.: Complete and send/fax the registration form to VFP. There will be a penalty of US$150, payable in advance, for changing workcamp selections after registering.

Notes: Citizens/residents of the United States and Canada may register through VFP. Placement of nationals of other countries may be possible, but if a partner organisation exists, the recruitment will be through the partner, not through VFP. **Programs for Teenagers**: Programs for 15–17-year olds in France and 16–17-year olds in Germany. Fees range from US$300–600. Family camps accepting parents with children are offered in Switzerland, Italy, Denmark and occasionally in other countries.

VSO – Voluntary Service Overseas

317 Putney Bridge Road
London SW15 2PN UK
Tel.: ++44 (20) 8780-7500
Fax: ++44 (20) 8780-7300
E-mail: enquiry@vso.org.uk
www.vso.org.uk

Desc.: VSO is an international development charity that works through volunteers. At any one time around 1,500 experienced professionals are sharing their skills with local colleagues in some of the world's poorest communities, working together to find realistic solutions to the problems they face. VSO responds to requests from governments and community organisations throughout Asia and Africa. The volunteers aim to pass on their expertise to local people so that when they return home their skills remain. Volunteers can be aged between 20 and 75 years old and must have a formal qualification and some work experience. VSO actively recruits volunteers all the time. The range of jobs is vast, and includes small business advisors, teachers, social workers, health professionals, management consultants, marine biologists, accountants and farmers.

.Sector: Agriculture, community development, education, environment, health, IT, skills training, small enterprise development.

Country: Africa (Cameroon, Eritrea, Ethiopia, Gambia, Ghana, Kenya, Malawi, Mozambique, Namibia, Nigeria, Rwanda, Sierra Leone, South Africa, Tanzania, Uganda, Zambia), Asia (Bangladesh, Cambodia, China, India, Kazakhstan, Maldives, Mongolia, Nepal, Philippines, Sri Lanka, Thailand, Vietnam), Latin America (Guyana), Oceania (Papua New Guinea, Vanuatu).

Qualif.: Most placements require volunteers with formal qualifications and a minimum of 2 years relevant experience.

Nonpro: Several Youth programs offered, including an Overseas Training program.

Age: Volunteers can be between 18 and 75 years old.

Duration: 2 weeks-2 years.

Lang.: English. Some placement require language skills. Language lessons are provided for all in their in-country orientation.

Benefits: Volunteers are provided with accommodation and a local level allowance as well as air fares and insurance.

Costs: No placement fee apply to any VSO placement.

Applic.: On-line form or contact VSO directly. Go to www.vso.org/volunteering or call the Response Unit on 020 8780 7500. Returned volunteers who have worked in a variety of projects and countries are available on the RV Hotline on 0845 603 0027 to answer calls every week night between 6 and 9 pm.

Notes: EU, Iceland and Norway residents only. Canadian and US volunteers should apply with VSO Canada (see listing).

VSO Canada

44 Eccles Street
Ottawa, Ontario K1S 6R4 Canada
Tel.: ++1 (613) 234-1364 (toll free in N. Am. 888-876-2911)
Fax: ++1 (613) 234-1444
E-mail: inquiry@vsocan.org
www.vsocan.org

Desc.: VSO is an international development agency that works through volunteers – the largest independent organization of its kind in the world. VSO promotes volunteering to fight poverty and disadvantage. Since 1958, more than 30,000 women and men have shared their skills through VSO. Volunteers work with local colleagues in more than 30 developing countries to share skills, creativity and learning to achieve shared goals. VSO recruits volunteers through agencies in Canada, India, Kenya, the Netherlands, the Philippines and the UK.

Sector: Community development, education, health, small-enterprise development, various.

Country: Africa (Cameroon, Eritrea, Ethiopia, Gambia, Ghana, Kenya, Malawi, Mozambique, Namibia, Nigeria, Rwanda, South Africa, Tanzania, Uganda, Zambia), Asia (Bangladesh, Cambodia, China, India, Indonesia, Kazakhstan, Maldives, Mongolia, Nepal, Pakistan, Philippines, Sri Lanka,Thailand), Latin America (Guyana).

Qualif.: Placements available to professionals from more than 60 occupations.

Nonpro: Most placements require qualifications in a field as well as 2 years of related work experience. High demand areas such as Education, Health and Management may need further work experience or a combination of skills.

Age: 21and over (VSO is obliged to respect the mandatory retirement requirements of countries in which we work.)

Duration: Most placements in the Volunteer Sending Program are for two years. Placements through the Youth Volunteer Program (Canada) and the VSO Business Partnership are for 6 – 9 months.

Lang.: English, French (Rwanda and Cameroon). In most programs, training and support given to learn local languages where needed for work.

Benefits: Assistance with travel costs to a VSO assessment day.

Pre-departure training which includes associated costs for travel, food and accommodation;

. costs of medical examination and required immunizations

return airfare to your country of placement ;

. pre-departure grant for purchase of supplies and equipment;

. costs associated with processing your visa application

health insurance;

. in-service grant and end of service grant;

. support for language training;

. quarterly payments to the volunteer's North American bank account (CAD$300 per quarter).

. A basic living allowance for necessities, paid in local currency.

Costs: No program fees, however volunteers are encouraged to raise CAD $,2000 through pre-departure fundraising to support the cost of their placement.

Applic.: Online form or request form via post. At the application stage, qualifications, work experience, and personal circumstances will be reviewed.. If an applicant's skills and experience match those required by VSO's overseas partners they will be invited to attend an assessment day in either Ottawa or Vancouver.

Notes: VSO Canada accepts applications from people who are living in Canada or the United States. Applicants who are living outside of North America should contact VSO - Voluntary Service Overseas in the UK (see listing).

Women's Aid Organisation

PO Box 493, Jalan Sultan, 46760 Petaling Jaya
Selangor Darul Ehsan, Malaysia
Tel.: ++6 (3) 7956-3488
Fax: ++6 (3) 7956-3237
E-mail: wao@po.jaring.my
www.wao.org.my

Desc.: This organisation's work concerns issues of violence against women. Volunteers organise activities for children and women (craft sessions, language classes, cooking lessons, computer skills, etc.), providing transport and accompanying women who need to make police reports, go the hospital, or run errands, as well as help out with administrative work.

Sector: Child welfare, women's issues.

Country: Asia (Malaysia).

Qualif.: Passion and interest in dedicating some time to volunteer in the Refugee and Child Care Centre.

Nonpro: Yes, with awareness of the relevant issues, good report writing and fundraising skills, ability to do research and study, good computer literacy, able to conduct programs, teach skills to women, and create activities for children,

Age: Minimum 18.

Duration: 8 weeks or more.

Lang.: English, spoken and written.

Benefits: None.

Costs: International airfare. Room and board (US$70–160 for a room per month and US$210–400 for an apartment per month). Utility bills (water and electricity) may amount to US$15–20 per month. Transportation costs vary (approx. US$80 per month). Living expenses (food, etc.) approximately US$130 per month. In Kuala Lumpur a comfortable budget is US$650–700 per month, a tight budget is US$315–400 per month.

Applic.: Request application form to return via e-mail (preferred), plus cover letter and CV, which should include relevant experience, research, and studies. Contact person: Annie/Didie.

Notes: A Visa is necessary under the responsibility of the volunteer.

WorldTeach

c/o Center for International Development, Harvard University
79 John F. Kennedy St., Box 122, Cambridge, Massachusetts 02138 USA
Tel.: ++1 (617) 495-5527 (toll free in N. Am 1-800-483-2240)
Fax: ++1 (617) 495-1599
E-mail: info@worldteach.org
www.worldteach.org

Desc.:	WorldTeach is a non-profit, non-governmental organisation based at the Centre for International Development at Harvard University, which provides opportunities for individuals to make a meaningful contribution to international education by living and working as volunteer teachers in developing countries. WorldTeach was founded by a group of Harvard students in 1986, in response to the great need for educational assistance in developing countries.
Sector:	Education.
Country:	Africa (Namibia, Rwanda, South Africa), Asia (Bangladesh, China, Mongolia), Europe (Poland), Latin America (Costa Rica, Ecuador, Chile, Guyana, Venezuela), Oceania (American Samoa, Marshall Islands, Micronesia).
Qualif.:	Native-English speakers. All year-long programs require a Bachelor's degree (BA/BS) or equivalent. The degree must be completed and diploma received prior to departure, but application accepted while still a college senior.
Nonpro:	Yes.
Age:	Minimum 18 for Summer Teaching Programs.
Duration:	1 year and summer positions. Time of year varies. depending on school calendars.
Lang.:	No requirement. Local language preferred.
Benefits:	Small stipend; room and board, usually with host family. Some programs fully or partially subsidized; see website.
Costs:	Year programs range from fully funded to US$5,990; summer programs US$3,990- 4,490. The fee covers international airfare, health insurance, room and board, materials and organisational support, intensive in-country orientation including teaching and language training and conferences. Full-time in-country field staff for all programs.
Applic.:	Application form on-line. See: www.worldteach.org/apply.

World Vision UK

Opal Drive, Fox Milne
Milton Keynes MK15 0ZR UK
Tel.: ++44 (1908) 841-000
Fax: ++44 (1908) 841-001
E-mail: info@worldvision.org.uk
www.worldvision.org.uk

Desc.: World Vision is one of the world's leading aid agencies, currently working in nearly 100 countries and helping over 75 million people in their struggle against poverty, hunger, and injustice. World Vision is a Christian organisation and a member of several major agency groups including the Disasters and Emergency Committee (DEC), British Overseas NGO's for Development (BOND), and the Consortium for Street Children (CSC).

Sector: Agriculture, disaster relief, education, health, human rights, hunger relief, small-enterprise development.

Country: Various countries in Africa, Asia, Europe, Latin America and the Middle East.

Qualif.: Job openings for highly qualified professionals on the website.

Nonpro: Yes, students in the Student Challenge program.

Age: 19–29 years old and either still studying or just graduated.

Duration: 4– 6 weeks; each year in late June through to the end of July or the beginning of August.

Lang.: English, French, or Spanish, depending.

Benefits: Flight, accommodation, food, internal travel, and full insurance for the Student Challenge. Long-term qualified professionals receive a stipend according to their experience.

Costs: GB£900–1,400 depending on destination for the Student Challenge. Personal expenses for long-term professionals.

Applic.: On-line form. See website for country contacts.

WWISA – Willing Workers in South Africa

PO Box 2413
Plettenberg Bay 6600
South Africa
Fax: ++27 (44) 534-8958
E-mail: info@wwisa.co.za
www.wwisa.co.za

Desc.: WWISA is a community development organisation aimed at facilitating international volunteer involvement in sustainable projects in Garden Route and in the Eastern Cape area of South Africa. WWISA believes that by responding to the identified needs of under-privileged communities, transferring skills or enhancing existing skills in local peoples, and acquiring new expertise to launch and further new projects promotes the development of productive communities.

Sector: Community development, education, environment, skills training, various.

Country: Africa (South Africa).

Qualif.: Professionals and students seeking experience are needed to help set-up projects and transfer skills to local people.

Nonpro: Yes.

Age: Minimum 18.

Duration: From 3 weeks to 12 months: volunteers can set their own timing. Some projects have a minimum stay requirement (see "projects" page on the website).

Lang.: English.

Benefits: Accommodation, food, Visa, airport transfer and project-related transport, fieldtrips, 3–5-day orientation. Accommodation varies from project to project.

Costs: Refer to information schedule on www.wwisa.co.za. Costs are from January to June GB£675 for 1 month or GB£180 for one week. From July to December costs are GB£710 for 1 month or GB£190 for one week.

Applic.: On-line form with GB£ 150 non-refundable deposit Documentation including credit details, insurance, passport photos, must be faxed or sent by registered post.

YAP – Youth Action for Peace

3, Avenue du Parc Royal
1020 Brussels, Belgium
Tel.: ++32 (2) 478-9410
Fax: ++32 (2) 478-9432
E-mail: info@yap.org
www.yap.org

Desc.:	YAP is an international youth movement, with branches mainly in Europe and associated group and partner organisations elsewhere worldwide. It struggles against the different forms of violence, exploitation, and injustice against networks of ideological religious, sexist, political, cultural, and economic oppression. YAP, thorough partner organisations, organises workcamps in about 50 countries in the world.
Sector:	Community development, environment, human rights, peacekeeping.
Country:	Europe (Albania, Algeria, Belgium, France, Germany, Hungary, Italy, Latvia, Portugal, Romania, Spain, Switzerland, United Kingdom), Latin America (Mexico, Peru), Middle East (Israel, Palestine). However YAP sends volunteers to more than 50 countries in the world.
Qualif.:	No particular skills are required for YAP workcamps.
Nonpro:	Yes.
Age:	Minimum 18 (though some projects may be for teenagers).
Duration:	Short-term projects are 1–4 weeks; medium- to long-term projects are 3 months to 1 year.
Lang.:	English, French, Spanish, Portuguese, German, depending on destination.
Benefits:	Accommodation, food.
Costs:	A small registration fee and travel costs.
Applic.:	Contact organisation (most convenient local branch—consult website).

YCI – Youth Challenge International

20 Maud Street, Suite 305
Toronto, Ontario M5V 2M5 Canada
Tel.: ++1 (416) 504-3370 (ext. 300)
Fax: ++1 (416) 504-3376
E-mail: generalinfo@yci.org
www.yci.org

Desc.:	YCI is a Canadian-based organisation that involves international youths in substantive overseas community development projects in Costa Rica, Guyana, Tanzania, Ethiopia and Vanuatu. Work projects include health education and Youth development. Adult volunteers are needed to accompany groups of youths.
Sector:	Community development, construction, education, environment, health.
Country:	Africa (Ethiopia, Ghana, Kenya, Tanzania), Latin America (Costa Rica, Grenada, Guatemala, Guyana), Oceania (Vanuatu).
Qualif.:	Adequate physical fitness level and ability to swim 200 metres. Leaders require previous field experience working with groups of youths aged 18–25, working in remote areas or developing countries.
Nonpro:	Yes.
Age:	18–30 dependent upon program.
Duration:	5–12 weeks. Upon review, volunteers can work for another placement period.
Lang.:	English; Spanish may also be required in Latin America.
Benefits:	Accommodations, food, insurance, and local travel.
Costs:	CAD$3,000-3,900, dependent upon program, plus airfare, vaccinations, and personal equipment.
Applic.:	On-line form to submit by e-mail or fax. Telephone the YCI office to verify application is received. Volunteer field staff can apply at any time. Canadian citizens, residents or landed immigrants only.

Youth Development Centre

PO Box 1659 or YMCA Building, 1 Durban Road
Pietermaritzburg 3200 South Africa
Tel.: ++27 (33) 3452970
Fax: ++27 (33) 3451583
E-mail: ydc@youthkzn.co.za
www.youthkzn.co.za

Desc.: The Youth Development Centre was established in 1996 to provide overseas volunteers the opportunity to serve at-risk and disadvantaged youth in South Africa. It now has volunteers in Durban, Pietermaritzburg, L'Abri, a wilderness training camp. Volunteers may be working in shelters for homeless youth, running programs at the local YMCA, facilitating leadership camps with school groups, working with youth who are living on the streets, leading classes and groups on youth issues with students, running workshops on HIV/AIDS, or coordinating a variety of programs in schools.

Sector: Child welfare, education, environment, health, women's issues.

Country: Africa (South Africa).

Qualif.: No particular qualifications needed. Certain volunteer positions require marketing, IT, PR, or computer skills.

Nonpro: Yes.

Age: Minimum 18.

Duration: 3–12 months, with longer periods available.

Lang.: English, however Zulu as their first language.

Benefits: Accommodation, food, training, project-related transportation, living expenses such as electricity, linen, equipment, etc., recreational trips relevant to the programme.

Costs: Approx. US$400/month. International travel, spending money (US$100/month), medical insurance. Application fee of US$30.

Applic.: On-line form. E-mail CV plus 2 letters of reference and a current photograph. Apply at least 6 months in advance.

Notes: Orientations are in January, April, July, and October. Volunteers must come 1–2 days prior to the orientation.

YPSA – Young Power in Social Action

House-F10(P), Road-13, Block-B, Chandgaon R/Area
Chittagong-4212, Bangladesh
Tel.: ++88 (31) 672-857 or 257 0916
Mob.: ++88 (1711) 825-068 or (1819) 321-432
Fax: ++88 (31) 257-0255
E-mail: info@ypsa.org or arif@ypsa.org or ypsa_arif@yahoo.com
www.ypsa.org

Desc.:	YPSA is a voluntary social development organisation playing an active role in empowering the poor and vulnerable people, especially women, through the active participation of organised groups of the grass-root level. YPSA is also working to activate and help young people , women, persons with the disabilities, indigenous people to become a skilled human resource and engaging them in development activities. YPSA acts as a catalyst in implementing sustainable development programs alongside the government as a supplementary force.
Sector:	Child welfare, community development, education, emergency, environment, health, housing, hunger relief, sanitation, small-enterprise development, women's issues.
Country:	Asia (Bangladesh).
Qualif.:	"A" level education completed with skills in any sector.
Nonpro:	Yes.
Age:	Minimum 18.
Duration:	3– 24 months (negotiable).
Lang.:	English.
Benefits:	No financial benefits . One Official certificate will be awarded after the successful completion of the assignment.
Costs:	A small cost is charged for food and accommodation for the local host family or official guest house (approx. US$125 - US$ 250 per month per person). Program registration one-time fee (US$100) . Volunteers are responsible for International airfare , insurances and personal expenses.
Applic.:	An application form will be sent upon request to be returned with full CV. See note on page 35.

YWTO – Youth World Travel Organization

PO Box KS 5283
Adum, Kumasi,
Ashanti 23351, Ghana
Tel.: ++(233) 2423-0943
E-mail: volunteers@ywto.org
www.ywto.org

Desc.:	YWTO offers short term and long-term voluntary projects in Ghana. Volunteers come from all over the world. The voluntary work projects are teaching, health care, agriculture, web page design, computer training, environmental projects and other social works.
Sector:	Agriculture, child welfare, community development, culture, education, environment, health, IT, skills training, small-enterprise development, women's issues, various.
Country:	Africa (Ghana).
Qualif.:	Volunteers may be placed where their skills are of most advantage.
Nonpro:	Yes.
Age:	Minimum 18.
Duration:	YWTO Voluntary Service offers short term and long term voluntary projects in Ghana.
Lang.:	English.
Benefits:	Project fee covers 1 meal, accommodation, preparatory materials and manuals, administrative expenses, and an experienced team leader and materials for the project.
Costs:	From US$100 per month plus personal expenses.
Applic.:	On-line form.
Notes:	Once accepted the applicant may request to be put in contact with former volunteers. See Note on page 35.

Zajel Youth Exchange Program

Public Relations Department, An-Najah National University
PO Box 7, Nablus, Palestine
Tel.: ++972 (9) 2345-113
Fax: ++972 (9) 2345-982
E-mail: youthexchange@najah.edu
www.najah.edu or www.youth.zajel.org

Desc.:	Zajel is the Arabic word for the carrier pigeon, used for many years as an important mean of communication. It represents the way this program sees its volunteers participate in its exchange programs: people that will deliver a message of peace and solidarity across the world. Zajel is an international self-financing, non-profit, educational program mainly supported by partner organisations. The Zajel Youth Exchange Program has developed an exchange program that assembles youth from diverse backgrounds to interact with Palestinians and learn about Palestinian society and political reality. The intention is to provide foreign youth and An-Najah National University students a venue to create a progressive learning environment for cultural enlightenment, experience sharing, and partnership to achieve a breakthrough in understanding and interpersonal respect.
Sector:	Culture, education, environment, IT,various.
Country:	Middle East (Palestine).
Qualif.:	Computer skills and strong motivation.
Nonpro.:	Yes.
Age:	Minimum 21.
Duration:	1–12 months, with longer periods available.
Lang.:	English.
Benefits:	Accommodation. Food and local transportation provided for the youth exchange volunteers.
Costs:	Contact the organisation. Volunteers must budget for food, travel, and personal expenses but no fees are charged.
Applic.:	Volunteers may apply at any time of year.
Notes:	Orientations are year round via the Internet.

APPENDICES

Analytical Table by geographical area and volunteer type

ORGANISATIONS	Africa	Asia	Caribbean	Europe	Latin America	North America	Middle East	Oceania	Nonpro	Short-term	Workcamps
Aang Serian "House of Peace"	X								X	X	
Abha Light Foundation	X									X	
ACDI / VOCA	X	X		X	X					X	
Action Against Hunger UK	X	X		X	X						
Adarsh Community Development Trust		X									
AFS International	X	X		X	X				X	X	
AFSAI – Association for Training and Inter-Cultural Activities and Exchange	X	X		X	X		X		X	X	X
AFSC – American Friends Service Committee					X		X		X	X	
AID India		X							X	X	X
AJUDE – Youth Association for the Dev. of Voluntary Service in Mozambique	X								X	X	X
AJWS – American Jewish World Service	X	X			X				X	X	
Alive Foundation	X								X	X	X
Alliance Abroad Group					X				X	X	
Amaudo UK	X								X	X	
Amazon-Africa Aid Organization					X				X	X	
AMIGOS – Amigos de las Américas					X				X	X	
Amizade, Ltd.	X	X	X	X	X	X		X		X	
Amnesty International	X	X	X	X	X	X	X			X	
AMURT Global Network	X	X	X	X			X		X	X	
APA-Onlus	X	X								X	
ARC – American Refugee Committee	X	X					X		X	X	
Australian Volunteers International	X	X			X		X	X	X	X	
AVSO – Association of Voluntary Service Organisations	X	X		X	X	X	X	X	X	X	X
AYAD – Australian Youth Ambassadors for Development		X						X	X	X	
Balkan Sunflowers				X					X	X	
BERDSCO – Benevolent Community Education and Rural Development Society	X								X	X	X
BMS World Mission	X	X		X	X				X	X	

Note. The organisations are in alphabetical order by name or acronym. Short-term volunteering is considered to be up to three months in duration. For nonpro explanation see page 29.

238

ORGANISATIONS	Africa	Asia	Caribbean	Europe	Latin America	North America	Middle East	Oceania	Nonpro	Short-term	Workcamps
Brethren Volunteer Service	X	X	X	X	X	X			X		
Bridge Foundation, the	X								X		
BUNAC	X	X			X				X	X	X
BWCA – Bangladesh Work Camps Association		X	X						X	X	X
Canada World Youth (Jeunesse Canada Monde)	X	X	X	X	X	X			X		
Canadian Crossroads International	X	X			X				X		
Casa de los Amigos					X	X			X	X	
Catholic Institute for International Relations		X		X	X		X		X		
Catholic Medical Mission Board	X	X	X	X	X					X	
CCIVS – Coordinating Committee for International Volunteers	X	X	X	X	X	X	X	X	X	X	X
CECI – Canadian Centre for International Studies and Cooperation	X	X			X		X				
CESVI – Cooperation and Development	X	X		X	X		X				
CFHI – Child Family Health International	X	X			X				X	X	
Chantiers Jeunesse		X		X	X				X	X	X
Chol-Chol Foundation for Human Development, the					X				X	X	X
Christian Peacemakers Corps					X	X	X		X	X	
CNFA – Citizens Network for Foreign Affairs				X			X		X	X	
Concern America	X				X						
Concern Worldwide	X	X	X								
Concordia	X	X		X	X	X			X	X	X
COOPI – Cooperazione Internazionale	X	X		X	X		X		X	X	X
CORD – Christian Outreach Relief and Development	X	X									
Cotravaux				X					X	X	X
Council for Mayan Communication in Sololá					X				X	X	
Cross Cultural Solutions	X	X	X		X				X	X	
CUSO	X	X			X			X	X		
Dakshinayan	X	X							X		

ORGANISATIONS	Africa	Asia	Caribbean	Europe	Latin America	North America	Middle East	Oceania	Nonpro	Short-term	Workcamps
Desteens Volunteering Services	X								X	X	
Development in Action	X	X							X	X	
EMERGENCY	X						X				
EnterpriseWorks/VITA	X										
EVS – European Voluntary Service	X			X	X				X	X	
Foundation for Sustainable Development	X	X			X				X	X	
Fundación Aldeas de Paz – Peace Villages Foundation				X	X				X	X	
Global Citizens Network	X	X			X	X			X	X	
Global Routes	X	X			X				X	X	
Global Service Corps	X	X							X	X	
Global Visions International	X	X	X	X	X				X	X	
Global Volunteer Network	X	X	X	X	X			X	X	X	
Global Volunteers	X			X	X	X		X	X	X	
Global Works, Inc.		X	X	X	X			X	X	X	
Globe Aware	X		X	X	X	X			X	X	
Good Shepherd Volunteers	X								X		
Goodwill Community Center	X						X		X	X	
Habitat for Humanity International	X	X	X	X	X	X		X	X	X	
Heifer International									X	X	X
Help2educate		X							X	X	X
IBO – International Building Organization				X					X	X	X
ICYE – International Cultural Youth Exchange	X	X		X	X			X	X	X	
ICYE-UK – Inter-Cultural Youth Exchange	X	X		X	X			X	X		
IESC Geekcorps	X	X		X						X	
IFESH – International Foundation for Education and Self-Help	X						X				
Info Nepal		X							X	X	X
InterConnection Virtual Volunteer Program	X	X	X	X	X	X		X	X	X	
International Executive Service Corps	X	X	X	X	X		X		X	X	
International Medical Corps	X	X		X			X			X	

ORGANISATIONS	Africa	Asia	Caribbean	Europe	Latin America	North America	Middle East	Oceania	Nonpro	Short-term	Workcamps
International Partnership for Service Learning and Leadership		X		X	X	X			X	X	
International Volunteer Program		X		X	X	X			X	X	
i-to-i Meaningful Travel	X	X		X	X				X	X	
IVDN - Interactive Voluntary Development Network	X	X							X	X	X
IVS – International Volunteer Service	X	X		X	X				X	X	
Jesuit Refugee Service	X	X	X	X	X		X	X	X	X	
Joint Assistance Centre, Inc.		X									
Kibbutz Program Center – Takam Artzi							X		X	X	
Kids Worldwide	X				X				X	X	X
LA-NO-CHE Orphanage	X								X	X	
MADRE - International Women's Human Rights Organization	X				X				X	X	
Makindu Children's Center	X								X		
MedAir	X	X									
Mercy Orphanage	X								X	X	
Mission Discovery	X		X		X	X			X	X	
Mission Doctors / Lay Mission Helpers Associations	X	X			X			X	X	X	
MondoChallenge	X	X		X	X				X	X	
MS – Mellemfolkeligt Samvirke	X	X		X	X				X	X	
MSF – Médicins Sans Frontiers	X	X	X	X	X		X	X			
Navti Foundation	X	X						X	X	X	
NetAid Online Volunteering	X	X	X	X	X	X	X	X	X	X	
Oikos	X								X	X	X
Olomayani Kindergarten	X								X	X	
Operation Crossroads Africa, Inc.	X								X	X	
Original Volunteers	X	X			X		X	X	X	X	
Oxfam International	X	X		X	X				X		
Pamoja International Voluntary Services	X								X		
Peace Brigades International		X	X		X		X	X	X		
Peace Corps	X	X	X	X	X		X	X	X		
Peacework	X	X		X	X	X			X		X

ORGANISATIONS	Africa	Asia	Caribbean	Europe	Latin America	North America	Middle East	Oceania	Nonpro	Short-term	Workcamps
Pitaya Suwan Foundation/Greenway International Workcamps	X	X							X	X	X
Projects Abroad	X	X		X	X				X	X	
Project Trust	X	X			X				X		
Quest Overseas	X				X				X	X	
Raleigh International		X			X				X	X	
RCDP-Nepal – Rural Community Development Program		X							X	X	
Recife Voluntário Brazil (Volunteer Centre of Recife)					X				X	X	
Red Cross – International Federation of Red Cross and Red Crescent Societies	X	X	X	X	X	X	X	X			
RedR UK	X	X	X	X	X	X	X	X			
Religious Youth Service	X	X	X	X	X	X		X	X	X	
Right to Play International	X	X					X		X		
Rokpa UK Overseas Projects		X							X		
RRN - Rural Reconstruction Nepal		X									
Safety Helping Hand Organisation	X	X	X	X	X	X	X		X	X	
Save the Children	X	X	X					X	X		
Save the Earth Network	X	X							X	X	
SCI – Service Civil International	X	X	X	X	X	X	X	X	X	X	X
SENEVOLU – Association Sénégalaise des Volontaires Unis	X								X	X	
Shekinah Care Centre	X										
Skillshare International	X	X									
SMILE Society		X							X	X	X
Sports Skills for Life Skills Foundation	X								X		
SPW – Students Partnership Worldwide	X	X							X		
STAESA – Students Travel and Exposure South Africa	X								X	X	X
Tearfund	X			X	X		X		X		
Terre des Hommes	X	X		X	X						
Ugunja Community Resource Centre	X									X	
UNA Exchange	X	X		X	X				X	X	X

ORGANISATIONS	Africa	Asia	Caribbean	Europe	Latin America	North America	Middle East	Oceania	Nonpro	Short-term	Workcamps
UNAREC – Union Nationale des Associations Régionales Etudes & Chantiers	X	X							X	X	X
UNICEF – United Nations International Children's Emergency Fund	X	X	X	X	X	X	X	X	X	X	
UNICEF Internship Programme	X	X	X	X	X	X	X	X	X		
United Action for Children	X								X	X	
United Children's Fund, Inc.	X								X	X	
United Planet	X	X		X	X				X	X	
UNV – United Nations Volunteers	X	X		X	X		X	X	X	X	
VIA	X	X							X		
VIP – Volunteers for International Partnership	X	X		X	X				X	X	
Visions in Action	X				X				X		
VOICA – Canossian International Voluntary Service	X	X		X	X				X		X
VOLU – Voluntary Workcamps Association of Ghana	X								X	X	
Volunteer Africa	X								X	X	
Volunteer in Africa	X								X	X	
Volunteer Latin America					X				X	X	
Volunteer Missionary Movement	X				X				X	X	
Volunteer Nepal – National Group		X							X		
Volunteers for Peace International	X	X		X	X	X	X	X	X	X	X
VSO – Voluntary Service Overseas	X	X			X			X	X	X	
VSO Canada	X	X			X				X		
Women's Aid Organisation		X							X		
WorldTeach	X	X		X	X	X		X	X	X	
World Vision UK	X	X		X	X		X		X	X	
WWISA - Willing Workers in South Africa	X								X	X	
YAP – Youth Action for Peace				X	X		X		X	X	
YCI – Youth Challenge International	X							X	X	X	
Youth Development Centre	X								X	X	
YPSA – Young Power in Social Action		X							X	X	
YWTO – Youth World Travel Organisation	X								X	X	
Zajel Youth Exchange Program							X		X	X	X

243

Analytical Table by sector

ORGANISATIONS	Agriculture	Child welfare	Community devel.	Construction	Culture	Education	Emergency	Environment	Health	Housing	Human rights	Hunger relief	IT	Peacekeeping	Refugee aid	Religious	Sanitation	Skills training	Small-enterp. devel.	Women's issues	Various
Aang Serian "House of Peace"	X		X	X				X											X		
Abha Light Foundation									X												
ACDI / VOCA	X		X					X											X		
Action Against Hunger UK	X		X					X	X			X							X		
Adarsh Community Development Trust		X	X	X	X	X			X	X							X			X	
AFS International		X	X	X	X	X		X													X
AFSAI – Ass. for Training and Inter-Cultural Activities		X	X		X	X		X			X										X
AFSC – American Friends Service Committee				X		X	X		X							X		X			
AID India	X	X	X		X	X		X	X		X								X	X	
AJUDE – Youth Ass. for Voluntary Servi. in Mozambique	X	X				X		X	X		X									X	X
AJWS – American Jewish World Service	X							X	X												X
Alive Foundation	X	X	X			X		X	X										X		X
Alliance Abroad Group	X	X			X	X		X	X									X	X		
Amaudo UK	X								X		X										
Amazon-Africa Aid Organization		X	X			X		X	X												
AMIGOS – Amigos de las Américas		X	X	X	X	X		X	X												
Amizade, Ltd.				X	X	X		X	X												
Amnesty International											X										X
AMURT Global Network			X			X			X	X		X									
APA-Onlus							X														
ARC – American Refugee Committee		X				X	X	X	X		X	X			X		X				X
Australian Volunteers International	X		X	X	X	X		X	X		X		X				X				X
AVSO – Ass. of Voluntary Service Organisations			X	X	X	X		X	X												X
AYAD – Australian Youth Ambassadors for Development			X	X	X	X		X	X								X			X	
Balkan Sunflowers		X	X		X	X	X				X										
BERDSCO –Community Education and Rural Dev.	X		X			X		X	X										X	X	X
BMS World Mission			X			X			X						X	X	X		X		X
Brethren Volunteer Service	X	X	X			X		X	X		X	X			X	X					X
Bridge Foundation, the		X	X			X			X				X			X			X	X	
BUNAC	X				X	X		X	X		X		X					X			X
BWCA – Bangladesh Work Camps Association	X			X		X		X	X				X								

Note: The organisations are in alphabetical order by name or acronym. See the meaning of the sectors on pages 26–27.

ORGANISATIONS	Agriculture	Child welfare	Community devel.	Construction	Culture	Education	Emergency	Environment	Health	Housing	Human rights	Hunger relief	IT	Peacekeeping	Refugee aid	Religious	Sanitation	Skills training	Small-enterp. devel.	Women's issues	Various
Canada World Youth (Jeunesse Canada Monde)	X		X			X		X	X									X	X	X	
Canadian Crossroads International			X						X									X	X		X
Casa de los Amigos			X																		X
Catholic Institute for International Relations			X			X			X		X							X	X	X	X
Catholic Medical Mission Board									X		X										
CCIVS – Coord. Committee for International Volunteers				X	X	X		X	X				X								
CECI – Canadian Centre for Int.Studies and Cooperation			X		X	X		X	X										X		X
CESVI – Cooperation and Development			X	X	X	X		X	X												
CFHI – Child Family Health International						X	X		X												
Chantiers Jeunesse			X	X	X	X		X													
Chol-Chol Foundation for Human Development, the											X			X	X	X		X	X	X	X
Christian Peacemakers Corps											X			X							
CNFA – Citizens Network for Foreign Affairs	X											X							X		
Concern America	X	X	X	X		X			X		X						X		X		
Concern Worldwide				X	X	X	X		X		X						X				
Concordia		X					X	X													
COOPI – Cooperazione Internazionale	X		X			X		X					X		X		X	X	X	X	X
CORD – Christian Outreach Relief and Development	X		X			X			X						X		X	X	X	X	
Cotravaux				X	X			X													X
Council for Mayan Communication in Sololà						X							X								X
Cross Cultural Solutions		X			X	X		X	X	X			X								X
CUSO	X				X	X		X	X	X	X		X						X		X
Dakshinayan			X			X			X				X						X		
Desteens Volunteering Services		X	X	X		X		X							X						
Development in Action		X	X					X					X						X	X	
EMERGENCY							X		X												
EnterpriseWorks/VITA	X	X	X		X	X		X					X				X	X	X		X
EVS – European Voluntary Service		X	X		X	X		X													X
Foundation for Sustainable Development		X	X			X		X	X		X								X	X	X

245

ORGANISATIONS	Agriculture	Child welfare	Community devel.	Construction	Culture	Education	Emergency	Environment	Health	Housing	Human rights	Hunger relief	IT	Peacekeeping	Refugee aid	Religious	Sanitation	Skills training	Small-enterp. devel.	Women's issues	Various
Fundacioón Aldeas de Paz – Peace Villages Foundation	X	X	X			X		X											X		
Global Citizens Network				X		X		X												X	
Global Routes				X		X		X													X
Global Service Corps	X		X			X			X												
Global Visions International					X	X		X	X												
Global Volunteer Network			X		X	X		X	X								X				
Global Volunteers			X		X			X													
Global Works, Inc.			X	X	X	X		X													
Globe Aware																					X
Good Shepherd Volunteers		X				X										X		X		X	
Goodwill Community Center		X	X										X			X			X		
Habitat for Humanity International				X						X											
Heifer International	X		X			X		X													
Help2educate						X															
IBO – International Building Organization			X	X						X	X		X								
ICYE – International Cultural Youth Exchange		X	X		X	X		X	X	X	X		X		X			X	X	X	
ICYE-UK – Inter-Cultural Youth Exchange		X	X		X	X		X	X		X							X	X	X	
IESC Geekcorps													X								
IFESH – Internat. Found. for Education and Self-Help	X					X			X				X								X
Info Nepal		X	X		X			X	X								X				
InterConnection Virtual Volunteer Program													X								
International Executive Service Corps	X												X								
International Medical Corps		X					X		X			X					X	X	X	X	X
Internat. Partnership for Service Learning and Leadership		X	X	X			X	X	X	X	X									X	
International Volunteer Program		X	X		X			X	X	X	X										
i-to-i Meaningful Travel	X	X	X	X	X	X		X	X										X		X
IVDN – Interactive Voluntary Development Network		X	X		X			X	X									X			X
IVS – International Volunteer Service				X	X			X						X							X
Jesuit Refugee Service		X				X	X				X				X			X			

ORGANISATIONS	Agriculture	Child welfare	Community devel.	Construction	Culture	Education	Emergency	Environment	Health	Housing	Human rights	Hunger relief	IT	Peacekeeping	Refugee aid	Religious	Sanitation	Skills training	Small-enterp. devel.	Women's issues	Various
Joint Assistance Centre, Inc.	X	X	X	X		X		X	X								X			X	
Kibbutz Program Center – Takam Artzi	X																				X
Kids Worldwide		X		X					X											X	
LA-NO-CHE Orphanage		X	X			X		X													
MADRE – Internat. Women's Human Rights Organization		X	X	X		X		X	X		X	X	X				X		X	X	X
Makindu Children's Center	X	X	X			X			X		X								X	X	
MedAir									X	X											
Mercy Orphanage		X	X			X			X	X							X				
Mission Discovery		X	X	X					X	X						X	X				
Mission Doctors / Lay Mission Helpers Associations			X	X					X								X			X	
MondoChallenge		X	X			X		X	X										X		X
MS – Mellemfolkeligt Samvirke	X		X					X	X		X							X			
MSF – Médicins Sans Frontiers							X		X						X						
Navti Foundation			X			X		X	X		X										X
NetAid Online Volunteering						X			X				X								
Oikos	X					X		X	X				X								
Olomayani Kindergarten		X				X															
Operation Crossroads Africa, Inc.	X		X		X	X		X	X												
Original Volunteers			X		X	X		X	X												
Oxfam International			X			X	X	X	X		X	X	X				X			X	X
Pamoja International Voluntary Services	X		X		X	X		X	X		X								X	X	X
Peace Brigades International											X			X							
Peace Corps	X		X			X			X					X					X		
Peacework		X	X	X	X	X										X	X		X		
Pitaya Suwan Foundation/Greenway Internat.Workcamps	X			X	X	X		X											X		
Projects Abroad	X		X		X	X			X		X								X		
Project Trust	X				X	X													X		X

ORGANISATIONS	Agriculture	Child welfare	Community devel.	Construction	Culture	Education	Emergency	Environment	Health	Housing	Human rights	Hunger relief	IT	Peacekeeping	Refugee aid	Religious	Sanitation	Skills training	Small-enterp. devel.	Women's issues	Various
Quest Overseas			X					X										X			X
Raleigh International		X	X					X													X
RCDP-Nepal – Rural Community Development Program		X	X			X		X													X
Recife Voluntário Brazil (Volunteer Centre of Recife)			X		X																
Red Cross – Int. Fed. Red Cross and Red Crescent Soc.				X			X		X			X									
RedR UK			X	X			X	X	X	X	X	X					X				X
Religious Youth Service			X	X		X		X	X								X				
Right to Play International		X	X																		
Rokpa UK Overseas Projects						X									X						
RRN - Rural Reconstruction Nepal	X	X	X	X		X		X	X		X						X			X	X
Safety Helping Hand Organisation		X	X	X	X	X			X												
Save the Children		X				X	X	X	X											X	
Save the Earth Network			X	X		X	X	X	X		X										X
SCI – Service Civil International		X	X	X		X		X							X						X
SENEVOLU – Ass. Sénégalaise des Volontaires Unis			X			X													X		X
Shekinah Care Centre									X												
Skillshare International			X			X		X	X				X					X	X		
SMILE Society		X	X	X		X		X	X												
Sports Skills for Life Skills Foundation					X																X
SPW – Students Partnership Worldwide			X	X	X	X		X	X				X						X		
STAESA – Students Travel and Exposure South Africa		X			X	X		X	X		X		X					X		X	
Tearfund	X		X			X									X		X				
Terre des Hommes		X	X		X						X										
Ugunja Community Resource Centre	X	X	X	X		X		X	X		X		X					X	X	X	X
UNA Exchange	X		X	X	X	X		X						X						X	X
UNAREC – Union Nat. des Ass. Régionales Et. Chantier		X	X	X			X														X
UNICEF – UN International Children's Emergency Fund						X			X		X	X	X				X	X	X	X	X
UNICEF Internship Programme											X										

ORGANISATIONS	Agriculture	Child welfare	Community devel.	Construction	Culture	Education	Emergency	Environment	Health	Housing	Human rights	Hunger relief	IT	Peacekeeping	Refugee aid	Religious	Sanitation	Skills training	Small-enterp. devel.	Women's issues	Various
United Action for Children		X	X			X			X								X		X	X	
United Children's Fund, Inc.	X	X		X		X														X	
United Planet		X	X		X	X			X	X	X	X	X	X	X		X	X	X	X	X
UNV – United Nations Volunteers	X	X	X			X		X	X												
VIA						X		X	X												
VIP – Volunteers for International Partnership		X	X			X		X	X	X	X	X	X		X				X	X	X
Visions in Action	X	X	X			X		X	X												
VOICA – Canossian International Voluntary Service			X	X		X			X							X					X
VOLU – Voluntary Workcamps Association of Ghana	X	X	X			X		X		X	X				X		X				X
Volunteer Africa			X		X	X															
Volunteer in Africa		X	X																		
Volunteer Latin America		X	X	X		X		X													X
Volunteer Missionary Movement	X	X	X	X		X			X		X					X					
Volunteer Nepal - National Group		X	X			X		X	X	X			X			X					X
Volunteers for Peace International	X		X	X	X	X		X	X	X	X				X						
VSO – Voluntary Service Overseas	X		X			X	X	X	X				X					X	X		X
VSO Canada		X	X															X	X		
Women's Aid Organisation		X				X	X													X	
WorldTeach						X															
World Vision UK	X		X			X		X	X		X	X						X	X		X
WWISA - Willing Workers in South Africa			X					X			X			X				X			
YAP – Youth Action for Peace				X				X	X		X								X		
YCI – Youth Challenge International			X			X		X	X												
Youth Development Centre		X				X	X	X	X			X					X			X	
YPSA – Young Power in Social Action		X	X		X	X	X	X	X											X	
YWTO – Youth World Travel Organisation	X	X	X		X	X	X	X	X				X					X	X	X	X
Zajel Youth Exchange Program		X			X	X	X	X	X				X						X	X	X

ORGANISATION ALPHABETICAL INDEX

Aang Serian 'House of Peace' 40
Abha Light Foundation 41
ACDI/VOCA 42
Action Against Hunger UK 44
Adarsh Community Development Trust 45
AFS International 46
AFSAI – Association for Training and Inter-Cultural
    Activities and Exchange 48
AFSC – American Friends Service Committee 49
AID India 50
AJUDE – Youth Association for the Development of
    Voluntary Service in Mozambique 51
AJWS – American Jewish World Service 52
Alive Foundation 54
Alliance Abroad Group 55
Amaudo UK 56
Amazon - Africa Aid Organization 57
AMIGOS – Amigos de las Américas 58
Amizade, Ltd. 59
Amnesty International 60
AMURT Global Network 61
APA-Onlus 62
ARC – American Refugee Committee 63
Australian Volunteers International 64
AVSO – Association of Voluntary Service Organisations 65
AYAD – Australian Youth Ambassadors for Development 66
Balkan Sunflowers 67
BERDSCO – Benevolent Community Education and Rural Development
    Society 68
BMS World Mission 70
Brethren Volunteer Service... 71
The Bridge Foundation.. 72
BUNAC.. 73
BWCA – Bangladesh Work Camps Association.. 74
Canada World Youth (Jeunesse Canada Monde) 75
Canadian Crossroads International.. 76
Casa de Los Amigos, A. C. 77
Catholic Institute for International Relations - Progressio 78
Catholic Medical Mission Board 79
CCIVS – Coordinating Committee for International Volunteers 80
CECI – Canadian Centre for International Studies and Cooperation........... 81

CESVI – Cooperation and Development......83
CFHI – Child Family Health International......84
Chantiers Jeunesse......85
The Chol-Chol Foundation for Human Development......86
Christian Peacemakercorps......87
CNFA – Citizens Network for Foreign Affairs......89
Concern America......90
Concern Worldwide......91
Concordia......92
COOPI – Cooperazione Internazionale......93
CORD – Christian Outreach Relief and Development......94
Cotravaux......95
Council for Mayan Communication in Sololà......96
Cross-Cultural Solutions......98
CUSO......99
Dakshinayan......101
Desteens Volunteering Services......102
Development in Action......103
Emergency......104
EnterpriseWorks/VITA......105
EVS – European Voluntary Service......106
Foundation for Sustainable Development......108
Fundaciòn Aldeas de Paz-Peace Villages Foundation......109
Global Citizens Network......110
Global Routes......111
Global Service Corps......113
Global Vision International......114
Global Volunteer Network......115
Global Volunteers......116
Global Works Travel......118
Globe Aware......119
Good Shepherd Volunteers......120
Goodwill Community Center......121
Habitat for Humanity International......122
Heifer International......123
Help2Educate......124
IBO – International Building Organization......125
ICYE – International Cultural Youth Exchange......126
ICYE-UK – Inter-Cultural Youth Exchange......127
IESC Geekcorps......128
IFESH – International Foundation for Education and Self-Help......129
INFO Nepal - Volunteer in Nepal......130
Interconnection Virtual Volunteer Program......131

International Executive Service Corps 132
International Medical Corps 133
International Partnership for Service Learning and Leadership 134
International Volunteer Program 135
i-to-i Meaningful Travel...136
IVDN – Interactive Voluntary Development Service..................................138
IVS – International Voluntary Service...139
Jesuit Refugee Service 140
Joint Assistance Centre, Inc. 141
Kibbutz Program Center – Takam-Artzi..142
Kids Worldwide 144
LA-NO-CHE Orphanage 146
MADRE – International Women's Human Rights Organization 147
Makindu Children's Center 148
Medair 150
Mercy Orphanage Primary and High School..151
Mission Discovery 153
Mission Doctors/Lay Mission Helpers Associations 154
Mondo Challenge 155
MS – Mellemfolkeligt Samvirke 156
MSF – Médecins Sans Frontières 157
NAVTI Foundation 158
NET AID Online Volunteering 159
Oikos 160
Olomayani Kindergarten, Eluwai 161
Operation Crossroads Africa, Inc. 162
Original Volunteers 163
Oxfam International 164
Pamoja International Voluntary Services 165
Peace Brigades International 166
Peace Corps 168
Peacework 170
Pitaya Suwan Foundation/Greenway Thailand 171
Projects Abroad 172
Project Trust 173
Quest Overseas 174
Raleigh International 175
RCDP-Nepal – Rural Community Development Program..........................176
Recife Voluntario Brazil (Volunteer Centre of Recife) 177
Red Cross – International Federation of Red Cross
        and Red Crescent Societies..178
RedR UK 180
Religious Youth Service 181

Right To Play International 182
Rokpa UK Overseas Projects 184
RRN – Rural Reconstruction Nepal 185
Safety Helping Hand Organisation 186
Save The Children 187
Save the Earth Network 188
SCI – Service Civil International.. 189
SENEVOLU – Association Sénégalaise des Volontaires Unis 190
Shekinah Care Centre.. 191
Skillshare International 192
SMILE Society... 193
Sport Skills For Life Skills Foundation.. 194
SPW – Students Partnership Worldwide 195
STAESA – Students Travel and Exposure South Africa 196
Tearfund 197
Terre des Hommes 198
Ugunja Community Resource Centre 199
UNA Exchange 200
UNAREC – Union Nationale des Associations
        Régionales Etudes & Chantiers 202
UNICEF – United Nations International Children's Emergency Fund 203
UNICEF Internship Programme 204
United Action for Children 205
United Children's Fund, Inc. 206
United Planet.. 207
UNV – United Nations Volunteers 208
VIA 210
VIP – Volunteers for International Partnership 212
Visions in Action 213
VOICA – Canossian International Voluntary Service 214
VOLU – Voluntary Workcamps Association of Ghana 215
Volunteer Africa 216
Volunteer in Africa 217
Volunteer Latin America 218
Volunteer Missionary Movement 219
Volunteer Nepal - National Group 220
Volunteers for Peace International 221
VSO – Voluntary Service Overseas 223
VSO Canada 225
Women's Aid Organisation 227
WorldTeach 228
World Vision UK 229

WWISA – Willing Workers in South Africa 230
YAP – Youth Action for Peace 231
YCI – Youth Challenge International 232
Youth Development Centre 233
YPSA – Young Power in Social Action 234
YWTO – Youth World Travel Organization 235
Zajel Youth Exchange Program 236

From the same publisher

(available from your bookstore or from the website www.greenvol.com)

Green Volunteers   The World Guide
to Voluntary Work in Nature Conservation
Over 200 projects worldwide for those vho want to experience active conservation work as a volunteer. Projects are worldwide, year round, in a variety of habitats, from one week to one year or more. From dolphins to rhinos, from whales to primates, this guide is ideal for a meaningful vacation or for finding thesis or research opportunities.
£ 10.99 € 16.00   US$ 14.95   CAN$ 21.00   Pages: 256

World Volunteers   The World Guide
to Humanitarian and Development Volunteering
Nearly 200 projects and organizations worldwide for people who want to work in international humanitarian projects but don't know how to begin. Opportunities are from 2 weeks to 2 years or longer. An ideal resource for a working holiday or a leave of absence. A guide for students, reitrees, doctors or accountants, nurses or agronomists, surveyors and teachers, plumbers or builders, electricians or computer operators... For everyone who wants to get involved in helping those who suffer worldwide.
£ 11.99 € 16.00   US$ 16.95   CAN$ 20.00   Pages: 256

Archaeo-Volunteers   The World Guide
to Archaeological and Heritage Volunteering
Listing 200 projects and organizations in the 5 continents for those who want to spend a different working vacation helping Archaeologists Placements are from 2 weeks to a few months. For enthusiastic amateurs, students and those wanting hands-on experience. Cultural and historical heritage maintenance and restoration and museum volunteering opportunities are also listed. The guide also tells how to find hundreds more excavations and workcamps on the Internet.
£ 10.99 € 16.00   US$ 14.95   CAN$ 21.00   Pages: 256